Structure and Meaning

Jeffrey C. Alexander has also written:

*Twenty Lectures: Sociological Theory
Since World War II*

and

*Action and Environments: Toward a
New Synthesis*

Structure and Meaning

Relinking Classical Sociology

Jeffrey C. Alexander

Columbia University Press

NEW YORK

LIBRARY OF CONGRESS
Library of Congress Cataloging-in-Publication Data
Alexander, Jeffrey C.
Structure and meaning : relinking classical sociology / Jeffrey C.
Alexander.
p.   cm.
Includes bibliographies and index.
ISBN 0-231-06688-0 (alk. paper)
1. Sociology.   2. Civilization, Modern.   I. Title.
HM24.A4649 1989   88-22019
301—dc19   CIP

63829

COLUMBIA UNIVERSITY PRESS
New York   Guildford, Surrey

Printed in the United States of America

Hardback editions of Columbia University Press books are Smyth-
sewn and printed on permanent and durable acid-free paper

Book design by Ken Venezio

Contents

Acknowledgments

"Sociology and Discourse: On the Centrality of the Classics" (chapter 1) first appeared in Anthony Giddens and Jonathan Turners, eds., *Social Theory Today* and is reprinted here by permission of the Polity Presss.

"The Dialectic of Individuation and Domination: Weber's Rationalization Theory and Beyond" (chapter 2) first appeared in Sam Whimster and Scott Lash, eds., *Max Weber and Rationality* and is reprinted here by permission of Allen and Unwin.

"The Cultural Grounds of Rationalization: Sect Democracy Versus the Iron Cage" (chapter 3) first appeared in *Sociological Theory* and is reprinted here by permission of the American Sociological Association.

"Rethinking Durkheim's Intellectual Development: On the Complex Origins of a Cultural Sociology" (chapter 4) first appeared in *International Sociology* and is reprinted here by permission of the International Sociological Association.

"Durkheimian Sociology and Cultural Studies Today" (chapter 5) first appeared in Jeffrey C. Alexander, ed., *Durkheimian Sociology: Cultural Studies* and is reprinted here by permission of Cambridge University Press.

"Culture and Political Crisis: 'Watergate' and Durkheimian Sociology" (chapter 6) first appeared in Jeffrey C. Alexander, ed., *Durkheimian Sociology: Cultural Studies* and is reprinted here by permission of Cambridge University Press.

"Habermas and Critical Theory: Beyond the Marxian Dilemma?" (chapter 7) first appeared in the *American Journal of Sociology* and is reprinted here by permission of the University of Chicago Press.

Each of these essays has been revised since their original publication.

Structure and Meaning

Introduction

These essays concern the relation between structure and meaning within both sociological theory and modern society.

Sociological theory deals with modernity. First Western, then world society has undergone a great transformation. What are the costs, and the gains? Since the nineteenth century there have been strains of liberal and technocratic theorizing that have emphasized the gains and underemphasized the costs. In the period after World War II, these strains became particularly pronounced. Classical sociology itself came to be read in this positive way. In the 1980s our view of modern society has become more realistic. Liberal theories of modernity must be reconstituted so they reflect this new realism; the classical grounding for contemporary thought must be reconsidered in a corresponding way.

The great classical figures of modern sociology were, in fact, more worried about the costs of modernity than they were confident about its gains. In varying degree, they viewed modernization as an emptying out of meaning. Throughout the writings of Marx, Weber, Simmel, and Durkheim we find assertions, and suggestions, that at the end of this modernizing process only hard and impersonal structures will be left. The promise of freedom appeared to be either meaningless or essentially unfulfilled, the hope for community even more remote. Industrialization and secularization, it seemed, had produced more harm than good. The first allowed structures to develop that were impervious to human will; the second prevented the new society from being meaningfully understood. Today, we know that modernity has been just this bad, indeed that it has exceeded the founding figures' worst nightmares. From the pessimistic sensibility of classical sociology, therefore, there is still much to be learned. To explore this dark side sets one agenda for this book.

Yet, as this great century of modernity draws to a close, it is important to stress that we have learned that there is a contrasting, lighter side as well. Some modern societies have not self-destructed; even though they have suffered great strains, they have not only survived but have been increasingly enriched. Many of the societies that came to naught in the process of modernization, moreover, have been able to establish new and much more promising foundations. Modernity, then, has not always been as bad as the classical figures suggested; it would appear that there is no deep structural reason for it eventually to come to ruin. Classical sociologists conceived ideas in a period of particularly sharp disruption, a period that, after two world wars and a half-century of crippling instability, we may now have the luxury of identifying as transitional. It is not surprising that their critiques betray a certain metaphysical nostalgia for the traditional world and a corresponding difficulty in seeing the possibilities for a modernity in a positive light. To demonstrate that there is hope for a modern society is to confront the dark side of the classical heritage. It is to demonstrate that meaningless is not the logical deduction from the death of god and that domination is not the inevitable corollary of industrialization. Freedom and community can survive in a "rational," postcosmological, and industrial world. To explore these more positive possibilities marks this book's other agenda.

The success of this more positive agenda depends on intertwining structure and meaning in both a formal and a substantive way. Substantively, it must be shown that positive social and cultural resources do exist. Formally, an analytical theory must be developed that shows how and why structure and meaning can be combined. The possibility of a good society cannot be established only by normative argument. There is a distinctive contribution that sociological theory can make. If we are to attain the "reflective equilibrium" that Rawls (1979: sec. 1.9) has established as a precondition not only for justice but for theorizing about justice, we need clear technical ideas about the empirical structures and real possibilities of social life. We cannot make do with moral reasoning writ large. This sociological theory, which has formal and substantive components, must tell us where, in the mundane but by no means entirely hopeless societies in which we actually live, the modern resources for meaning, community, and the democratic control of power lie.* In the

---

*I take this sociological turn to be an implication of the "internalist" moral theorizing that

collection of essays that forms a companion for this volume (Alexander 1988a), I have addressed these issues through efforts at empirical explanation and systematic theory.* In the current collection I do so by returning to the classics.

The base line for these reflections is established by "The Dialectic of Individuation and Domination: Max Weber's Rationalization Theory and Beyond," the second essay in this collection. The distinctive tone of Weber's sweeping but precise account of civilizational history—sober about imminent danger yet courageously determined to press on—seems peculiarly appropriate for the tense and contradictory history of modern times. In the present period, the ebullience of postwar American liberalism seems naively out of place. Modernity is not an end point that will be imminently achieved. It is a process that, one hopes, will go on without end. In the early postwar period, the only alternative to early American optimism seemed to be Marxist critique or existentialist despair. I prefer Weber to Marx because he is neither millenial nor apocalyptic. By showing that within "bourgeois" society there are significant resources for moral responsibility, Weber restores a dialectic missing from Marx's work. He does not, however, neglect the reality of either domination or despair. Individual moral courage is the only antidote to these scourges of modernity that Weber can find. In the last pages of this essay I argue that more properly sociological alternatives exist. The challenge is to expand on the liberating side of Weber's dialectic without losing sight of modernity's ever-present dangers and constraints. Durkheim went far beyond Weber in this regard, as did Parsons, Keynes, Habermas, and Piaget.

The aim of the subsequent essays is to explore the resources for developing this fuller dialectic, following the traditions of Durkheim, Habermas, and Weber himself. In "The Cultural Grounds of Rationalization: Sect Democracy and the Iron Cage," Colin Loader and I reconstruct a kernel from Weber's giant corpus that has been almost completely ignored. We suggest that in the aftermath of Weber's first and only trip to America he briefly considered an alternative to the notion that modernity implied a domination impervious to human control. The source for such

has evolved in reaction to the strains of abstract deduction—the "externalism"—in Rawls' theory. For social scientists, the most important elaboration of internalism is Michael Walzer's (1983) work.

*In a subsequent essay, "The New Theoretical Movement" (Alexander 1988b), I argued that the intertwining of structure, action, and meaning has recently emerged as a leading theme throughout the schools of contemporary theoretical work.

an alternative, Weber believed, lay in the unique sect organization of American religious life, which allowed America to secularize and industrialize without become "Europeanized." Rather than rationalization being presented as a univocal universal theory—the main thrust of his later comparative and historical work—Weber here suggests that it can take different paths. The "switchman" that determines which track will be taken is the religious experience of a nation in its formative years. If church has been replaced by Protestant sect, then there is some chance that the modern society which follows can be meaningfully integrated and democratically controlled.

These unexpected conclusions are premised on the possibility that religion, and the secular belief systems that follow in its wake, continue to exert a profound influence on the modern age. In the remaining four essays, I elaborate and generalize this premise through my interpretations of Durkheim's and Habermas's work, and I demonstrate its practical viability by a detailed analysis of Watergate, one of the most prototypically modern events in recent times.

Weber's unexpected and unpursued premise, I suggest, was at the very heart of Durkheim's later work. Durkheim's aim from the very beginning of his intellectual life was to challenge the conceptual necessity for an iron cage—even if, for what he believed to be transitory historical reasons, domination tended to be an empirical fact. In the last two decades of his career, Durkheim believed that he finally had worked out the foundations for this new conceptual scheme. He developed a "religious sociology" that could redefine the structures of modern society in terms of symbolic codes, rituals, and solidarities. Until recently the very existence of this project was lost to professional social science. In "Rethinking Durkheim's Intellectual Development: On the Complex Origins of a Cultural Sociology," I show how it is now possible, given recent theoretical and scholarly developments, to set this error right. The problems that Durkheim faced, I argue, are not at all dissimilar to those that confront social science. If we can understand his tentative solutions, we can gain important resources for resolving problems of our own. In the essay that follows, "Durkheimian Sociology and Cultural Studies Today," I show that in important disciplines outside of social science narrowly construed there have been significant elaborations of Durkheim's late program. These developments are exemplars for a more culturally sensitive sociology.

In the penultimate essay, "Culture and Political Crisis: 'Watergate' and

Durkheimian Sociology," I apply the agenda derived from Weber and Durkheim to a major crisis in contemporary society, developing in much more detail a conceptual scheme for the cultural analysis of modern societies.* To do so involves much more than mapping the internal logic of cultural systems, although this is something I certainly try to provide. It involves also linking the operation of these collective codes to institutions, power, and social actors, and to the contingent aspirations for rationality that distinguish modern life.

In the concluding essay, "Habermas and Critical Theory: Beyond the Marxian Dilemma?" I confront a theorist who is more closely identified with the project of rational modernity than any contemporary. At an earlier point in his career, Habermas pursued this project within a revised version of Marxian thought. In his later work he has tried to find a more meaning-related, noninstrumental theory within which rationality can be articulated. He turns on its head Marx's sharp distinction between calculating means-ends activity and expressive communication. Rather than accepting calculation as the basis of our theory of contemporary society, we are urged to consider action from the perspective of communication. In doing so, Habermas believes, we must acknowledge that every action contains an effort at consensual understanding. This movement toward consensus provides an immanent standard for critical rationality, even within the confines of "bourgeois" life.

The problem is that in elaborating this communicative theory Habermas reproduces the very dichotomy he has sought to avoid. On the one hand, he acknowledges that reaching understanding depends on shared normative criteria. To pursue the latter, he has turned back to the same traditions that are the object of this book, to Weber and Durkheim, and also to Parsons and Piaget. He has read these figures to understand the historical evolution of moral communities and the institutionalization of values in social systems. On the other hand, Habermas insists that modern communication not only involves the norm of rationality but that in empirical practice it can and should be completely transparent, its aims and terms consciously available for dispute. To pursue this possibility, Habermas relies on theories that understand communication as pragmatic speech acts. This move blunts his more cultural turn. In semiotic terms, in so far as norms and values are important, communication must be

---

*I draw here upon the approach I developed in Alexander (1988a):301–333.

related to the arbitrary symbolic systems of language, not the situational and contingent processes of speech. In the end, Habermas has not fully escaped a radical, dichotomizing understanding of secularization. He cannot conceive of rationality being pursued without a symbolic world that remains grounded in some arbitrary and particularistic way. My own argument in these essays is to the contrary: this is the only way that rationality can be conceived.

I have introduced these essays by talking about the empirical and theoretical issues to which they are addressed, ignoring the peculiar medium through which their address is made. This, of course, is the medium of classical work. But while I have ignored this medium, many readers will not. Ever since Merton crystallized the distinction, empiricist social science has argued for the strict separation of systematic from historical approaches to sociological theory. Let historians study, and interpret, the nature of the classics; we sociologists will study, and explain, the nature of society.

These essays take exactly the opposite approach. They talk about modernity, power, culture, and explanation by interpreting the meaning of other people's writing. They do not do so by studying empirical society or even, for the most part, by producing systematic and testable theories out of studies that have been conducted by others. I establish the plausible linkage of modernity and domination in the process of "discovering" the sub-rosa theme of discipline in Weber's historical and comparative studies. I sketch a counter-theory of democratic control by reconstructing Weber's seldom noted text on sect religion, and I qualify this optimism by making explicit and coherent the latent theory of irresponsibility and flight from the world found in his essays on vocation. My effort to deepen the cultural dimension of sociological theory—and, indeed, to argue for the empirical importance of contemporary symbolic codes—begins from a radical reinterpretation of the phases and meaning of Durkheim's intellectual career.

In the lengthy first essay of this collection, I develop an explicit justification for this merging of history and systematics. This mode seems peculiar for social science, I suggest, only from a normative perspective that takes natural science practice as our proximate goal. It is not peculiar, however, in any empirical sense; indeed, merging is normal and typical of actual social science practice. This is not because the goals of social science are any less rational than those of the physical sciences. The latter's self-consciously empirical focus masks but does not neutralize the more general metaphysical commitments that lie beneath. Social science is different, not because it is less rational, but because it is less consensual. Endemic disagreement makes nonempirical commitments much more visible. These disagreements occur explicitly at every level of generality, and in the process social science often takes the form of discursive argument, rather than empirical explanation.

Discourse demands adjudicating standards that are both outside of itself and more consensual than any empirical reference can be. This is where the classics come in. Works become classics by the virtue of the consensual admiration they engender. Disputation about the meaning of these classics has at least some chance of being understood by other members of the disciplinary community. To argue successfully vis-à-vis a classic, therefore, has much the same impact as having argued about the nature of empirical reality itself.

This is the functional reason for the centrality of the classics. There are intellectual reasons as well. Sociological insight is an unevenly distributed gift; it must be preserved as surely as classical works of art. The thinkers we have designated as classical sociologists powerfully illuminated the dangers of modernity; we return to them also, however, to assess modernity's strengths. It is in classical sociology that the case for structural domination in contemporary life is most indelibly made; yet it is to the great classical works that we return to qualify this structural approach in subjective and cultural ways. If we are to embrace both structure and meaning, there is no better way to begin than by rethinking the achievements and limits of our classical works.

RESOURCES

Alexander, Jeffrey C. 1988a. *Action and Its Environments*. New York: Columbia University Press.

——1988b. "The New Theoretical Movement." In Neil J. Smelser, ed., *Handbook for Sociology*. Los Angeles and London: Sage.

Rawls, John. 1971. *A Theory of Justice*. MA: Harvard University Press.

Walzer, Michael. 1983. *Spheres of Justice*. New York: Basic Books.

Sociology and Discourse:
On the Centrality of the Classics

The relationship between social science and the classics is a question which opens up the deepest issues not only in sociology but in the human sciences more generally.

In the essay which follows I argue for the centrality of the classics in contemporary social science. This position is challenged from what, at first glance, appear to be two entirely different camps. Among social science practitioners, of course, there has always been skepticism toward "the classics." For those of the positivist persuasion, indeed, the very question of the relation between social science and the classics leads immediately to another, namely, whether there should be any relationship at all. Why do disciplines which profess to be oriented to the empirical world and to the accumulation of objective knowledge about it need recourse to texts by writers who are long dead and gone? According to the canons of empiricism, after all, whatever is scientifically relevant in these texts should long ago have been either verified and incorporated into contemporary theory, or falsified and cast into the dustbin of history.

Yet it is not only "hard" positivists who argue against interrelating the interpretation of the classics and contemporary social science; it is humanists as well. Recently there has emerged a powerful argument against the injection of contemporary concerns into the consideration of classical texts. Classical texts, so this argument goes (e.g., Skinner 1969), must be considered in historical terms. This historicist position on the classics

Steve Seidman, David Sciulli, Mark Gould, and Charles Lemert provided helpful comments on earlier drafts.

converges with the empiricist, insofar as both camps argue against inter-mingling the concerns of contemporary social science with the discussion of historical texts.

To answer the question about the relation between social science and the classics, then, one must think about exactly what empirical social science is and how it relates to the science of nature. One must also think about what it means to analyze the classics and about what relation this kind of presumptively historical activity might have to the pursuit of contemporary scientific knowledge.

Before taking these questions up, however, I will offer a pointed defi-nition of just what a classic is. Classics are earlier works of human exploration which are given a privileged status vis-a-vis contemporary explorations in the same field. The concept of privileged status means that contemporary practitioners of the discipline in question believe that they can learn as much about their field through understanding this earlier work as they can from the work of their own contemporaries. To be accorded such a privileged status, moreover, implies that, in the day-to-day work of the average practitioner, this deference is accorded without prior demonstration; it is accepted as a matter of course that, as a classic, this work establishes fundamental criteria in the particular field. It is because of this privileged position that exegesis and reinterpretation of classics—within or without a historical context—become conspicuous currents in various disciplines, for what is perceived to be the "true meaning" of a classical work has broad repercussions. Western theologians have taken the Bible as their classic text, as have those who practice the Judeo-Christian religious disciplines. For students of English literature, Shakespeare is undoubtedly the author whose work embodies the highest standards in their field. For 500 years, Aristotle and Plato have been accorded a classical status in political theory.

The Empiricist Challenge
to the Centrality of the Classics

What stimulates the argument against the classics' centrality from the side of social science seems obvious enough. As I have defined the term, the genre of "classics" does not exist today in the natural sciences. Whitehead ([1917] 1974:115), certainly one of the most sophisticated philosophers of science in this century, wrote that "a science which hesitates to forget its founders is lost." This pronouncement seems undeniably true, insofar, at least, as science is taken in its Anglo-American sense as equivalent to *Naturwissenschaft*. As an historian of science has observed, "every college freshman knows more physics than Galileo knew, whose claim is higher than any other's to the honor of having founded modern science, and more too than Newton did, whose mind was the most powerful ever to have addressed itself to nature" (Gillispie 1960:8).

This fact is undeniable. The problem is what does it mean? For adherents to the positivist persuasion, it means that in the long run social science must do without the classics as well. And in the short run, attention to the classics must be severely delimited. They should be mined simply for empirical information. Exegesis and commentary— which are the sure marks of privileged status—have no place in the social sciences. These conclusions are based on two presumptions. The first is that the absence of classical texts in natural science indicates the latter's purely empirical status; the second is that natural and social science are basically the same. I will argue below that neither of these presumptions is true. Before doing so, however, I will examine in a more systematic way the empiricist argument which they inform.

In an influential essay Merton ([1947] 1967:1–38) argued against what he called the merging of the history and systematics of sociological theory. His model for systematic theorizing was the natural sciences. It consisted, apparently, of codifying empirical knowledge and constructing covering laws. What is systematic about scientific theory is that it tests covering laws through experimental procedures and, thereby, steadily accumulates true knowledge. Insofar as accumulation occurs, there is no need for classical texts. "The severest test of truly cumulative knowledge," Merton ([1947] (1967:27) argues, "is that run-of-the-mill minds can solve problems today which great minds could not begin to solve earlier." In a real science, therefore, the "commemoration of the great contributors of the past is substantially reserved to the history of the discipline" (p. 28). Investigation of earlier figures is an historical activity which has nothing to do with scientific work. This is a job for historians, not social scientists. This radical distinction between science and history is dramatically contrasted by Merton (p. 28) with the situation which holds in the humanities, where "by direct contrast, each classical work—each poem, drama, novel, essay, or historical work—tends to remain a part of the direct experience of succeeding generations."

While Merton acknowledges (p. 29) that sociologists are "poised between the physical and life scientists and the humanists," his prescription for a position closer to the natural sciences is clear enough. He (pp. 28–29) invokes Weber's confident assertion that "in science, each of us knows that what he has accomplished will be antiquated in ten, twenty, fifty years" and Weber's insistence that "every scientific [contribution] asks to be 'surpassed' and outdated." That, fifty years after Weber's death, neither Weber's sociological theories nor his assertions about science had actually been "surpassed" is an irony which, it seems, passes Merton by. To the contrary, he insists that while sociology's intermediate position between science and humanities may be a fact, it must not be made into a normative position. "Efforts to straddle scientific and humanistic orientations typically lead to merging the systematics of sociological theory with its history" (p. 29), a merging which, for Merton, is tantamount to making the accumulation of empirical knowledge impossible. The problem, from Merton's point of view, is that sociologists are cross-pressured, a structural position which typically leads to deviance from legitimate role expectations. Most sociologists succumb to these pressures and develop deviant roles. They "oscillate" between social science and humanities. Only a few are able to "adapt to these pressures by acting wholly the scientific role" (p. 29).

It is deviance (my term, not Merton's) from the scientific role which leads to what Merton calls the "intellectually degenerative tendencies" (p. 30) that merge systematics with history. An attempt at what might be called historical systematics is degenerate because—precisely in the sense in which I have defined a "classic"—it privileges earlier work. One finds a "reverence" for "illustrious ancestors" and an emphasis on "exegesis" (p. 30). Worst of all, because erudition becomes important to understanding the meaning of earlier, often difficult works, one finds an emphasis on "erudition versus originality." Merton does not characterize erudite investigation into classical texts as interpretation. To do so, I believe, would imply that such investigation involves a creative theoretical element which is generative (as opposed to degenerative) in the contemporary scientific sense. Generativity would contradict the slavish attitude toward earlier works which Merton sees as inherent in the historical investigation of classical texts, for it is not just reverence but "uncritical reverence" (p. 30) which he believes to be involved.* Interpretation and the creativity it implies would also contradict the mechanistic epistemology which under-girds his argument. For Merton historical systematics simply provide contemporaries with mirrors in which earlier texts are reflected. They are "critical summaries" (pp. 2, 4), "mere commentary" (pp. 30, 35), "largely sterile exegesis" (p. 30), "chronologically ordered set[s] of critical syno-poses of doctrine" (p. 35; cf. p. 9).

Earlier texts, Merton insists, simply should not be looked at in this "deplorably useless" (p. 30) way. He offers two alternatives, one from the side of systematics, the other from the side of history. From the point of view of social science, he argues that earlier texts must be treated in a utilitarian rather than classical way. True, the present situation is not ideal—there has not been the kind of empirical accumulation which social science has every right to expect. Rather than dwelling on this situation, however, the proper response is to convert now classic texts into simple sources of data and/or untested theories, that is, to make them into vehicles for further accumulation. They must be treated as sources of "previously unretrieved information" which can be "usefully employed as new points of departure" (p. 35). Such texts can then point toward the scientific future rather than the humanistic past. In this way, the study of earlier texts can itself become scientific. By "following up and developing theoretical leads" (p. 30), it can be devoted to "retrieving relevant cumu-lative knowledge . . . and incorporating it in subsequent formulations" (p. 35).

The alternative to merging from the point of view of history is, in fact, not much different. Rather than using texts as mines of unretrieved information, the texts can be studied as historical documents in them-selves. Once again, the point here is to avoid textual exegesis. "A genuine *history* of sociological theory," Merton (p. 35; italics in original) writes, "must deal with the interplay between theory and such matters as the

---

*Such a fawning, demeaning attitude to classical authors—the full quote is "uncritical reverence toward almost any statement made by illustrious ancestors" (Merton 1967:30)—must be sharply distinguished from the deference and privileged status which accrue to classics according to the definition I have offered above. I will argue below that while deference defines the formal attitude, continuous critique and reconstruction are what the real substance of historical systematics is all about. Merton's extremism on this matter is typical of those who deny the relevance of classical investigations to social science, for it views these investigations as antiscientific and uncritical.

social origins and statuses of its exponents, the changing social organization of sociology, the changes that diffusion brings to ideas, and their relations to the environing social and cultural structure." It is the environment of the ideas, not the ideas themselves, which a good historian of social science should study. The historian's aims, it is assumed, are fully as empirical as those of the sociological, who studies the same texts for the purposes of accumulation. Merton's rejection of the merging of science and history, then, is based not only on the demand for scientific sociology but for scientific history as well.

The first assumption upon which the empiricist challenge to the centrality of the classics depends is that the absence of classics in natural science stems from its empirical and cumulative nature; the second is that in these respects social and natural science are basically the same. In Merton's essay against the merging of history and systematics, the empiricist perspective on natural science is an unstated assumption. His account of the history of science is a purely progressive one. Rather than a relativistic and historical treatment of earlier scientific texts, which in the spirit of post-Kuhnian sensibilities emphasizes the formative power of suprascientific cultural and intellectual frameworks, Merton (pp. 8–27) looks on earlier work as a series of "anticipations," "adumbrations," and "prediscoveries" of what is known in the present day. We know, moreover, from Merton's systematic protocols for the sociology of science (e.g., Merton [1942] 1973) that this impression is not a mistake. For Merton, disciplinary and methodological commitments are the only nonempirical factors which impinge on scientific work, and neither of these is conceived as having any direct effect on scientific cognition of the object world.

That in its primarily empirical referent social science resembles natural science is the other fundamental assumption upon which Merton's argument rests. This second point, however, is a little more difficult for Merton to make. We know from his essay on middle range theory (Merton 1967:39–72)—which, not incidentally, immediately follows the work on the merging of history and systematics in Merton's collection, *Social Theory and Social Structure*—that Merton does not view social science as paradigm-bound in Kuhn's sense. Because it is problem rather than paradigm driven, social science is organized by empirical specialty rather than by school or tradition. But why, if sociologists are empiricists, do they straddle science and the humanities? Why, moreover, do they merge history and systematics if they are not intent on forming and sustaining schools? As I have earlier suggested, even while Merton acknowledges these unavoidable facts he insists they are deviant anomalies, not inherent tendencies. Insisting that "sociology adopts the orientation and practice of the physical sciences," he claims (pp. 29–31) that social science "research moves from the frontiers advanced by the cumulative work of past generations."

Indeed, despite the degenerate tendency for engaging in what I have called historical systematics, Merton believes that our knowledge about how to study the history of scientific thought is itself scientific and cumulative! He employs the terminology of progressive science—adumbration, prediscovery, anticipation—to make his case for the right kind of progressive scientific history. Arguing against progressive histories which rest only upon the formal, published descriptions of scientific work, he suggests (pp. 4–6) that such accounts rest on a conception of history which "lags extraordinarily far behind long-recognized reality." It was Bacon who first "observed" that the process of objective discovery is more creative and intuitive than the formal logic of scientific proof suggests. That there have been independent discoveries of this fact must confirm it—"perceptive minds have repeatedly and, it would seem, independently made the same kind of observation." The scientific theory which covers, or explains, these empirical observations has developed in due course—"this observation has been generalized" by later thinkers. It is because this empirical logic has held that Merton is confident that the history of science will make inevitable progress—"the failure of sociology to distinguish between the history and systematics of theory will eventually be wiped out."

These are the basic assumptions of Merton's (now classic?) argument against the centrality of the classics. There seems, however, to be a third, auxiliary one as well, one which is implied by the two central assumptions rather than standing on its own. This is the notion that the meaning of significant earlier texts is there for all to see. I have shown how in condemning historical systematics Merton characterizes it as producing merely summarizing synopsis. I have also demonstrated how the sociological history he prefers will focus on the environment of scientific theories rather than on the nature of the ideas themselves. This inclination, by the way, is also found in the challenge to the centrality of the classics, which has been issued by the humanities—a challenge I will consider in due course below.

In the section which immediately follows, however, I direct my argument against the empiricist challenge to the centrality of classical texts and the two central assumptions upon which it rests.

The Positivist View of Science

The argument against the centrality of the classics assumes that to the degree a discipline is empirical it will be cumulative, and to the degree it is cumulative it will not produce classics. I will argue, to the contrary, that whether a discipline has classics depends not on its empiricism but upon the consensus within that discipline about nonempirical things.

In *Theoretical Logic in Sociology* (Alexander 1982a:5–15), I suggested that the positivist persuasion in the social sciences rests on four major postulates. The first is that a radical, epistemological break exists between empirical observations, which are held to be specific and concrete, and nonempirical statements, which are held to be general and abstract. Only because this break is taken for granted can the second postulate be made: more general and abstract concerns—philosophical or metaphysical ones —do not have fundamental significance for the practice of an empirically-oriented discipline. Third, questions which are of a generalized, abstract, and theoretical nature can be evaluated only in relation to empirical observations. This suggests that, whenever possible, theory should be stated in propositional form and, further, that theoretical conflicts are decided through empirical tests and crucial experiments. Finally, because these first three postulates supply no ground for structured scientific disagreement, the fourth postulate suggests, scientific development is "progressive," that is, linear and cumulative. Differentiation in a scientific field, then, is taken to be the product of specialization in different empirical domains rather than the result of generalized, nonempirical disagreement about how to explain the same empirical domain.

While these four postulates still accurately reflect the common sense of most practicing social scientists—especially those of the American variety —they have been sharply challenged by the new wave of postpositivist philosophy, history, and, indeed, sociology of natural science which has emerged over the last two decades (Alexander 1982a:18–33). Whereas the postulates of the positivist persuasion effectively reduce theory to fact, those of the postpositivist position rehabilitate the theoretical.

1. The empirical data of science is theoretically informed. The fact/theory distinction is neither epistemological nor ontological, that is, a distinction between nature and thought. It is an analytical distinction. As Lakatos (e.g., 1969:156) has written, describing some statements as observations is a manner of speech, not an ontological reference. *Observations* refers to statements informed by those theories about which we feel the most certainty.

2. Scientific commitments are not based solely on empirical evidence. As Polyani (e.g., 1958:92) convincingly demonstrates, the principled rejection of evidence is the very bedrock upon which the continuity of science depends.

3. General, theoretical elaboration is normally dogmatic and horizontal rather than skeptical and progressive. The more generalized the claim, the less Popper's falsification theorem holds. Theoretical formulation does not proceed, as Popper ([1934] 1959:42) would then have it, according to the law of "the fiercest struggle for survival." To the contrary, when a general theoretical position is confronted with contradictory empirical evidence which cannot be ignored, it proceeds to develop ad hoc hypotheses and residual categories (Lakatos 1969:168–176). In this manner, new phenomena can be "explained" without surrendering the general formulations.

4. Fundamental shifts in scientific belief occur only when empirical changes are matched by the availability of convincing theoretical alternatives. Because such theoretical shifts are often in the background, they are less visible to those engaged in scientific work. It is for this reason that empirical data give the appearance of being concretely induced rather than analytically constructed. In truth, however, as Holton (1973:26, 190) observes, the struggle between general theoretical commitments is "among the most powerful energizers of empirical research," and it must be placed "at the heart of major changes in the natural sciences."

If generalized, nonempirical considerations play such a decisive role, then Merton's first assumption—about the character of natural science—does not hold. Neither, in my view, does his second, for in crucial respects the practices of social and natural science are not particularly alike. This conclusion may seem surprising. Once we have established the nonempirical dimension of natural science, it might seem that the status of classical works would be unchallenged. The fact remains, however, that natural science does not have recourse to classics. The challenge is to explain this fact in a nonempiricist way.

Why There Are No Classics in Natural Science: A Postpositivist View

The epistemology of science does not determine the particular topics to which scientific activity is allocated in any given scientific discipline. Yet, it is precisely the allocation of such activity which is responsible for any discipline's relative empirical "feel." Thus, even outspoken anti-empiricists have acknowledged that an explicit focus on empirical questions is what distinguishes natural from human sciences.[1] For example, while Holton has painstakingly demonstrated that arbitrary, supra-empirical "themata" affect modern physics, he (1973:330–331, italics added) insists that it has never been his intention to argue for the introduction of "thematic discussions . . . into the *practice* of science itself." He suggests, indeed, that "only when such questions were ruled out of place in a laboratory did science begin to grow rapidly." Even the forthrightly idealist philosopher Collingwood (1940:33), who has insisted that scientific practice rests upon metaphysical assumptions, allows that "the scientist's business is not to propound them but only to presuppose them."

The allocation of scientific activity depends upon what is considered by practitioners to be scientifically problematic. Because in the modern era natural scientists tend to agree about the generalized commitments which inform their craft, it is more empirical questions which usually receive their explicit attention. This, of course, is precisely what allows "normal science," in Kuhn's phrase (1970), to proceed as an activity of empirical puzzle solving and specific problem solutions. Taking normal science to characterize natural science as such, Habermas (1971:91), too, has identified consensus as what differentiates "scientific" as compared to "nonscientific" activity.

We term information scientific if and only if an uncompelled and permanent consensus can be obtained with regard to its validity . . . The genuine achievement of modern science does not consist primarily in producing truth, that is, correct and cogent statements about what we call reality. Rather, it distinguishes itself from traditional categories of knowledge by a method of arriving at an uncompelled and permanent consensus of this sort about our views.

Only if there is disagreement about the background assumptions which inform a science do these nonempirical issues come explicitly into play. Kuhn calls this a paradigm crisis. It is in such crises, he believes, that there is "recourse to philosophy and to debate over fundamentals."

It is because attention is usually directed to the empirical dimensions of natural science that classics are absent. The nonempirical dimensions are camouflaged, and it appears that speculative hypotheses can be decided by reference either to sense data which are relatively accessible or to theories whose specificity makes their relevance to such data immediately apparent. Classics, by contrast, imply a privileged position for earlier theories. Earlier theories, not just contemporary ones, are seen as having explanatory status; indeed, classical texts often are considered to be capable of supplying relevant data as well. My point is that natural science is no less apriori than its social counterpart. A nonapriori, purely empirical stance is not the explanation for "classic-less" natural science. Rather, it is a matter of the form which the mixture of prior and contingent knowledge takes.

Thus, rather than classics, natural science has what Kuhn called exemplars. With this term, Kuhn (1970:182) means concrete examples of successful empirical work—examples of the kind of powerful problem solutions which define paradigmatic fields. While exemplars embody metaphysical and nonempirical commitments of various kinds, in themselves they are models of how specifically to explain the world. Of necessity, they include definitions and concepts, but they direct those who study them to questions of operationalization and technique. Yet for all their specificity, exemplars themselves play an apriori role. They are learned in textbooks and laboratories before neophytes are capable of testing for themselves whether or not they are really true. They are, in other words, internalized because of their privileged position in the socialization process rather than because of their scientific validity. The learning processes are the same in social science; what is different is that social scientists internalize classics at least as often as they internalize exemplars.

The Postpositivist Case for the Classics

The ratio of exemplars to classics is so much different in social science because in its social application science produces so much more disagreement. Because there is persistent and widespread disagreement, the more general background assumptions which remain implicit and relatively invisible in natural science here come vividly into play.* The conditions which Kuhn defines for paradigm crisis in the natural sciences are routine in the social. I am not suggesting that there is no "objective" knowledge in the social sciences, nor even that there is no possibility for successful predictions or covering laws. It is possible, it seems to me, to gain real cumulative knowledge about the world from within different and competing points of view, and even to sustain relatively predictive covering laws from within general orientations which differ in substantial ways. What I am suggesting, however, is that the conditions of social science make consistent agreement about the precise nature of empirical knowledge— let alone agreement about explanatory covering laws—highly unlikely. In social science, therefore, arguments about scientific truth do not refer only to the empirical level. They cut across the full range of nonempirical commitments which sustain competing points of view.

There are cognitive and evaluative reasons for the vast differences in level of consensus. I will mention here only the most fundamental.†

1. Insofar as the objects of a science are located in the physical world outside of the human mind, its empirical referents can, in principle, more easily be verified through interpersonal communication. In social science, where the objects are either mental states or conditions in which mental states are embedded, the possibility for confusing mental states of the scientific observer with mental states of those observed is endemic.

2. Resistance to simple agreement on empirical referents emerges from the distinctive evaluative nature of social science as well. There is a symbiotic relationship between description and evaluation. The findings

---

*Mannheim (1936:102–03) puts this distinction well: "No one denies the possibility of empirical research nor does anyone maintain that facts do not exist . . . We, too, appeal to 'facts' for our proof, but the question of the nature of facts is in itself a considerable problem. They exist for the mind always in an intellectual and social context. That they can be understood and formulated implies already the existence of a conceptual apparatus. And if this conceptual apparatus is the same for all the members of a group, the presuppositions (i.e., the possible social and intellectual values), which underlie the individual concepts, never become perceptible . . . However, once the unanimity is broken, the fixed categories which used to give experience its reliable and coherent character undergo an inevitable disintegration. There arise divergent and conflicting modes of thought which (unknown to the thinking subject) order the same facts of experience into different systems of thought, and cause them to be perceived through different logical categories."

†For a sophisticated and detailed review of the differences between natural and social science in an axiomatic form, see Sztompka 1979:60–64.

of social science often carry significant implications for the desireable organization and reorganization of social life. In natural science, by contrast, "changes in the content of science do not usually imply changes in social structures" (Hagstrom 1965:285). The ideological implications of social science redound to the very descriptions of the objects of investigation themselves. Often, the very characterization of states of mind or institutions—e.g., Is society called "capitalist" or "industrial"? Has there been "proletarianization," "individuation," or "atomization"?—reflects an estimation of the implication, for political values, of an explanation of a phenomenon that is yet to occur. While Mannheim overestimated evaluative as opposed to cognitive assumptions, he was certainly sensitive to this point. Every definition, he (1936:196–97) wrote, "depends necessarily upon one's perspective, i.e., it contains within itself the whole system of thought representing the position of the thinker in question and especially the political evaluations which lie behind this system of thought." His conclusion, in this regard, seems accurate: "The very way in which a concept is defined and the nuance in which it is employed already embody to a certain degree a prejudgment concerning the outcome of the chain of ideas built upon it."

   3. Needless to say, insofar as it is difficult, for cognitive and evaluative reasons, to gain consensus about even the simple empirical referents of social science, about the abstractions from such concrete referents which form the substance of social theory there will be even less. Hagstrom suggests (1965:256–58) that possibilities for scientific consensus significantly depend upon the degree of quantification that is consistent with the discipline's scientific goals. Insofar as empirical referents are not clear and abstractions subject to constant dispute, efforts to mathematicize social science can only be efforts at disguising or promoting particular points of view.

   4. Insofar as neither empirical referents nor covering laws generate agreement, the full range of nonempirical inputs to empirical perception become objects of debate. Because there is such endemic disagreement, moreover, social science will invariably be differentiated by traditions (Shils 1970) and schools (Tiryakian 1979). For most members of the social scientific community, moreover, it is apparent that such "extra-scientific" cultural and institutional phenomena are not simply manifestations of disagreement but bases upon which scientific disagreements are

promoted and sustained. This realization further sensitizes social scientists to the nonempirical dimensions of their field.

For all of these reasons, discourse—not just explanation—becomes a major feature of the social science field. By discourse, I refer to modes of argument which are more consistently generalized and speculative than are normal scientific discussions. The latter are directed in a more disciplined manner to specific pieces of empirical evidence, to inductive and deductive logics, to explanation through covering laws, and to the methods by which these laws can be verified or falsified. Discourse, by contrast, is ratiocinative. It focuses on the process of reasoning rather than the results of immediate experience, and it becomes significant when there is no plain and evident truth. Discourse seeks persuasion through argument rather than prediction. Its persuasiveness is based on such qualities as logical coherence, expansiveness of scope, interpretive insight, value relevance, rhetorical force, beauty, and texture of argument.*

Foucault (1973) identifies intellectual, scientific and political practices as "discourses" in order to deny their merely empirical, inductive status. In this way, he insists that practical activities are historically constituted and shaped by metaphysical understandings that can define an entire epoch. Sociology, too, is a discursive field. Still, one finds here little of the homogeneity that Foucault attributes to such fields; in social science, there are discourses, not a discourse. These discourses are not, moreover,

---

*Thus, in their vigorous defense of the contemporary empirical relevance of Parsonian sociology, Holton and Turner (1986) insist on the need to confront, through interpretion and criticism, the mass of secondary discussion of Parsons, which obviously is not directly empirical: "The aim of . . . this book [is] to offer a defence, where necessary, against criticism which is often spurious and finally to indicate aspects of [Parsons'] sociology which are of enduring importance to the social sciences" (p. 183). They explain their own goal as critical in turn, and they define criticism in a discursive manner. "Criticism is ultimately concerned with what can be said and hence with the coherence, scope and presuppositions of any discourse. To discourse is to move backwards and forwards. To criticise discourse is to ask whether any theoretical movement is valid. The validity of any argument has to do with consistency between primary assumptions and the conclusions drawn from them . . . We may accept the assumptions of a theory, but argue that the conclusions are incompatible with its assumptions; the argument is thus internally inconsistent and the critique is internalist. We may argue that theory is perfectly consistent with its presuppositions but reject the theory because we cannot accept the initial premises; the theory is incompatible with a set of preferred assumptions and the critique is externalist. To criticise is to uncover the crisis . . . which threatens to disrupt the flow of a discourse, in terms of conditions which are neither internal or external" (pp. 182–183).

closely linked to the legitimation of power, as Foucault in his later work increasingly claimed. Social scientific discourses are aimed at truth, and they are constantly subjected to rational stipulations about how truth can be arrived at and what that truth might be. Here I draw upon Habermas' (e.g., 1984) understanding of discourse as part of an effort that speakers make at achieving undistorted communication. If Habermas underestimates the irrational qualities of communication, let alone action (see essay 7, below), he certainly has provided a way to conceptualize its rational aspirations. His systematic attempts to identify modes of argument and criteria for arriving at persuasive justification show how rational commitments and the recognition of supra-empirical arguments can be combined. Between the rationalizing discourse of Habermas and the arbitrary discourse of Foucault—this is where the actual field of social science discourse uneasily lies.

It is because of the centrality of discourse that theory in the social sciences is so multivalent and that compulsive efforts (e.g., Wallace 1983) to follow the logic of natural science are so misguided. Followers of the positivist persuasion sense the tension between such a multivalent conception and their empiricist point of view. To resolve it they try to privilege "theory" over "metatheory," indeed, to exclude theory in favor of "explanation" narrowly conceived. Thus, complaining that "far too much social theory consists of the history of ideas and general hero worship of Marx, Weber, [and] Durkheim," Turner (1986:974) argues for "doing theory as opposed to . . . providing yet another metatheoretical analysis of the early theoretical masters."* And Stinchcombe (1968:3, italics added) describes Marx, Durkheim, and Weber as "those great *empirical* analysts . . . who did not work mainly at what we now call *theory*." He insists that they "worked out *explanations* of the growth of capitalism, or of class conflict, or of primitive religion." Rather than being concerned with discursive theory, in his view, "they used a wide variety of theoretical *methods*."

*This pejorative characterization of metatheory as hero worship recalls Merton's (1967:30) claim of "uncritical reverence" which I discussed in the note on p. 12. Obsequiousness, of course, is the obverse of scientific skepticism, and it is ultimately in order to deny a scientific role to classical investigations that such negative claims are made. It seems clear, to the contrary, that what I earlier called historical systematics consists of the critical reconstruction of classical theories. Ironically, empiricists like Turner and Merton are able to gain some legitimacy for their accusations because such reconstruction does, in fact, often occur within a framework which explicitly denies any critical ambition. I will try to account for this "naive attitude" of participants in classical debate in the section which follows.

These distinctions, however, seem more like "utopian" efforts to escape from social science than real efforts to understand it. Generalized discourse is central, and theory is inherently multivalent. Indeed, the centrality of discourse and the conditions which produce it make for the overdetermination of social science by theory and its underdetermination by fact. Because there is no clear, indisputable reference for the elements which compose social science, there is no neat translatability between different levels of generality. Formulations at one level do not ramify in clear-cut ways for the other levels of scientific concern. For example, while precise empirical measurements of two variable correlations can sometimes be established, it is rarely possible for such a correlation to prove or disprove a proposition about this interrelationship which is stated in more general terms. The reason is that the existence of empirical and ideological dissensus allows social scientists to operationalize propositions in a variety of different ways.*

Let us briefly consider, for example, two of the best recent efforts to move from data to more general theory. In Blau's attempt to test his newly developed structural theory, for example, he starts with a proposition he calls the size theorem—the notion that a purely ecological variable, group size, determines outgroup relations (Blau, Blum, and Schwartz 1982:46). Drawing from a data set that establishes not only a group's size but its rate of intermarriage, he argues that a relationship between intermarriage rates and group size verifies the size theorem. Why? Because the data demonstrate that "group size and the proportion outmarried are inversely related" (p. 47). But outmarriage is a datum that does not, in fact, operationalize "outgroup relations." It is one type of outgroup relation among many others, and as Blau himself acknowledges at one point in his argument it is a type into which enter factors other than group size. Outgroup relation, in other words, does not have a clear-cut referent. Because of this, the correlation between what is taken to be its indicator and group size cannot verify the general proposition about the relation between group size and outgroup relations. Blau's empirical data, then, are disarticulated from his theory, despite this effort to link them in a theoretically decisive way.

In Lieberson's (1980) ambitious study of black and white immigrants to the U.S. since 1880, similar problems emerge. He begins with the less

*For a powerful demonstration of the inevitability of empirical underdetermination which is tied to an historical indictment of contemporary quantitative work, see S. Turner 1987.

formally stated proposition that the "heritage of slavery" is responsible for the different economic achievement levels of black and European immigrants. In order to operationalize this proposition, Lieberson takes two steps. First, he defines heritage in terms of "lack of opportunity" for former slaves, rather than in cultural terms. Second, he operationalizes "opportunity" in terms of the data he has developed about varying rates of education and residential segregation. Finding a correlation between these rates and differential economic achievement, he concludes that his proposition has been tested and proved. But has it? Both Lieberson's definition and his operationalization are highly contestable. Other social scientists might not only define the heritage of slavery in very different terms, but also conceive of opportunities in ways other than education and residence. As a result, no necessary empirical relationship exists between these three elements (heritage, opportunity, and rates), so it is uncertain that Lieberson's data demonstrate the more general proposition. The rates and the measured correlation, of course, stand on their own as "facts." These data, however, cannot test the theory at which they are aimed. This is the overdetermination of "theory" by "facts."

It is far easier to find examples of the contrasting problem, the overdetermination of empirical "facts" by theory. In virtually every broader, more theoretically gauged study, the sampling of empirical data is open to dispute. In *The Protestant Ethic and the Spirit of Capitalism,* for example, Weber's ([1904–5] 1958) operationalization of "capitalism" via seventeenth- and eighteenth-century English entrepreneurs has been widely disputed. If the Italian businessmen in the early modern city states were also capitalists, then Weber's correlation between capitalist and Puritan is based on a restricted sample. If these Italians also manifested the captalist spirit, as Trevor-Roper (1965) once claimed, then an entirely different theory must be advanced. One reason the 'Weber thesis' has never been completely falsified is that, like every other middle range theory, the empirical data it refers to are overselected by its theoretical scheme.

In Smelser's famous study, *Social Change in the Industrial Revolution* (1959), a similar distance between general theory and empirical indicator can be found. In his theory, Smelser argues that shifts in familial role divisions, not industrial upheavals per se, were responsible for the radical protest activities by English workers which developed in the 1820s. In his narrative historical account, Semlser describes fundamental shifts in family structure as having occurred in the sequence he has suggested. His specific presentations of archival data (Smelser 1959:188–99) seem to indicate, however, that these family disturbances did not develop until one or two decades later. Smelser's theoretical concern with the family overdetermined the presentation of his narrative history (and his archival data underdetermined his theory in turn.)*

In Skocpol's (1979) more recent effort at documenting an historical and comparative theory, the same kind of overdetermination is exercised by a very different theory. Her search is for the empirical data of revolution, and the only apriori she acknowledges is her commitment to the comparative method (pp. 33–40). At the same time, she announces early in the book (p. 18) that she proposes to take an "impersonal and nonsubjective viewpoint" on revolutions, which gives causal significance only to "the institutionally determined situations and relations of groups." Not surprisingly, what Skocpol finds in her subsequent empirical investigation are, for the most part, material and "structural" causes for revolution. Residual categories, however, do manage to poke through. When she acknowledges at various points that local traditions and rights do play a role (e.g., pp. 62, 138), and that political leadership and ideology must (however briefly) be essayed (pp. 161–73), the theoretical overdetermination of her data becomes apparent. Her structural presuppositions have led her to leave out of her account of relevant data the entire intellectual and cultural contest of revolution.†

Empirical underdetermination and theoretical overdetermination go hand in hand. From the most specific factual statements up to the most abstract generalizations, social science is essentially contestable. Every conclusion is open to argumentation by reference to supraempirical considerations. Here is the specifically social-scientific version of the thematization which, Habermas (1984) has shown, must lay behind every effort at rational argument.

Every kind of social scientific statement is subject to the demand for justification by reference to general principles. In other words, I need not —and social scientists as a community simply will not—limit an argu-

---

*It demonstrates Smelser's conscientiousness as an historical researcher that he himself presented data that, as it were, went beyond his own theory. (Walby [1986] relies on Smelser's data, for example, in her Marxist-feminist reconstuction of the same period.) This is not usually the case, for the overdetermination of data by theory usually makes countervailing data invisible, not only to social scientists themselves but often to their critics.

†Sewell (1985) has forcefully demonstrated this gap in Skocpol's data for the French case.

ment against Blau to an empirical demonstration that structural considerations are only one of several which determine outmarriage; I can,
instead, demonstrate that the very stipulation of such structural causation
rests upon presuppositions about action which are of an excessively rationalistic kind. In considering Lieberson's work I can bracket the empirical question of the relation between education and objective opportunity
in a similar way. Instead, I can try to suggest through discursive argument that Lieberson's exclusive focus on the heritage of slavery reflects
ideological considerations and a prior commitment to models generated
by conflict theory. In turn, Smelser's work can be effectively criticized in
terms of logical adequacy or by demonstrating that his early functionalist
model overemphasizes socialization. And Skocpol's argument—without
any reference to empirical material—can be negatively evaluated for the
implausible manner in which it limits "purposive theories," which she
applauds, to the instrumental model of purposive-rationality her theory
implies.

To make such arguments—indeed, merely to engage in the kind of
discussion I have just employed—is to engage in discourse, not explanation. As Seidman (1986) has emphasized, discourse does not imply the
abandonment of claims to truth. Truth claims, after all, need not be
limited to the criterion of testable empirical validity (Habermas 1984).
Each level of supraempirical discourse has embedded within it distinctive
criteria of truth. These criteria go beyond empirical adequacy to claims
about the nature and consequences of presuppositions, the stipulation and
adequacy of models, the consequences of ideologies, the meta-implica-
tions of models, and the connotations of definitions. Insofar as they
become explicit, they are efforts, in short, to rationalize and systematize
the intuitively grasped complexities of social analysis and social life.
Current disputes between interpretive and causal methodologies, utilitarian and normative conceptions of action, equilibrium and conflict models
of societies, radical and conservative theories of change—these are far
more than empirical arguments. They reflect efforts by sociologists to
articulate criteria for evaluating the "truth" of different nonempirical
domains.

It is no wonder that the discipline's response to important works bears
so little resemblance to the neat and confined responses that advocates of
the "logic of science" suggest. Skocpol's *States and Social Revolutions,*
for example, has been evaluated at every level of the sociological contin-

uum. The book's presuppositions, ideology, model, method, definitions, concepts and, yes, even its facts have been clarified, disputed, and praised in turn. At stake are the truth criteria Skocpol has employed to justify her positions at each of these levels. Very little of the response to this work has involved controlled testing of its hypotheses or the reanalysis of its data. Decisions about the validity of Skocpol's structural approach to revolution certainly will not be decided on these grounds.[2]

At the beginning of this section, I suggested that the proportion of classics to contemporaries is so much greater in social than natural science because endemic disagreement makes the background assumptions of social science more explicit. It is this obvious quality of background assumptions, in turn, that makes discourse so central a quality of social scientific debate. What remains is to explain why this discursive form of argument so often takes a "classical" turn. The existence of generalized, nonempirical debate does not logically imply any privileged position for earlier works. Nonetheless, the very conditions which make discourse so prominent also make the classics central. There are two reasons for this centrality, the functional and the intellectual, or scientific.

Because disagreement is so rife in social science, serious problems of mutual understanding arise. Without some baseline of minimal understanding, however, communication is impossible. For disagreement to be possible in a coherent, ongoing, and consistent way, there must be some basis for a cultural relationship. This can exist only if the participants in a disagreement each have a fair idea of what the other is talking about.

This is where the classics come in. The functional necessity for classics develops because of the need for integrating the field of theoretical discourse. By integration, I do not mean cooperation and equilibrium but rather the boundary maintenance, or closure, which allows systems to exist (Luhmann 1984). It is this functional demand that explains the formation of disciplinary boundaries which from an intellectual standpoint often seem arbitrary. It is the disciplines of social science, and the schools and traditions of which they are composed, which have classics.

To mutually acknowledge a classic is to have a common point of reference. A classic reduces complexity (cf. Luhmann 1979). It is a symbol which condenses—"stands for"—a range of diverse general commitments. Condensation, it seems to me, has at least four functional advantages.

In the first place, of course, it simplifies, and thereby facilitates, theoretical discussion. It does so by allowing a very small number of works to substitute for—to represent by a stereotyping or standardizing process—the myriad of finely-graded formulations which are produced in the course of contingent intellectual life. When we discuss in classical terms the central issues which affect social science, we are sacrificing the ability to embrace this finely graded specificity. We gain, however, something very important. By speaking in terms of the classics, we can be relatively confident that those whom we address will at least know whereof we speak, even if they do not recognize in our discussion their own particular and unique position. It is for this reason that if we wish to make a critical analysis of capitalism we will more than likely draw from Marx's work. Similarly, if we wish to evaluate the variety of critical analyses of capitalism which exist today, we will probably typify them by comparing them to Marx's original. Only by doing so can we be relatively confident that others will be able to follow, and perhaps be persuaded by, our ideological and cognitive judgments.

The second functional advantage is that classics allow generalized commitments to be argued without the necessity for making the criteria for their adjudication explicit. Since such criteria are very difficult to formulate, and virtually impossible to gain agreement upon, this concretizing function of the classics is very important. Rather than having to define equilibrium and the nature of systems, one can argue about Parsons, about the relative "functionality" of his early and later works, about whether his theory (whatever that may precisely be) can actually explain conflict in the real world. Or, rather than explicitly exploring the advantages of an affective or normative perspective on human action, one can argue that such a perspective was, in fact, actually taken by Durkheim's most important works.

The third functional advantage is an ironic one. Because a common classical medium of communication is taken for granted, it becomes possible not to acknowledge the existence of generalized discourse at all. Thus, because the importance of the classics is accepted without argument, it is possible for a social scientist to begin an empirical study—in, for example, industrial sociology—by discussing the treatment of labor in Marx's early writings. While it would be quite illegitimate for him to suggest that nonempirical considerations about human nature, let alone utopian speculations about human possibility, form the baseline for industrial sociology, this is precisely what he has implicitly acknowledged by referring to Marx's work.

Finally, because the condensation provided by classics gives them such privileged power, reference to the classics becomes important for purely strategic and instrumental reasons. It is in the immediate self-interest of every ambitious social scientist and every rising school to be legitimated vis-a-vis the classical founders. Even if no genuine concern for the classics exists, they still must be criticized, reread, or rediscovered if the discipline's normative criteria for evaluation are to be challenged anew.

These are the functional, or extrinsic reasons for the privileged status accorded by social science to a small and select number of earlier works. But there are, I believe, intrinsic, genuinely intellectual reasons as well. By intellectual, I mean that certain works are given a classical position because they make a singular and continuing contribution to the science of society. My argument here begins from the proposition that the more generalized a scientific discussion, the less cumulative it can be. Why? Because, while generalized commitments are subject to truth criteria, it is impossible to anchor these criteria in an unequivocal way. Generalized evaluations are sustained less by qualities in the object world—upon which minimum agreement can often be reached—than by the relative tastes and preferences of a particular cultural community. Generalized discourse, then, relies on qualities of personal sensibility—aesthetic, interpretive, philosophical, observational—which are not progressive. In this sense, variations in social science reflect not linear accumulation—an issue which can be calculated temporally—but the essentialy random distribution of human ability.[3] Producing great social science is a gift which, like the capacity for creating great art (cf., Nisbet 1976), varies transhistorically between different societies and different human beings.*

* It is the idiosyncrasy of the capacity for creativity, of course, that is the usual reason cited for the centrality of classics in the arts. In his writing on the formation of canonical literary works, Kermode (1985) has shown that this view attributes too much to accurate information about a work and too little to uninformed group opinion and "irrational" value commitments. The artistic eminence of Botticelli, for example, was re-established in late nineteenth century circles on grounds that have since turned out to be highly spurious. His defenders used arguments whose vagueness and indirection could not, in themselves, have justified his art on aesthetic grounds. In this sense, Kermode introduces functional reasons for canonical works. Indeed, he (1985:78) concludes that "it is hard to see how the normal

Dilthey (1976:183) wrote that "life as a starting-point and abiding context provides the first basic feature of the structure of the human studies; for they rest on experience, understanding and knowledge of life." Social science, in other words, cannot simply be learned by imitating an empirical problem solution. Because its object is life, it depends on the scientist's own ability to understand life. It depends on idiosyncratic abilities to experience, to understand, and to know. There are, it seems to me, at least three different ways in which such personal knowledge distinguishes itself.

1. *Through the interpretation of states of mind.* Any generalization about the structure or causes of a social phenomenon—an institution, religious movement, or political event—depends upon some conception of the motives involved. To understand motives accurately, however, requires highly developed capacities for empathy, insight, and interpretation. All other things being equal, the work of social scientists who manifest such capacities to the highest degree become classics from which those with more mundane capacities must refer for insight into the subjective inclinations of humankind. The strength of Durkheim's later 'religious sociology" depends, to an important degree, on his remarkable ability to intuit the cultural meaning and psychological import of ritual behavior among the Australian Aborigines. Similarly, it is not Goffman's inheritance of interactionist theory or his empirical methods which has made his theorizing so paradigmatic for the micro-analysis of social behavior; it is his extraordinary sensitivity about the nuances of human behavior. Few contemporaries will ever be able to achieve Goffman's level of insight. His works are classical because one must return to them in order to experience and to understand just what the nature of interactional motivation really is.

2. *Through the reconstruction of the empirical world.* Because disagreement on background issues makes even the objective empirical referents

---

operation of learned institutions . . . can manage without them." At the same time, Kermode insists that some intrinsic dimension for canonization remains. Thus, while he acknowledges that "all interpretations are erroneous," he (p. 91) argues that "some, in relation to their ultimate purpose, are good nevertheless." Why? "Good enough interpretation is what encourages or enables certain necessary forms of attention. What matters . . . is that ways of inducing such forms of attention should continue to exist, even if they are all, in the end, dependent on opinion." The notion of "good enough" will be historicized in my discussion of sociological arguments about classics below.

of social science open to doubt, the complexity of the object world cannot here be reduced via the matrix of consensual disciplinary controls. Hence the social scientist's singular capacity for selection and reconstruction becomes correspondingly important. Here, once again, one finds the same kind of creative and idiosyncratic capacity for representation typically associated with art. As Dawe (1978:366) writes about the classics, "through the creative power of their thought . . . they reveal the historical and human continuity which makes their experience representative of ours."

It is not only insightfulness but that evanescent thing, "quality of mind," upon which the capacity for representation depends. Thus, contemporaries may be able to list the ideal-typical qualities of urban life, but few will be able to understand or represent anonymity and its implications with the richness or vivacity of Simmel himself. Has any Marxist since Marx been able to produce an economic-political history with the subtlety, complexity, and apparent conceptual integration of *The Eighteenth Brumaire?* Has any social scientist, indeed, been able to communicate the nature of "commodities' as well as Marx himself in the first chapter of *Capital?* How many contemporary analyses of feudal society approach the complex and systematic account of economic, religious, and political interrelations which Weber produces in the chapters on patrimonialism and feudalism in *Economy and Society?* This is not to say that in significant respects our knowledge of these phenomena has not surpassed Marx's and Weber's own. It is to say, however, that in certain critical respects our knowledge has not. Indeed, the particular ideas I have just cited were so unusual that they simply could not be understood —much less critically evaluated or incorporated—by Marx's and Weber's contemporaries. It has taken generations to recapture, piecemeal, the structure of these arguments—with their intended and unintended implications.* This, of course, is exactly what may be said for the most important aesthetic works.

---

*After an exhaustive review of studies about the relation between religion and the origins of capitalism that have followed in the wake of Weber's work, Marshall writes: "My broad appraisal of the controversy . . . is that the masterly argument of *The Protestant Ethic and the Spirit of Capitalism* has but sporadically been matched in quality during the course of the debate occasioned by this text. [Weber] attempts to deal theoretically, historically, and empirically with the complex relationships . . . Few who have taken up Weber's argument have displayed his resourcefulness and skills. Working often with a crude and bastardized version of his thesis, most critics have pursued inadmissible data in the wrong time and places" (1982:168).

3. *Through the formulation of moral and ideological evaluations.* The more general a social scientific statement, the more it must provide a compelling interpretation of the "meaning of life." This is its ideological function in the broadest sense of that term. Even if such an ideological reference were undesirable—which in my view it is not—it would not be possible to cleanse even the most scrupulous of social scientific practice of its effects. Effective ideology, moreover (Geertz 1964), depends not only on a finely-tuned social sensibility but on an aesthetic ability to condense and articulate "ideological reality" through appropriate rhetorical tropes. Ideological statements, in other words, can assume a classical status as well. The soulless character of rationalized modernity is not just reflected in Weber's concluding pages in *The Protestant Ethic;* it is created by it. To understand rationalized modernity, one cannot merely observe it; one must return to Weber's early work in order to understand and experience it once again. Just so, what is oppressive and suffocating about modernity may never be quite so firmly established as in Marcuse's *One Dimensional Man.*

These functional and intellectual considerations make the classics—not just generalized discourse per se—central to the practice of social science. It is because of these considerations that earlier works are accorded a privileged status, that they are so venerated that the meaning attributed to them is often considered equivalent to contemporary scientific knowledge itself. Discourse about a work so privileged becomes a legitimate form of rational scientific dispute; investigation into the "new meaning" of such texts becomes a legitimate way to point scientific work in a new direction.* Which is to say that once a work is "classicized," its interpre-

---

After so attesting to the intellectual reasons for Weber's classical status, Marshall concludes with a cautionary note on accumulation: "In sum, after nearly three-quarters of a century of sustained research, commentary, and debate, we are scarcely better placed now than were combatants at the outset to offer informed arbitration between those who view Weber's account . . . as in immensely important and durable insight, and those for whom it remains in imaginative but wholly unsubstantiated flight of speculation." (1982: 169).

*After having worked for more than a decade on his comparative study of historic civilizations, Eisenstadt devoted a paper to Weber and Chinese society. He begins (Eisenstadt 1985:168) by asserting the linkage between classical interpretation and contemporary knowledge: "In this paper we shall attempt to indicate that a critical analysis of Weber's famous *Konfuzianismus und Taoismus* (or in the English translation: *The Religion of China*) can shed, even today, and almost seven decades after its original publication, very important light on some of the basis characteristics and dynamics of Chinese civilization—especially in the framework of a comparative analysis of world civilizations."

tation becomes a key to scientific argument. Indeed, because classics are central to social science, interpretation must be considered as one major form of theoretical argument.

Merton was quite right to suggest that social scientists tend to merge the history and systematics of sociological theory. He (1967:29) was also thoroughly justified in attributing this merging to "efforts to straddle scientific and humanistic orientations." He was wrong, however, to suggest that the merging, or the straddling which produced it, is pathological. In this sense Merton has not himself been empirical enough. From the beginning of the systematic study of society in ancient Greece, merging and straddling have been endemic to the practice of social science. To read this situation as abnormal reflects unjustified speculative preconceptions, not an understanding of the empirical facts.

The first unjustified preconception is that social science is a youthful and immature enterprise in comparison to natural science, with the implication that, as it matures, it will grow increasingly to resemble the sciences of nature. I have argued, to the contrary, that there are endemic, irrepressible reasons for the divergence between natural and social science; moreover, the "maturity" of the latter, it seems to me, has been firmly set for quite a long time. The second preconception is that social science—again, supposedly like its natural science counterpart—is a purely empirical discipline which can shed its discursive and generalized form. I have argued, however, that there is nothing to suggest that such a pristine condition will ever be achieved. Indeed, I have suggested that the science of nature upon which such hopes are modeled can itself never be separated from (usually camouflaged) commitments of an equally generalized kind.

Merton (1967:2) complains that "almost all sociologists see themselves as qualified to teach and to write the 'history' of sociological theory—after all they are acquainted with the classical writings of an earlier day." This, it seems to me, is all to the good. If sociologists did not see themselves as qualified in this way, it would not be merely a "vulgarized" history of sociology which would be eliminated, but the very practice of sociology itself.*

---

*I should also acknowledge that there are significant ambiguities in Merton's essay, which make it possible to construe his argument in significantly different ways. (I have found this to be true of his work on middle range theory as well, see, viz., Alexander 1982a:11–14). For example, on the penultimate page of this essay, Merton (1967:37) suggests the following

Phenomenological Naivete: Why Classical
Debates Must Be Deconstructed

In the preceding sections I have made a theoretical argument that the split between history and systematics cannot exist. In the section which follows, I will show empirically that it does not exist. Before doing so, however, I want to acknowledge that there is one place where the split is, after all, very real. This is in the minds of social scientists themselves.

While they continually engage in discourse about classical work, social scientists—on the whole—acknowledge neither that they are doing so in order to make scientific arguments nor that in the process they are committing acts of interpretation. The question of why they are discussing the classics is rarely broached. Instead, the discussion is taken for granted as the most natural kind of professionally sanctioned activity. As for its theoretical and interpretive character, these possibilities are rarely conceived. As far as the participants are concerned, their effort is simply one of seeing classics as they "really" are.

This lack of self-awareness is not a reflection of theoretical naivete. To the contrary, it characterizes some of the most sophisticated interpretive discussions that social science has produced.

The most famous example is Parsons' (1937) presentation of his convergence thesis in *The Structure of Social Action*. An interpretive tour de force, this work argued that all the major social scientific theories in the turn-of-the-century period emphasized the role of social values in the integration of society. Parsons sustained this reading by creative conceptualization and dense citation, but what is so striking is that he does not acknowledge that it is an interpretation at all! He insists (Parsons 1937:697) that he has conducted an empirical inquiry that is "as much a question of fact as any other." Indeed, rather than being the result of new questions

---

systematic "function for the classics"—"changes in current sociological knowledge, problems, and foci of attention enable us to find new ideas in a work we had read before." He acknowledges, moreover, that these changes could stem from "recent developments in our own intellectual life." This could well be read as endorsing just the kind of systematic need for presentist references to the classics (that is, for historical systematics) against which the main part of Merton's essay was written. For this reason, perhaps, Merton immediately qualifies this suggestion with a new version of his empiricist, accumulationist argument. It is because "each new generation accumulates its own repertoire of knowledge" that "it comes to see much that is 'new' in earlier works."

being asked by Parsons himself, it is changes in the object world that have produced Parsons' new analysis of the classics' work. The classics discovered values, and this discovery is the new empirical datum for Parsons' scientific work. His analysis, therefore (Parsons 1937:721), "has followed [largely] from their new empirical discoveries." The same bracketing of theoretical intent and interpretive practice can be seen in the arguments against Parsons' position. In *Capitalism and Modern Social Theory,* Giddens (1972, preface) presents his neo-Marxian argument as responding to empirical developments like "recent scholarship" and the discovery of new Marxian texts. Roth ([1968] 1978:xxxiii-xc) claims that his anti-Parsonian reading of Weber follows from his access to until-recently untranslated sections of *Economy and Society,* just as Mitzman (1970) argues that his Marcusean rereading of Weber proceeds from the discovery of new biographical material.

In light of what I have argued above, of course, it is clear that such an empiricist self-conception serves to obfuscate the relativism which the very centrality of the classics implies. I want to suggest, however, that to provide this camouflage is precisely the classics' functional role. If those who engage in classical debates knew that their investigations—whether "interpretive" or "historical"—were really theoretical argument by another name, such arguments could not succeed in reducing complexity. They would feel compelled to justify their positions through direct, systematic discourse. It is the same for empiricist self-understanding more generally. If practioners were aware and self-conscious about the degree to which their work was guided by presuppositions and the need to reinforce theoretical schools, it would be more difficult to engage in long-term, fruitful empirical work.

By definition, in other words, social scientists have to adopt in relation to their classics what Husserl (e.g., [1931] 1977) called the naive attitude. Immersed in classical formulations and disciplined by their legacies, social scientists cannot realize that it is they themselves, through their theoretical interests and their theoretical intentions, who make texts classical and give to each classical text its contemporary meaning. By complaining that the "concept of the history of theory" which pervades social science "is in fact neither history nor systematics but a poorly thought out hybrid," Merton, himself an empiricist, has once again not been nearly empirical enough. This hybrid, which has for so long been essential to social science, must of necessity be poorly thought out.

I have argued that it is because they express their systematic ambitions through such historical discussions that social scientists need classics. It is this scientific "intention," in the strict phenomenological sense, which creates the reality of the classics for social scientific life. Husserl showed that the objectivity of social life—its "realness" vis-à-vis the actor—rests upon the actor's ability to bracket, to make invisible to his own consciousness, his intentional creation of objectivity. Just so, in the discussion of the classics the intentionality of social scientists is hidden not just from outsiders but usually from the actors themselves. The intentions which make the classics what they are—theoretical interests and interpretive practices—are placed in phenomenological brackets. It follows, then, that to explore these theoretical interests and interpretive practices is to exercise what Husserl called the phenomenological reduction. Rather than acceding to common sense practice and bracketing subjective intention, we must engage in the scientific practice of bracketing the "objectivity" of the classics themselves. This is a reduction because it seeks to demonstrate that, at any given moment, the "classics" can be seen as projections of the theoretical and interpretive interests of the actors involved. It is because they can be so reduced that the split between history and systematics does not exist.

Building upon Husserl, among others, Derrida has suggested that every text is an intentional construction, not a reflection of some reality. Reflection theory is based on the notion of presence, that a given text can contain—can make present—within itself the key elements of the reality to which it refers, indeed, that there is a reality which is itself present in some ultimate way. If intentionality is acknowledged, however, then it is absence as much as presence which determines the nature of any text. Every description of reality must select from it; by leaving certain elements out, it produces not just the "presences" of what it includes but the absences of what it excludes. The myth of the present text, Derrida suggests, becomes the ideology of the text qua text. Texts are considered to be legitimate because they can be trusted to be reflections of the events or ideas they report. If texts rest upon absences, however, they cannot be accepted at face value. It is because they do rest on absences that texts must be deconstructed. "To 'deconstruct' philosophy," Derrida (1981:6–7, altered translation) writes at one point, is not only to investigate the history of its key concepts but to determine, from a position which is "external" to the writer's own, "what this history has been able to conceal or forbid, constituting itself as history through this repression in which it has a stake."

If the centrality of the classics is to be demonstrated, social scientific discussions about the classics must be deconstructed. Only if the subtle interplay between absence and presence is understood can one see the theoretical function of the classics, and the interpretive practices through which this theorizing proceeds.

Interpretation of the Classics as Theoretical Argument: Talcott Parsons and His Critics in the Postwar Period

It is possible to conceive sociological theory in the period extending roughly from World War II to the early 1980s as possessing a relatively coherent form (Alexander 1987). The beginning of this period was marked by the emergence of structural-functional theory, and until at least the late 1960s this approach exercised a certain dominance over the scientific field. As early as the late 1950s and early 1960s, however, significant challenges to functionalist theory had developed. By the mid-1970s, functionalism had diminished and its one-time challengers had become dominant tendencies. By the early 1980s, these established orientations had themselves begun to come under scrutiny. At the present time, an entirely new theoretical field may well be in the process of emerging; it may certainly be said that the "coherent form" of the last forty years is in the process of breaking down.

That this theoretical movement has provided the framework within which "normal" empirical social science has been conducted is an assumption for all that follows, but I will not try to demonstrate it here. What I do want to argue is that this systematic theoretical movement has informed, and been informed by, far-reaching arguments over the nature and meaning of sociology's classical works.

Through the period of the First World War, of course, European theory played a dominant role. In the interwar period, for a variety of social and intellectual reasons, the locus of sociology began to shift away from Europe toward America. In America before World War II, the Chicago school and institutionalist, quasi-Marxist theorizing played the significant roles. The emphases here were individual interaction, group conflict, and ecological/material environment, and the classics which informed them were American pragmatists, like Cooley and Mead, institutionalists like Veblen, and Europeans like Simmel. Structural-functionalism emerged against these traditions. It depended not only on the writings of Parsons but also on the work of an unusually wide range of talented students, students whose work had already begun to exert influence in the 1930s. In what follows, however, I will concentrate on Parsons as the leader of the tradition.

It is true, of course, that there were extrascientific, social reasons which contributed to the positive reception of functionalist work. In the first instance, however, this work was evaluated and received on what were considered to be scientific grounds. As the empiricist perspective would have it, these grounds included the theoretical scope and explanatory power of Parsons' work. But it was not limited to that. Indeed, Parsons did not rest his claim to scientific dominance on his systematic scientific work alone. He rested it on the authority of the classical texts. He argued that the classical texts directed scientific activity toward the kind of systematic theorizing which he himself devised.

When Parsons began his theoretical career in the 1920s, he was committed to the blend of pragmatism, evolutionism, and institutionalism which characterized the American tradition (Wearne 1985). In the work which began the ascent of functionalist theory, however, the classics associated with this tradition were notably absent. In *The Structure of Social Action,* Parsons (1937) claimed to define the most important results of the previous generation of sociological theorizing. Not only were the American pragmatists and institutionalists missing, but so were Simmel and Marx. They would not be found by systematic sociological theory for many years. The "presences" in Parsons' reconstruction were Marshall, Pareto, Durkheim, and Weber. Parsons claimed that it was they—and Durkheim and Weber more than the other two—who formed the classical tradition from which all future sociology must draw.

It was not only this selection from the field of earlier texts but his construction of those selected that made Parsons' 1937 work so important. He argued, somewhat ambiguously to be sure (Alexander 1983), that these sociologists had emphasized cultural values and social integration. Because of the sharpness of his conceptual insight and the density of his textual argument, Parsons was able to defend this interpretation in an extremely powerful way. It was his interpretive practice, in other words, not—as he himself had suggested (see above)—the empirical nature of his discovery, that made his argument about the classics so successful.

This interpretation, in turn, was informed by theoretical interests. It is only in retrospect that it has become apparent to the sociological community how incomplete was Parsons' reading, how it skewed the interpretation of these classical authors toward the very kind of systematic theoretical argument which Parsons had later claimed it justified in turn.

In his crucial discussion of *The Division of Labor in Society,* Durkheim's first major work, for example, Parsons construed the fifth chapter of Book I—the now famous discussion of the noncontractual elements of contract —as an argument for normative and cultural control in economic life. It can be argued, to the contrary (Alexander 1982b:124–140), that Durkheim's intention in this chapter was to underscore the need for a relatively autonomous, regulatory state. Furthermore, Parsons entirely ignored *The Division of Labor's* second book, in which Durkheim presented an ecological, even materialist analysis of the causes of social change. Parsons also suggested that Durkheim's last work, *The Elementary Forms of Religious Life,* represented an idealist deviation from the multidimensional treatment of solidarity which had emerged in his preceding writing. Because Parsons actually overlooked large parts of this preceding writing, however, he was hardly in a position to draw this conclusion. It seems much more likely that Durkheim's later writings were of a piece. If so, the idealism which Parsons claimed to be a deviation would be broadly characteristic of Durkheim's most mature work. Parsons' hasty reading had the effect of allowing the one-sided normative emphasis of the last twenty years of Durkheim's work to escape largely unscathed.

Parsons' interpretation of Durkheim then—not despite but because of its luminous quality—was informed by the theoretical interests which, in the period after the publication of *Structure,* served to establish the major lines of functionalist work. This was even more true of his analysis of Weber. In the first place, Parsons ignored the unresolved tension between normative and instrumental theorizing which permeates even Weber's sociology of religion. More significantly, however, he failed even to recognize the substantive political sociology Weber developed in *Economy and Society*—the historical discussions of the transition from patriarchal household to feudal and patrimonial systems which revolve almost exclusively around anti-normative considerations. Only because he ignored this major segment of Weber's work could Parsons construe Weber's political sociology as focusing on the problem of legitimacy in moral and symbolic terms.

In the years following World War II Parsons' selection and interpretation of the classics came to be widely accepted. His veneration for these classical writers was personal and unabashed, and he was instrumental in convincing his contemporaries to feel the same way. He insisted, at every step in his subsequent theoretical development, that functional theory followed logically from the path which these forefathers had laid out. Indeed, with each new phase of his later theorizing Parsons carefully "revisited" Weber and Durkheim, and with each rereading he found himself able to understand the promise and problems of their work in terms of the newer functional framework which was about to appear.

In the long introduction to his joint translation of Weber's *Theory of Social and Economic Organization,* Parsons (1947) found that Weber had correctly emphasized the value context of markets and the cultural backdrop for authority, but that his theory of bureaucracy had overemphasized hierarchy because it neglected socialization and professional norms. These were, of course, the very subjects of *The Social System* (Parsons 1951), which appeared four years later. Similarly, in the midst of his own analysis of the internal differentiation of social systems, Parsons investigated Durkheim's approach to social integration (Parsons [1960] 1967). He found that Durkheim was much more concerned with the differentiation of goals, norms, and values than he had realized in the interpretation of thirty years before. Once again, when Parsons began the task of conceptualizing an evolutionary theory of social change, he demonstrated through an extensive investigation of Weber's sociology of religion that Weber had an evolutionary approach as well, a point that Bellah (1959), one of Parsons' ablest students, had worked to demonstrate in the case of Durkheim several years before.

Finally, there is the case of the theorist whose classical status Parsons came to recognize only at a later date, and whose earlier absence, therefore, he urgently sought to correct. In Parsons' mature functionalist theorizing, which first appeared in 1950, socialization played a major role, and he approached the phenomenon in a psychoanalytic way. In his preface to later editions of *The Structure of Social Action,* Parsons expressed his regret that he had not included Freud in that selection of classical writers. Indeed, not doing so had by the 1950s become dangerously anomalous. Because the classics are so central, Parsons' failure to provide an authoritative discussion of Freud left his psychoanalytic functionalism open to serious challenge. Anti-functionalist Freudians could argue that psychoanalytic theory had nothing to do with socialization, that, to the contrary, it emphasized the disorganization of the personality and its rebellion against civilization. Beginning in 1952, Parsons ([1952] 1964), [1954] 1964), 1955) devoted a series of essays to demonstrating that Freud saw object introjection as the basis for personality development; object introjection, of coure, was simply value internalization by another name.

When the theoretical and empirical movement against functionalism emerged in the late 1950s, Parsons' construction of the classics became one of its primary targets. Again, this challenge was not a self-conscious effort at deconstruction, that is, a movement which revealed the theoretical interests behind classical argument as such. It was, rather, an argument aimed for the most part simply at "setting the historical record straight." Insofar as theoretical interests and interpretive strategies were acknowledged, moreover, they were attributed only to Parsons himself; toward their own investigations his challengers had, of necessity, to keep their naive attitude intact.

It is a testimony to Parsons' power that in the early stages of this process the most gaping absences in his classical construction received the least attention. Hinkle (1963, 1980) defended the legitimacy of early American theory, both institutional and pragmatic, suggesting that it be seen as a sophisticated body of theory in its own right. Yet this argument can actually be seen as defending Parsons' theoretical construction by shoring up his construction of history, as the title to Hinkel's early article —"Antecedents of the Action Orientation in American Sociology Before 1935"—suggests. Coser argued much more aggressively against Parsons' selectivity in his Ph.D. dissertation on the conflict orientation of early American sociology, pointing to its problem orientation and institutionalist theory. Only a brief summary of this argument, however, ever appeared in print (Coser 1956: 15–31).

Levine's 1957 Ph.D. dissertation compared Simmel and Parsons and implied, at the very least, an equivalent importance between Parsons and an important earlier author whom he had completely ignored. For more than twenty years, however, this dissertation was also unpublished. When it finally saw the light of day—in an offset series devoted to unpublished disseratations and out-of-print books—Levine ([1957] 1980) made the implications of his introduction of Simmel more critical and explicit. In a new introduction, he scored Parsons' decision to drop from the final manuscript of *The Structure of Social Action* a chapter which he had completed on Simmel. This demonstrated, in Levine's view, that Parsons had selected among the classics in a manner to support his "biased," apriori theoretical interest. Parsons excluded Simmel because to have included him would have spread an antifunctionalist influence. While Levine is justified, of course, in noting this ommision, what he makes of it is not. His argument that simply to include Simmel would be to present an antifunctionalist view rests on the empiricist assumption that Simmel's work has an unequivocal meaning.

The most conspicuous absence in Parsons' construction, however, the figure of Karl Marx, did not receive concerted attention in this early phase. Indeed, it was only through disputation within the confines of the Parsonian pantheon and under the guise of "conflict theory" that Marx first began to be discussed. Only after functionalism had been more or less replaced by its challengers was Marx's work recognized as classical. When, in 1968, Zeitlin turned Parsons' construction upside down by arguing that Parsons' classical figures were conservatives whose work could only be understood as reactions against Marx, his argument still attracted relatively little attention.*

What did become the focus of the emerging antifunctionalist movement were the more subtle absences in Parsons' interpretations of Durkheim, Weber, and Freud. The primary theoretical interest here was in restoring a more power-oriented, economically-centered sociological theory; a secondary interest was in restoring the importance of contingent action against what was conceived to be Parsons' focus on collective order as such. Thus, in the mid-1950s, Gouldner (1958) edited the first English translation of Durkheim's *Socialism and Saint-Simon,* a work of the middle period to which Parsons had never referred. Gouldner claimed that this work demonstrated the existence of a radical and materialist Durkheim which was totally at odds with the one of functionalist lore. That his interpretive practice was crude and unsubstantiated compared to Parsons' no doubt explains the book's relative lack of success, but the theoretical interests behind Gouldner's claim are what is important to see. Giddens (1972) later made the same point in a much more turbulent

---

*Need I emphasize here that I am only talking about discussion in the discipline of sociology as it is rather narrowly defined? In France and Germany, of course, Marx had never stopped being the focus of widespread intellectual debate. One need think here only of Sartre and the Frankfurt School.

period and through a more sophisticated interpretion. His argument that Durkheim converged with rather than diverged from Marx's economic and institutional focus—indeed, that Durkheim was never concerned with the Parsonian "problem of order" at all—played a significant role in the movement away from functionalist theory at that later time. In fact, in the process of elaborating the neo-Marxist argument for structural analysis to which he was devoted at the time, Giddens flatly denied Parsons' developmental view of Durkheim's work; inverting Parsons' analysis, he downgraded the *The Elementary Forms* and argued that it was *The Division of Labor* which actually represented Durkheim's most important work. Martindale (1960) and Bendix (1971) argued against Parsons' voluntaristic interpretation in a different way. Weberians who emphasized power, political movements, and contingency, they insisted that Durkheim actually represented an organicist, anti-individualist approach.

It was Bendix of course, who devoted himself to demonstrating that the "real" Weber had practically nothing in common with the normative portrait to be found in Parsonian work. Bendix claimed that Parsons' Weber rested upon idealist mistranslations of key concepts, for example Parsons' rendering of *Herrschaft* as "imperative coordination" rather than more literally as "domination." He also argued that Parsons underplayed Weber's political sociology and his writings about patrimonial control. For Bendix, this argument over Weber was simply the other side of his effort to construct a historically-specific comparative sociology (e.g., Bendix 1978). It has been the lifework of Bendix's student, Guenther Roth, to demonstrate this alternative Weber in a more scholarly and detailed way. That there was a clear theoretical ambition behind Roth's ([1968] 1978) scholarly reconstruction of Weber's *Economy and Society* is demonstrated by his emphasis, in the long introduction, on the conflict-group orientation of Weber's work. At about this same time, Coser's student, Arthur Mitzman (1970), suggested that, far from being oriented toward values and integration, Weber's mature work must be viewed as a Nietzchean struggle against rational value domination. Earlier, Wrong (1961) had made a similar revision in Parsons' interpretation of Freud, but in a much more explicit way. He had argued that Parsons profoundly underestimated the emphasis on repression in Freud's conception of the superego and the autonomous capacity for anti-social rebellion which Freud gave to the id.

But the mounting effort to break free from the hegemony of function-alist theorizing involved more than finding new ways to interpret the classics and new classics themselves. It also involved the development of theoretical schools which could provide a systematic alternative to what were conceived as functionalism's characteristic emphases. Thus there emerged conflict theory, exchange theory, symbolic interactionism, eth-nomethodology, and a specifically sociological form of humanistic or radical social theory. These schools had to define their own classics, and they did so not only in opposition to Parsons's interpretations but in opposition to Parsons himself. For in the course of the post-war period which marked Parsons' rise, his own work had become classical in a contemporary sense. It had become enveloped in a numinous charisma such that Parsons' statements came to be venerated in themselves, to be accepted not for their theoretical power but simply because they were his. In response, the interpretation of Parsons' work became a minor industry (see Alexander 1983:289–310), for to prove that Parsons did or did not say something became equivalent to making a theoretical argument per se.

The schools which developed in the wake of the antifunctionalist chal-lenges, therefore, had a double interpretive task. They had to find new classics and they had to get rid of this newly classicized contemporary. In the establishment of every new theoretical school we can see this double movement. Parsons and the older classics had to be separated. This was accomplished, first, by arguing that the classics were not what Parsons said they were and, second, by arguing that Parsons was not what he was put up to be. When Pope (1973) and his colleagues (Cohen, Hazelrigg, and Pope 1975) called, in a series of widely discussed essays, for "de-Parsonsizing" the classics, this double-sided intention was neatly ex-pressed.

Consider, for example, the emergence of conflict theory. The key texts in this movement were Rex's, *Key Problems in Sociological Theory* (1961), Dahrendorf's *Class and Class Conflict in Industrial Society* (1959), and Coser's *The Functions of Social Conflict* (1956). In order to argue that systematic sociological theory should be centered on conflict, they had to argue that functionalist theory centered on stability. Rather than arguing this simply at the level of systematic theory or empirical work, each also made the argument through an interpretation of the "meaning" of Par-sons' work. On the one hand, the theoretical interest they brought to this task allowed significant weaknesses in Parsons' work to be revealed; on the other hand, it merely produced a new semiotic field of absences to replace Parsons' own.

Conflict readings of Parsons ignored, for example, the whole series of "functionalist" essays devoted to power and change which Parsons had published between 1938 and 1950, and, more significantly perhaps, the fact that Parsons had turned directly to the problem of change after the publication of *The Social System* in 1951. This destruction of Parsons was symbiotically tied to the construction of Weber and Marx. Rex lauded Marx as an anti-superstructural theorist of conflict; Dahrendorf produced a Weber who was interested only in a theory of coercive power. Coser's construction of the classics differed because he claimed Simmel and Freud for the master theorists of conflict and change. One year before the publication of Coser's book, the groundwork for this argument had been laid in the English-speaking world by Bendix, Parsons' critic from the Weberian side, who published a translation of Simmel's *Conflict and the Web of Group Affiliation* (1955). The most important systematic theorist of the conflict school, Collins (e.g., 1968, 1975, 1986) has continued to challenge the classicization of Parsons and to restructure the older classical tradition in much the same way.

Exchange theory made its first appearance with Homans' (1958) contribution to the issue of the *American Journal of Sociology* commemorating the anniversary of Simmel's birth. After Homans elaborated the systematics of this theory in *Social Behavior* (1961), he defended its legitimacy through reinterpreting the reigning contemporary classic in his presidential address to the American Sociological Association three years later. This address, "Bringing Men Back In" (Homans 1964), established a reading of Parsons as theorizing "anti-human action"—and of one of his best students (Smelser) as secretly anti-Parsonian—which became the single most important polemical justification for individualistic theorizing in the years which followed. It was not until years later that the classical roots of exchange theory were established in a more positive way through arguments (e.g., Lindenberg 1983) for the centrality of Adam Smith's political economy.

The interpretive situation of ethnomethodology was at first quite different. Both because Garfinkel's central axioms were—as for many years he was the first to admit—merely succinct paraphrases of earlier phenomenological work, and because his theoretical ambition in those early years was not yet sufficiently developed, Garfinkel (1963) tried at first to force Schutz into the classical pantheon beside Weber and Parsons. As Garfinkel's intention to create the school of ethnomethodology became explicit, however, his relation to the classics became much more complex. It was not enough to read Schutz in an individualistic way, a manner which camouflaged Schutz's sympathy for Weber's emphasis on social values. Even references to Schutz's work became rare, for ethnomethodology (Garfinkel 1967) was being presented as emerging from empirical studies alone. At the same time, Garfinkel's interpretation of Parsons underwent an inversion. To argue for an alternative to Parsonian theory required Garfinkel to undermine Parsons' classical stature. He was forced to do so in any case, for his shifting theoretical interests caused him to see Parsons in a different way. Garfinkel now insisted that for Parsons actors were "cultural dopes" who conformed to norms in an unthinking and uncritical way. Henceforth, those who valued the creative and rebellious elements of human action would be compelled to do "anti-Parsonian" kinds of phenomenological work.

The same effect was produced by Blumer's (1969) scarcely veiled polemics against Parsonian theory, which helped resuscitate Mead as a patron for symbolic interactionism (cf. Strauss 1964). At about the same time, other interactionists (Stone and Farberman 1967) claimed that Durkheim's later work, far from being an endorsement of the moral order, actually pointed to a "rapproachement" with the individualist thrust of pragmatist thought.

Radical sociology gained ground, particularly in the United States, in much the same way. The key books here, both published in 1970, were Friedrichs' *A Sociology of Sociology* and Gouldner's *The Coming Crisis of Western Sociology*. Operating from within the liberal American context, neither theorist argued directly for the centrality of the classical theorist whom Parsons had left out, that is, for Marx. Instead, they argued against the ideological validity of Parsons. If Parsons could be proved to be on the side of the political establishment, the possibilities for an alternative and radical sociology would be legitimated thereby. Thus, whereas earlier theorists (e.g., Hacker 1961) had pointed to the tension between Parsons' supposedly organicist theories and his liberal, reformist ideals, Friedrichs tried to interpret Parsons as an ideologist of the bureaucratic-technocratic state, and Gouldner aligned him with pre-bureaucratic, individualistic capitalism. Gouldner's reinterpretation paved the way for ten years of left-oriented systematic empirical and historical work. Much of this work appeared in the pages of Gouldner's journal, *Theory and Society,* which tried to "renew" sociology in the light of the classics of conflict theory, ethnomethodology, and Gouldnerian critical theory. It was not until the end of this period that Gouldner (1980) actually tried to make Marx present in the classical pantheon in an ambitious way. It is revealing of the intimate relation between history and systematics that by the time he had composed this late work—at a time when his theoretical and ideological interests had become distinctly anti-Stalinist—Gouldner had begun to read the contemporary political implications of Parsons' work in a more sympathetically liberal way (Gouldner 1979, 1980:355–373).

It seems fitting that the final phase of this destruction of Parsons' construction of the classics involved an historicist attack on the factual foundations of Parsons' 1937 work. This argument maintained that Parsons had distorted the classics because he had pursued a presentist method; that is, his readings of earlier texts were "biased" because they had not discarded contemporary theoretical concerns in favor of a truly historical account. Jones (1977) claimed that Parsons was ignorant of Durkheim's intellectual milieu, and he suggested that knowledge of this environment revealed a theorist concerned not with general theoretical questions but with the detailed facts of Aboriginal religious life. Camic (1979) and Levine (1980) aimed closer to *Structure's* theoretical heart. An historically responsible examination of utilitarianism, they suggested, would reveal that it was hardly the individualistic and rationalistic theory against which, Parsons had insisted, the value-oriented theories of classical sociology correctly were aimed. They argued that utilitarianism had itself been a morally-oriented theory and that for this reason Parsons' entire reconstruction of the "advances" of the classical sociological tradition was flawed in a fundamental way. Their claim was launched, typically, under the banner of historical objectivity, and they presented their accounts as simple expositions which were without theoretical presuppositions. As Hirschman's (1977:108–110) influential intellectual history had already demonstrated, however, it is thoroughly possible for an equally "objective" investigator to read even Adam Smith's work on moral sentiments as paving the way for the individualistic rationalism of utilitarian thought. Just as the more systematic efforts which preceded them, these historicist arguments depended on theoretical interests which lay behind interpretation, not on a neutral reading of the historical literature itelf.

With the help of these arguments over the classics, the new theoretical schools came, by the mid-1970s, to be more or less in control of generalized sociological discourse. Parsons' reconstructions no longer compelled. His absent classics had reemerged; his present classics had been "represented" in significant ways. In 1972, Lukes published an intellectual biography of Durkheim which was hailed as the major intepretative work of recent times. In his apparently conscientious review of the disputes over Durkheim's work, Lukes simply failed to engage Parsons' interpretation altogether.

It was only now, when the challenge to Parsons' hegemony was nearly completed, that Marx finally emerged as a classic in his own right. For European and younger American theorists, indeed, Marx seemed the only classic to which social science need have recourse at all. The play of presence and absence in Marx intepretations held center stage. Humanists like Avineri (1969) and Lukacians like Ollman (1971) argued for the early Marx, but Althusser's (1969, and Althusser and Balibar 1970) much more systematic and demanding understanding of the centrality of the later work eventually gained wide acceptance. Works like the *Grundrisse,* Marx's early draft for *Capital,* were translated and immediately subject to controversy (e.g., compare Nicholas 1973 with McClellan 1971)* in terms of their implications for this dispute. Whether the early or the later work held pride of place played a crucial role in determining the empirical focus —class formations or ideational superstructures, economic processes or alienation, old working classes or new—of a wide range of investigations.

In England, for example, there emerged a robust movement of empirical work called "cultural studies" (e.g., Clark et al., eds., 1979; Hall et al., eds., 1980; Bennet et al., eds., 1981). Focusing on symbols and their

---

*In 1971, McClellan, who favored the more phenomenological Marx and the link between early and late writings, produced a translation of some 100 of the more than 800 pages of the *Grundrisse.* In his introduction (1971:12) he establishes the theoretical relevance of the text which follows: "The continuity between the *Manuscripts* [i.e., *The Economic and Philosophical Manuscripts* of 1844, which typified the "early" Marx] and *Grundrisse* is evident . . . One point in particular emphasizes this continuity: the Grundrisse is as 'Hegelian' as the *Paris Manuscripts* [of 1844]." While Nicholaus's translation appeared two years later, it had the obvious scholarly virtue of being annotated and complete. That the document is, nonetheless, a vehicle to demonstrate his theoretical opposition to the early writings is made clear from the first page of his sixty page forward, which announces (Nicholaus 1973:1) that the following manuscript "display[s] the key elements in Marx's . . . overthrow of the Hegelian philosophy."

relation to class and social conflict, this movement tooks its inspiration (see Hall 1981; Cohen 1980) almost entirely from classics within the Marxist tradition, from Williams' distinctively British version to Althusser's more orthodox theorizing about ideological state apparatuses. Neither Durkheim, who in Parsons' construction was the father of symbolic theory, nor Weber, nor indeed Parsons himself was considered by these British researchers to have exemplary status. An instructive contrast can be found in the earlier, American movement of cultural analysis which produced Bellah's civil religion analysis (e.g., Bellah and Hammond 1980). Because it had been derived from Durkheim and Parsons, it differed from the British tradition in fundamental empirical, ideological, and theoretical ways. Few contrasts provide more compelling evidence for the central force of classical works.

Not only had Parsons' constructions been overthrown, but Parsons himself was increasingly absent from the classical scene. In micro-sociology, debates about Homans, Blumer, Goffman, and Garfinkel replaced debates about Parsons; it was disputes over the meaning of their work which were now taken as the equivalents of systematic theorizing. In macro-sociology, an amalgam of conflict and critical theories had so powerfully displaced Parsons that the new "structural" approach could deny nonempirical and classical foundations altogether (e.g., Treiman 1977, Skocpol 1979, Lieberson 1980). A watermark in this declassicization was reached with the publication of Giddens' *New Rules of Sociological Method* in 1976, which declared not only that Parsons' ideas were inimical to good theory but that Parsons' classics, Durkheim and Weber, were the greatest stumbling blocks to theoretical progress in the future. Giddens (1979, 1981) set out to develop an entirely different stable of classical figures, and eventually his broom swept out Marx as well.

At this writing, however, it appears that the effort to entirely supersede Parsons' construction should be seen as a pendulum movement rather than a progressive succession. Early efforts to "stem the tide" which were written entirely from within the Parsonian tradition—Eisenstadt (1968) on Weber, Smelser (1973) on Marx, Bellah (1974) on Durkheim—clearly failed. Yet more recent efforts to maintain not only the centrality of Parsons' classics but his distinctive concern with the cultural dimensions of their theories have been more successful (Schluchter 1981; Alexander 1982b; Seidman 1983b; Habermas 1984; Traugott 1985; Whimpster and

Lash 1986; Wiley 1987). The depiction of American theory as an individ-ualistic alternative to the collectivism of the European classics has also begun to be sharply questioned (see especially Lewis and Smith 1980, but also Ekeh 1974 and Joas 1985). A movement is even underway to resuscitate the classical stature of Parsons' himself. In a remarkable about face, Habermas (1981:297) has argued that "no social theory can be taken seriously today which does not—at the very least—clarify its relationship to Parsons." My own work (1983) has suggested much the same and, in-deed, in recent years a surprising range of theorists (e.g., contributors to Alexander 1985 and Holton and Turner 1986) have begun to argue that a "neofunctionalist" tradition based on a reconstructed Parsons and his classical foundations remains possible. Finally, the presuppositions of the "new structuralism" are being explicated and criticized (Alexander 1988; Sewell 1985); indeed, in the view not only of theorists (Thompson 1985 and forthcoming; Alexander 1988) but also of important empirical analysts in this tradition (e.g., O'Connor 1980; Fenton 1984; Traugott 1984; Hunt 1988) Durkheim's ideas on structure may yet play a significant role.

This examination of classical debate in the postwar period has necessar-ily been a partial one. If space permitted, for example, the manner in which classical discussions helped to structure the empirical subfields of sociology would have to be explored.* Even within the confines of my discussion, moreover, I have had the opportunity neither to display the nuances of classical argument nor to demonstrate in a detailed manner how each discussion actually entered systematic theorizing, let alone em-pirical work. Despite these limitations, however, I believe that my analyt-ical point has been substantially documented. In the major "systematic" theoretical discussion which marked the postwar period, "historical" ar-gument about the meaning of classical works played a pivotal role.

In establishing a new pantheon for postwar theoretical discussion, Parsons' investigation of the classical authors was both intellectual and strategic. By immersing himself in the writings of Durkheim, Pareto, and Weber, he gained genuinely new insights into the structure and process

---

*In this regard, see the promising work by Thompson. In "Rereading the Classics: the Case of Durkheim" (1985; cf., Thompson, forthcoming), he demonstrates how in the development of the field of industrial sociology divergent interpretations of Durkheim's Division of Labor in Society have played a major role in specific empirical disputes. I have greatly benefited from Thompson's (1985) theoretical discussion of classical centrality, which in part responded to an earlier version of the present essay.

of the social world. By arguing that these authors were the only real founders of sociology, moreover, he could undermine the foundations of theories which he had come to consider badly mistaken. Parsons' claim to have "discovered" the classics was motivated by theoretical interest; at the same time, given the necessary background conditions, his interpretive practice was strong enough to convince the social scientific community that these classical positions actually foreshadowed his own.

The link between historical and contemporary systematics was so strong that Parsons' theoretical hegemony could be challenged only if his version of classical history was overturned as well. An alternative version was established and this occurred as much by rereadings of Parsons' classics as by creating new ones. The intellectual reasons for this are clear enough —with powerful theories there is insight enough for ample interpretive space. But the acceptance of common classics was functionally effective as well, for it allowed post-Parsonian theorists to make their arguments in terms which were more or less widely understood. Ironically, the classicization of Parsons' own work facilitated his theoretical eclipse, for it, too, provided a relatively well-understood medium through which to argue against the merits of functionalist ideas. Because post-Parsonian theory was built in part upon Parsons, morever, recent attempts to supercede it have returned not only to earlier classical texts but to Parsons' work as well, and they have done so not only for intellectual but also for strategic reasons.

Humanism and the Classics:
Why the Historicist Challenge Is Wrong

To defend the centrality of the classics in a strong way is to argue for an inextricable relationship between contemporary theoretical interests and investigations about the meaning of historical texts. In the first part of this essay I argued for this position in the realm of sociological theory. In the preceding section I have tried to substantiate it by looking at how sociological discussions about the classics actually proceed. In conclusion, I will defend this position against the challenge to classical centrality which has emerged from within the humanities itself. This is the historicist approach to intellecutual history associated with the work of Quentin Skinner, which—often in combination with self-styled Kuhnian histories of science—has made significant intrusions into sociological discussion as well (e.g., Stocking 1965; Peel 1971; Jones 1977).

This challenge is particularly important because it is the humanities which has usually offered the alternative to the social scientific reduction of cultural studies to contemporary empirical intent. In terms of the classics, as Merton himself posed the dichotomy, it has been the humanities which has traditionally defended the uniqueness and permanent importance of their contributions. The humanities are associated with interpretation rather than explanation: it was, after all, from within the humanities that this very distinction was first formalized and advanced. It has been within the humanistic disciplines, moreover—from nineteenth-century historical studies of religion to contemporary literary theory—that the methodology of interpretation and the investigation and reinvestigation of the meaning of classical texts has been most developed. Finally, it is the denial of the relevance of textual interpretation for the social sciences which underlies not only the empiricist injunction against the classics but the common sense of classical discussions themselves.

Whereas Merton's injunction against merging history and systematics seeks to cleanse systematics of historical baggage, Skinnerian theory argues against merging in order to purify history of the taint of systematics. The intent is to transform discussions of earlier texts into presupposition-less, purely historical investigations, investigations which would, ironically, be more explanatory than interpretive in form. Yet, while Skinner approaches the problem from an opposite angle, the effect of his argument would be exactly the same. If history can be atheoretical, then theory can be ahistorical. If the classics can be studied without shouldering the burden of interpretation, then interpretation certainly need not intrude into the practice of classic-less social science. Skinner provides the kind of intellectual history that Merton needed but could not find.* It seems to me, however, that his historical theory suffers from the same abstract, antiempirical quality as Merton's; it fails to account for the central role of interpretive debate in cultural studies today, and for much

---

*It is worth noting that the traditional "history of ideas" is an object of condemnation by Skinner and Merton as well. For both, not surprisingly, it is criticized as being too presentist in nature. In the first section of this paper, I criticized Merton's proposal for an alternative approach to intellectual history as itself pre-Kuhnian in form. Once again, Skinner would provide just the alternative to historical systematics which Merton was unable properly to envision. What one might call his preferred *"history* of ideas"—as contrasted to the "history of *ideas*—perfectly matches the stereotype which empiricist social scientists have of classical inquiry, namely that it is purely historical and, because of this, irrelevant to contemporary theoretical concerns. Thus, in Turner's attack on "metatheory" which I noted about, he (1986:974) contrasts "doing theory" with "tracing the history of ideas."

the same reason: it suffers from an empiricism which denies to presuppositions a central role in the study of social life. It makes this claim in the name of defending reason against relativism. In my view, howevever, it is only by acknowledging apriori interests that reason can bring them to task.

What historicism abhors is the anachronistic introduction of contemporary concerns into the understanding of earlier texts. Skinner complains (Skinner 1969:6–7) that this "priority of paradigms" can result only in "mythologies" rather than in the discovery of the texts themselves. Such a complaint rests, of course, on the implicit claim that the hermeneutical circle can be broken. What sustains historicism is the belief that the real world, in its pristine and original glory, can be revealed to the investigator if only he knows where and how to look. Historicism provides this knowledge through its emphasis on context and intention. The unmediated availability to cultural studies of intellectual context and authorial intention are the most important assumptions upon which historicism rests. From these follow a third assumption which, while implicit, might well be the most important of all. This is the notion that motivated, historically-situated texts can themselves be read and understood without any particular problem at all. This, we recall, was precisely the latent assumption in Merton's social scientific attack on the classics as well. To defend the "difficulty" of classical texts and their "relative autonomy" vis-à-vis intention and context is, therefore, to defend the practice of interpretation itself. It is, ultimately, just because interpretation is central that a merging of history and systematics must be made.

In what follows, I will criticize in turn each of the assumptions upon which historicism rests.

1. *Singular versus infinite context.* Historicism contends that the linguistic conventions of a given period reveal the intellectual universe for any particular historical work. "It follows from this," Skinner (1969:49) argues, "that the appropriate methodology for the history of ideas must be concerned, first of all, to delineate the whole range of communications which could have been conventionally performed on the given occasion by the utterance" (cf., Jones 1986; Stocking 1965:8; Peel 1971:264). No particular misgivings are expressed about the retrievability of this milieu. Jones (1974:355) blithely suggests, for example, that it is possible to achieve "an understanding of the total sociohistorical context within which sociological theories have emerged." It seems to me, however, that it is

precisely this capacity for history to mirror society which must be put into question. If Skinner's nominalism is maintained, then every significant statement in an historical period would have to be recorded and analyzed, a clearly impossible task. Total sociohistorical context is a chimera. On the other hand, if a more realist position is assumed, it must be acknowledged that generalizations are made which are necessarily selective. Selection, of course, always involves comparison to some prior standard. There is one anomalous point in his more recent writing where Skinner himself seems to see that the need for selection refutes the contextualist position he has tried to lay out.

Before we can hope to identify the context which helps to disclose the meaning of a given work, we must already have arrived at an interpretation which serves to suggest what contexts may most profitably be investigated as further aids to interpretation. The relationship between a text and its appropriate context is in short an instance of the hermeneutic circle. (Skinner 1976:227)

2. *Transparent versus opaque intention.* Historicism, however, is not a form of social determinism; it seeks to take authorial will fully into account. Context provides only the background for a text; it is the author's own intentions that reveal which conventions he aimed his text to support and supersede. Once again, this claim rests upon an empiricist confidence in the transparency of the social world. Intentions are considered as recoverable as contexts. Skinner (1969:22) is not troubled by the problem of discovering intent; one must simply look at "what the author himself meant to say." The counterargument "that it is actually impossible to recover a writer's motives and intentions" is, Skinner (1972:400) insists, "straightforwardly false." To find intentions and motive, one needs recourse (Skinner 1969:30) simply to "commonplace, but [heretofore] amazingly elusive, facts about the activity of thinking."

It is, of course, exactly the commonplace nature of thinking which has been subject to radical questioning throughout most of the twentieth century. Psychoanalysis has demonstrated that the full intentions of actors are unknown even to themselves, let alone to others who do not know them well. The mind fends off emotional discomfort by constructing defense mechanisms that drastically narrow the actor's conscious understanding (Freud 1950). While the pseudoscientific claims of psychoanalysis have been sharply scrutinized, its skepticism toward rational self-understanding has permeated intellectual opinion about interpretation and literary method. For example, it was psychoanalytic ideas which largely inspired the attack by New Criticism on contextual and intentionalist interpretation. Because profound ambiguity lies at the origin of most powerful imaginative works, Empson argued (1930), texts are filled with unresolved contradictions and readers are forced to invent interpretations about meaning and authorial intent. This points ineluctably to the autonomy of text, for it becomes clear that the author himself is not in conscious control. My work on the contradictory character of great social theory (e.g., Alexander 1982b:301–306, 330–343) suggests, similarly, that "unconscious deceit" is endemic to such theorizing; in light of this, to pursue the meaning of a theory through the author's conscious intent would surely be barking up the wrong tree.

Inspired not only by psychoanalysis but by cultural theory as well, structuralism and semiotics have made the same point. Arguing against Sartre's intentionalism, Lévi-Strauss (1966:252) insists that structural linguistics demonstrates the existence of a "totalizing entity" which is "outside (or beneath) consciousness and will" and that such linguistic formations are prototypes for every cultural text. Ricoeur argues similarly. Written discourse is possible, he suggests, only because there are symbolic resources available which transcend situational specificity and immediate intent. For the immediate situation of composition can scarcely be known by those who encounter written texts after they have been composed: "The text's career escapes the finite horizon lived by its author. What the text says now matters more than what the author meant to say" (Ricoeur 1971:534). Hermeutical philosophy supports this conclusion from the point of historical method itself. Gadamer argues that whether authorial intent and textual meaning coincide is irrelevant, for intent is something which it is impossible for the historian to recover. Making virtue from necessity, he expounds a dialogical perspective in which texts can reveal themselves only through interlocution in an historical context: "The real meaning of a text, as it speaks to the interpreter, does not depend upon the contingency of the author and whom he originally wrote for. It is partly determined also by the historical situation of the interpreter and hence by the totality of the objective course of history" (Gadamer 1975:264).

3. *Explicit versus multivalent texts.* The unstated assumption which informs historicism's exclusive concentration on context and intention is that it is unecessary to study the meaning of a text in itself, that is, to

concentrate on the text qua text. Behind this assumption is a pragmatic, anti-semiotic theory of meaning. Historicists claim that the meaning of any given text is dertermined and exhausted by its use on a particular occasion. Practice, not textual meaning, becomes the object of investigation—in Skinner's words (1969:50; italics added), "the *use* of the relevant sentence by a particular agent on a particular occasion with a particular intention (*his* intention) to make a particular *statement.*" Inverting Ricoeur, Skinner insists (1969:50) that a text is "specific to its situation in a way that it can only be naive to try to transcend." This is an agentic, nominalist approach. Texts are means for intellectual action; to study them is to find out "what genuine historical agents did think" (Skinner 1969:29).

But if context is far from definite and intention impossible to pin down, texts must be given a relative autonomy. They must be studied, that is, as intellectual vehicles in their own right. This is not to deny authorial intention; it is to assert that intention can only be discovered in the text itself. As Hirsch (1967:22) puts it, "there is a difference between meaning and consciousness of meaning." It is from such beliefs about the complex, camouflaged nature of authorial intention that arguments for textual autonomy emerge, for the intentions of the unconscious author can be discovered only through an indepependent examination of the text itself. For Ricoeur (1976), texts have a "surplus of meaning." Freud (1913) insists on the "overdetermination" of dream symbolism. Foucault (1970) argues that hidden discourses structure the written documents of history. This extra meaning accrues to a given text because of the organizing principles inherent in that particular cultural form. Ricoeur sees surplus as produced by myth and metaphor. Freud finds overdetermination in the devices of dream construction like displacement and condensation. Foucault's discourses rest on modalities which establish the archeology of knowledge.

A text is a system of symbols which fixes the meaning of an author as much as the author invests meaning in it. To study the meanings of a particular text, then, one must study that particular system's rules. The investigator must know the rules that govern that particular kind of imaginative activity—how displacement and condensation operate in dreams, how structural logic (Barthes 1977) undergirds the narrative form. These rules, which literary theorists (e.g., Hirsch 1967:74, 80) call the rules of genre, are embedded in the consciousness of authors but they are rarely invented by authors themselves. It is, indeed, because they are socially constituted and transmitted rules that texts allow interpersonal communication to proceed.

The purpose of critical debate is to make these rules explicit and to show how it is these presuppositions rather than others which produce the meaning of texts. If cultural reasoning is bound to be relative, Skinner's attempt to maintain reason by empiricist escape is doomed from the start.[4] Reason can be preserved only by making presuppositions explicit and subjecting them to disciplined debate. Standards of evaluation are proposed, not discovered; it is only persuasion which can lead the participants in discourse to accept them as valid. It is for this reason that interpretation and theoretical argument go hand in hand. "To recognize the impossibility of demonstrating an axiom system," Raymond Aron (1961:106) once wrote, "is not a defeat on the mind, but the recall of the mind to itself."

NOTES

1. The distinction I am employing between natural and human science obviously can have only an ideal-typical status. My purpose is to articulate general conditions, not to explain the situation of particular disciplines. At the general level, it is certainly fair to say that the conditions for and against having classics broadly correspond to the division between the sciences of nature and the sciences concerned with the actions of human beings. Specific analysis of any particular discipline would require specifying the general conditions in each case. Thus, natural science is typically broken down into the physical and the life sciences. The latter are less subject to mathematization, less consensual, and more often subject to explicit extraempirical dispute. In some instances this can extend to the point where debate over the classics has a continuing scientific role, as in the dispute over Darwin taking place in evolutionary biology.

In the human studies, too, disciplines differ in the degree to which they typically manifest the conditions I will describe. In the United States, sociology and anthropology most closely follow the ideal-typical form I am describing here. In history, by contrast, classical texts do not play a central role. This does not mean, however, that historical discussion proceeds without supraempirical references anchored in earlier debates. It seems, rather, that these discursive interests, as I will later call them, center upon the interpretation of critical events.

Historians present theoretical arguments through interpretations of the past. These arguments, which involve theories and debates with other historians, often are not directly linked to events in the past. Yet written history always presents theory in terms of these events. [This] reflects [the] historian's view of past events as 'classic texts,' which have a 'privileged status' in relation to all other evidence and interpretations. Because historians attach a special significance to events, successful intepretation of one is necessary to legitimate a historical argument. (Towers 1987)

Variation in these disciplinary conditions—economics would constitute yet another set—can be analyzed in terms of variations in the theoretical conditions for classical centrality that are established below.

2. In this section I have illustrated the overdetermination of social science by theory and its underdetermination by fact through discussion of single important works. It could also be illustrated by examining specific "empirical" subfields. In social science, even the most narrowly defined empirical subfields are subject to tremendous discursive argument. Discussion at a recent national conference on the state of disaster research (Symposium on Social Structure and Disaster: Conception and Measurement, College of William and Mary, Williamsburg, Virginia, May 1986), for example, revealed that even in this very concrete field there is vast disagreement simply abut the empirical object of study. "What is a disaster" is disputed and argued about by virtually every researcher in the field. Some argue for a criterion related to objective and calculable costs but disagree over whether these costs should be related to the geographical expanse of the event, the numbers of people involved, or the financial costs of rebuilding. Others argue for criteria that are more subjective but disagree over whether it is the larger society's consensus that a social problem has occurred which is decisive or the perceptions of the victims themselves. Given the extent of such conflict over the simple empirical referent of the field, it is not surprising that sharp discursive disputes rage at every level of the scientific continuum. There are presuppositional disagreements about individual versus social levels of analysis and about economizing versus interpreting actors; there are ideological struggles over whether disaster research should be governed by broad responsibilities to the community or by narrower professional concerns; there are many disputes over definitions, e.g., what is an "organization," and over the very value of exercises in definition and taxonomies. For a good summary of these disputes see Drabek 1986 and forthcoming, and Kreps 1988.

3. In the introduction to his strikingly original studies on the relationship between social class and linguistic codes. Basil Bernstein (1971) talks about his graduate student encounter with Durkheim. His account reveals the intuitive character of the relationship between classic and contemporary, the importance of personal sensibility and the relative unimportance of such positivist criteria as the balance of evidence and cumulative theoretical debate.

I read Durkheim and although I did not understand him it all seemed to happen. I did not care that he was a naughty functionalist with an oversocialized concept of man, that he neglected the institutional structure and the sub-strata of conflicting interests . . . In a curious way I did not care too much about the success of his various analyses. It was about the social bond and the structuring of experience. (p. 3)

Bernstein (p. 171) later reiterates this point. "Durkheim's work is truly magnificent . . . [He] attempted to derive the basic categories of thought from the structuring of the social relation. It is beside the point as to his success."

The unusual character of this relationship between Bernstein and Durkheim—unusual, that is, from a positivist perspective—has been pointed out by Coser (1988), whose essay first brought these statements to my attention. In his examination of the continuing centrality of Durkheim for the "sociology of knowledge," Coser (p. 85) writes of Durkheim and Mauss's *Primitive Classification:* "Although the methodology of the work, as well as the logic of the argument, was submitted to a strong, in fact devastating critique, the book has inspired the work of a number of contemporary or near-contemporary social scientists."

4. It is precisely this doomed quality of empiricism, in my view, which explains the series of what can only be called retractions which have been issued by Skinner and his associates in response to the critical debate over their work. Skinner (1972), for example, eventually tried to separate motive from intention, arguing that, while the former cannot really be known, the latter can. This marked an implicit acknowledgment of the autonomy of texts, for he now argued that intention could be discovered only through an understanding of what the actual act of writing involved. Yet this, too, is further qualified, and in an ambiguous way. Skinner (1972:405) insists that he has "been concerned only with the . . . point that whatever a writer is doing in writing what he writes must be relevant to interpretation," not that the writer's intention must be the basis of interpretation per se. He has reduced his claim to the notion that "amongst the interpreter's tasks must be the recovery of the writer's intentions in writing what he writes," and he indicates that intention may well be disregarded. While "it must always be dangerous . . . for a critic to override a writer's own explicit statements about what he was doing in a given work," he acknowledges, "the writer himself may have been self-deceiving about recognizing his intentions, or incompetent at stating them." The recent work of Jones, Skinner's most important follower in sociology, is also marked by critical equivocations and retractions. He now suggests (Jones 1986:17), for example, that "the contextual availability (or unavailability) of descriptive or classificatory terms is not the criterion by which our statements about an historical agent are rendered anachronistic or otherwise." And he appears to accept the unalterable presentism of textual investigation: "The practice of social science itself (history included) not only benefits from but repeatedly requires the imposition, upon agents whose beliefs and behavior we wish to understand, of concepts and categories wholly alien to them." While Jones and Skinner continue to make arguments for the historicist position, if these admissions were seriously taken, they would undermine the validity of the position. I am grateful to Seidman's (1983b, 1986) work in this area for bringing to my attention such contradictions, and, more generally, for its illumination of the problems considered in this essay.

REFERENCES

Alexander, Jeffrey C. 1982a. *Positivism, Presuppositions, and Current Controversies.* Vol. 1 of *Theoretical Logic in Sociology.* Berkeley and Los Angeles: University of California Press.

——1982b. *The Antinomies of Classical Thought: Marx and Durkheim.* Vol. 2 of *Theoretical Logic in Society.* Berkeley and Los Angeles: University of California Press.

——1983. *The Modern Reconstruction of Classical Thought: Talcott Parsons.* Vol. 4 of *Theoretical Logic in Sociology.* Berkeley and Los Angeles: University of California Press.

——1987. *Twenty Lectures: Sociological Theory Since World War II.* New York: Columbia University Press.

——1988. "Social-Structural Analysis: Presuppositions, Ideologies, Empirical Debates." In Alexander, *Action and Its Environments: Toward a New Synthesis* pp. 11–45 New York: Columbia University Press.

Alexander, Jeffrey C., ed. 1985. *Neofunctionalism.* Beverly Hills and London: Sage Publications.

——1988. *Durkheimian Sociology: Cultural Studies* New York: Cambridge University Press.

Althusser, Louis. 1969. *For Marx.* London: New Left Books.

Althusser, Louis, and Etienne Balibar. 1970. *Reading "Capital."* London: New Left Books.

Aron, Raymond. 1961, "Max Weber and Michael Polanyi." In Marjorie Grene, ed., *The Logic of Personal Knowledge: Essays Presented to Michael Polanyi,* pp. 99–116. Glencoe, Ill,: Free Press.

Avineri, Shlomo. 1969. *The Social and Political Thought of Karl Marx.* London: Cambridge University Press.

Barthes, Roland. 1977. "Introduction to the Structural Analysis of Narratives." In Barthes, *Image, Music and Text,* pp. 79–124. London: Fontana.

Bellah, Robert. 1959. "Durkheim and History." *American Sociological Review* 24:447–461.

——1973. Introduction to *Emile Durkheim on Morality and Society,* ed. by Bellah. Chicago: University of Chicago Press.

Bellah, Robert, and Phillip Hammond. 1980. *Varieties of Civil Religion.* San Francisco: Harper and Row.

Bendix, Reinhard. 1961. *Max Weber: An Intellectual Portrait.* New York: Doubleday Anchor.

——1971. "Two Sociological Traditions." In Bendix and Guenther Roth, *Scholarship and Partisanship,* pp. 282–298. Berkeley and Los Angeles: University of California Press.

——1978. *Kings or People.* Berkeley and Los Angeles: University of California Press.

Bennett, Tony, et al., eds. 1981. *Culture, Ideology, and Social Process*. London: Open University Press.

Bernstein, Basil. 1971. *Class, Codes, and Control*. New York: Schocken Books.

Blau, Peter M., Terry C. Blum, and Joseph E. Schwartz. 1982. "Heterogeneity and Intermarriage." *American Sociological Review* 47:45–62.

Blumer, Herbert. 1969. "The Methodological Position of Symbolic Interactionism." In Blumer, *Symbolic Interactionism*, pp. 1–60. Englewood Cliffs, N.J.: Prentice-Hall.

Camic, Charles. 1979. "The Utilitarians Revisited." *American Journal of Sociology*. 85:516–550.

Clarke, John, et al., eds. 1979. *Working Class Culture*. London: Hutchinson Press.

Cohen, Jere, Lawrence Hazelrigg, and Whitney Pope. 1975. "De-Parsonsizing Weber: A Critique of Parson's Intepretation of Weber's Sociology." *American Sociological Review* 40:229–241.

Cohen, Stanley. 1980. "Symbols of Trouble: Introduction to the New Edition." In Cohen, *Folk Devils and Moral Panics*, pp. 1–8. Oxford: Martin Robertson.

Collingwood, Charles. 1940. *Metaphysics*. Oxford: Clarendon Press

Collins, Randall. 1968. "A Comparative Approach to Political Sociology." In Reinhard Bendix, ed., *State and Society: A Reader in Political Sociology*, pp. 42–67. Berkeley and Los Angeles: University of California Press.

——1975. *Conflict Sociology*. New York: Academic Press.

——1986. *Weberian Sociological Theory*. New York: Cambridge University Press.

Coser, Lewis A. 1956. *The Functions of Social Conflict*. New York: Free Press.

——1988. *"Primitive Classification* Revisited." *Sociological Theory* 6(1):85–90.

Dahrendorf, Ralf. 1959. *Class and Class Conflict in Industrial Society*. Stanford: Stanford University Press.

Dawe, Alan. 1978. "Theories of Social Action." In Tom Bottomore and Robert Nisbet, eds., *The History of Sociological Analysis*, pp. 362–417. New York: Basic Books.

Derrida, Jacques. 1981. *Positions*. Chicago: University of Chicago Press.

Dilthey, Wilhelm. 1976. "The Construction of the Historical World in the Human Studies." In Dilthey, *Selected Writings*, ed. H.P. Richman, pp. 168–263. Cambridge: Cambridge University Press.

Drabek, Thomas E. 1986, "Taxonomy and Disaster: Theoretical and Applied Issues." Paper presented at symposium, Social Structure and Disaster: Conception and Measurement, College of William and Mary, Williamsburg, Va.

——Forthcoming. *Human System Response to Disaster: An Inventory of Sociological Findings*. New York, Heidelberg, and Berlin: Springer-Verlag.

Eisenstadt, S. N. 1968. "Charisma and Institution Building: Max Weber and Modern Sociology." In Eisenstadt, ed., *Max Weber on Charisma and Institution Building*, pp. ix–lvi. Chicago: University of Chicago Press

——1985 "This Worldly Transcendentalism and the Structuring of the World:

Weber's *Religion of China* and the Format of Chinese History and Civilization." *Journal of Developing Societies* 1:168–186.

Ekeh, Peter. 1974. *Social Exchange Theory: The Two Traditions.* Cambridge, MA: Harvard

Empson, William. 1930. *Seven Types of Ambiguity.* London: Chatto and Whindus.

Fenton, Steve, ed. 1984. *Durkheim and Modern Sociology.* London: Cambridge University Press.

Foucault, Michel. 1970. *The Order of Things.* London: Tavistock Publications.

Freud, Anna. 1950. *The Ego and the Mechanisms of Defense.* London: International Universities Press.

Freud, Sigmund. 1913. *The Interpretation of Dreams.* London: G. Allen.

Friedrichs, Robert. 1970. *A Sociology of Sociology.* New York: Free Press.

Gadamer, Hans-Georg. 1975. *Truth and Method.* New York: Crossroads.

Garfinkel, Harold. 1963. "A Conception of and Experiments with 'Trust' as a Condition of Concerted Stable Actions." In O.J. Harvey, ed., *Motivation and Social Interaction,* pp. 187–238. New York: Ronald Press.

——1967. *Studies in Ethnomethodology.* Englewood Cliffs, N.J: Prentice-Hall.

Geertz, Clifford. 1964. "Ideology as a Cultural System." In David Apter, ed., *Ideology and Discontent,* pp. 47–76. New York: Free Press.

Giddens, Anthony. 1972. *Capitalism and Modern Social Theory.* Cambridge: Cambridge University Press.

——1976. *New Rules of Sociological Method.* New York: Basic.

——1979. *Central Problems in Social Theory.* Berkeley and Los Angeles: University of California Press.

——1981. *A Contemporary Critique of Historical Materialism.* Vol. 1. Berkeley and Los Angeles: University of California Press.

Gillispie, Charles C. 1960. *The Edge of Objectivity: An Essay in the History of Scientific Ideas.* Princeton: Princeton University Press.

Gouldner, Alvin. 1958. Introduction to *Socialism and Saint-Simon,* by Emile Durkheim. Yellow Springs, Ohio: Antioch University Press.

——1970. *The Coming Crisis of Western Sociology.* New York: Equinox.

——1979. "Talcott Parsons." *Theory and Society* 8:299–301.

——1980. *The Two Marxisms.* New York: Seabury.

Habermas, Jurgen. 1971. *Knowledge and Human Interests.* Boston: Beacon Press.

——1981. *Zur Kritik der Funktionalistischen Vernunft.* Vol. 2 of *Theorie des Kommunikativen Handelns.* Frankfurt: Suhrkamp.

——1984. *Reason and the Rationalization of Society.* Vol. 1 of *The Theory of Communicative Action.* Boston: Beacon.

Hacker, Andrew. 1961. "Sociology and Ideology." In Max Black, ed., *The Social Theories of Talcott Parsons,* p. 289–310.

Hagstrom, Warren. 1965. *The Scientific Community.* New York: Free Press.

Hall, Stuart. 1981. "Cultural Studies: Two Paradigms," In Bennett et al.,

Culture, Ideology and Social Process, pp. 19–37. London: Open University Press.

Hall, Stuart, et. al., eds. 1980. *Culture, Media, Language.* London: Hutchinson University Press.

Hinkle, Roscoe. 1963. "Antecedents of the Action Orientation in American Sociology before 1935." *American Sociological Review* 28:705–715.

——1980. *Founding Theory of American Sociology, 1881–1915.* London: Routledge and Kegan Paul.

Hirsch, E. D. 1967. *Validity in Interpretation.* Bloomington, Ind.: Indiana University Press.

Hirschman, Albert. 1977. *The Passions and the Interests.* Princeton: Princeton University Press.

Holton, Gerald. 1973. *Thematic Origins of Scientific Thought: Kepler to Einstein.* Cambridge: Harvard University Press.

Holton, Robert J., and Bryan S. Turner. 1986. *Talcott Parsonson Economy and Society.* London and New York: Routledge and Kegan Paul.

Homans, George. 1958. "Social Behavior as Exchange." *American Journal of Sociology* 62:597–606.

——1961. *Social Behavior: Its Elementary Forms.* New York: Harcourt, Brace, and World.

——1964. "Bringing Men Back In." *American Sociological Review* 29:809–818.

Hunt, Lynn. 1988. "The Sacred and the French Revolution." In Jeffrey C. Alexander, ed., *Durkheimian Sociology,* pp. 25–43. New York: Cambridge University Press.

Husserl, Edmund. [1931] 1977. *Cartesian Meditations.* The Hague: Martinus Nijhoff.

Joas, Hans. 1985. *G. H. Mead: A Contemporary Re-Examination of His Thought.* Cambridge, England: Polity Press.

Jones, Robert Alun. 1974. "Durkheim's Response to Spencer: An Essay toward Historicism in the Historiography of Sociology." *Sociological Quarterly* 15:341–358.

——1977. "On Understanding a Sociological Class." *American Journal of Sociology.* 88:279–319.

——1986. "Second Thoughts on Privileged Access." *Sociological Theory.* 3 (1):16–19.

Kermode, Frank. 1985. *Forms of Attention.* Chicago: University of Chicago Press.

Kreps, Gary, ed. 1988 *Social Structure and Disaster.* Newark, Del: University of Delaware Press.

Kuhn, Thomas. 1970. *The Structure of Scientific Revolutions.* 2d ed. Chicago: University of Chicago Press.

Lakatos, Imre. 1969. "Criticism and the Methodology of Scientific Research Programmes." *Proceedings of the Aristotelian Society* 69:149–186.

Levine, Donald. [1957] 1980. "Introduction to the Arno Press Edition." In

Levine, *Simmel and Parsons: Two Approaches to the Study of Society,* pp. iii–lxix. New York: Arno Press.

Lévi-Strauss, Claude. 1966. *The Savage Mind.* Chicago: University of Chicago.

Lewis, J. David, and Richard Smith. 1980. *American Sociology and Pragmatism: Mead, Chicago Sociology and Symbolic Interactionism.* Chicago: University of Chicago Press.

Lieberson, Stanley. 1980. *A Piece of the Pie.* Berkeley and Los Angeles: University of California Press.

Lindenberg, Siegward. 1983. "Utility and Morality." *Icyklos* 36:450–468.

Luhmann, Niklas. 1979. *Trust and Power.* New York: Wiley.

——1984. *The Differentiation of Society.* New York: Columbia University Press.

Lukes, Steven. 1972. *Emile Durkheim: His Life and Work.* New York: Harper and Row.

McClellan, David, ed. 1971. Introduction to *The Grundrisse: Karl Marx,* ed. by McClellan. New York: Harper and Row.

Mannheim, Karl. 1936. *Ideology and Utopia.* New York: Harcourt, Brace, and World.

Marshall, Gordon. 1982. *In Search of the Spirit of Capitalism: An Essay on Max Weber's Protestant Ethic Thesis.* New York: Columbia University Press.

Martindale, Don. 1960. *The Nature and Types of Sociological Theory.* New York: Houghton Mifflin.

Merton, Robert K. [1942] 1973. "The Normative Structure of Science," In Merton, *The Sociology of Science,* Norman W. Storer, ed., Chicago: University of Chicago Press.

——1947. "Discussion of 'The Position of Sociological Theory.' " *American Sociological Review* 13:164–168.

——1967. *Social Theory and Social Structure.* New York: Free Press.

Mitzman, Arthur. 1970. *The Iron Cage.* New York: Knopf.

Nicholas, Martin. 1973. Forward to *Grundrisse,* by Karl Marx. New York: Random House.

Nisbet, Robert. 1976. *Sociology as an Art Form.* London: Oxford University Press.

O'Connor, James. 1980. "The Division of Labor in Society." *Insurgent Sociologist* 10:60–68.

Ollman, Bertell. 1971. *Alienation.* London: Cambridge University Press.

Parsons, Talcott. 1937. *The Structure of Social Action.* New York: Free Press.

——1947. Introduction to *Theory of Social and Economic Organization,* by Max Weber. New York: Free Press.

——1951. *The Social System.* New York: Free Press

——[1952] 1964. "The Superego and the Theory of Social Systems. In Parsons, *Social Structure and Personality,* pp. 17–33. New York: Free Press.

——[1954] 1964. "The Father Symbol: An Appraisal in the Light of Psychoanalytic and Sociological Theory." In Parsons, *Social Structure and Personality,* pp. 34–56. New York: Free Press.

———1955. "Family Structure and the Socialization of the Child." In Parsons et al., *Family, Socialization, and Interaction Process*, pp. 35–122. New York: Free Press.

[1960] 1967. "Durkheim's Introduction to the Theory of the Integration of Social Systems." In Parsons, *Sociological Theory and Modern Society*, pp. 3–34. New York: Free Press.

Peel, J.D. 1971. *Herbert Spencer*. New York: Basic Books.

Polanyi, Michael. 1958. *Personal Knowledge*. New York: Harper and Row.

Pope, Whitney. 1973. "Classic on Classic: Parsons' Interpretation of Durkheim." *American Sociological Review* 38:399–415.

Popper, Karl. [1935] 1949. *The Logic of Scientific Discovery*. New York: Basic Books.

Rex, John. 1961. *Key Problems in Sociological Theory*. London: Routledge and Kegan Paul.

Ricoeur, Paul. 1971. "The Model of the Text: Meaningful Action Considered as a Text." *Social Research* 38:529–562.

——— 1976. *Interpretation Theory: Discourse and the Surplus of Meaning*. Fort Worth: Texas Christian University Press.

Roth, Guenther. [1968] 1978. Introduction to *Economy and Society,* by Max Weber, ed. by Roth and Claus Wittich. Berkeley and Los Angeles: University of California Press.

Schluchter, Wolfgang. 1981. *The Rise of Western Rationalism: Max Weber's Developmental History*. Berkley and Los Angeles: University of California Press.

Seidman, Steven. 1983a. *Liberalism and the Origins of European Social Theory*. Berkeley and Los Angeles: University of California Press.

——— 1983b. "Beyond Presentism and Historicism: Understanding the History of Social Science." *Sociological Inquiry* 53:79–94.

———1986. "The Historicist Controversy: A Critical Review with a Defense of a Revised Presentism." *Sociological Theory* (1):13–16.

Sewell, William Jr. 1985. "Ideologies and Social Revolutions: Reflections on the French Case." *Journal of Modern History* 57:57–85.

Shils, Edward. 1970. "Tradition, Ecology, and Institution in the History of Sociology." *Daedalus* 99:798–820.

Simmel, George. 1955. *Conflict and the Web of Group Affiliations*. New York: Free Press.

Skinner, Quentin. 1969. "Meaning and Understanding in the History of Ideas." *History and Theory* 8:3–52.

——— 1972. "Motives, Intentions, and the Interpretation of Texts." *New Literary History* 3:393–408.

———1976. "Hermeneutics and the Role of History." *New Literary History* 7:209–232.

Skopol, Theda. 1979. *States and Social Revolutions*. New York: Cambridge University Press.

Smelser, Neil. 1959. *Social Change in the Industrial Revolution*. Chicago: University of California Press.

—— 1973. Introduction to Smelser, ed., *Karl Marx on Society Change*. Chicago: University of Chicago Press.

Stinchcombe, Arthur. 1968. *Constructing Social Theories*. Baltimore: Johns Hopkins University Press.

Stocking, George. 1965. "On the limits of 'Presentism' and 'Historicism' in the Historiography of the Behavioral Sciences." *Journal of the History of the Behavioral Sciences* 1:211–217.

Stone, Gregory, and Havey Farberman. 1967. "On the Edge of the Reapprochement. Was Durkheim Moving toward the Perspective of Symbolic Interaction?" *Sociological Quarterly* 8:149–164.

Strauss, Anselm. 1964. Introduction to *George Herbert Mead on Social Psychology*, ed. by Strauss. Chicago: University of Chicago Press.

Sztompka, Piotr. 1979. *Sociological Dilemmas*. New York: Academic Press.

Thompson, Kenneth. 1985. "Rereading the Classics: The Case of Durkheim." Paper, delivered at the Department of Sociology, University of California, Los Angeles.

—— Forthcoming. *Durkheim and Sociological Methods*. Beverly Hills and London: Sage Publications.

Tiryakian, Edward. 1979. "The Significance of Schools in the Development of Sociology." In William E. Snizek, et al., eds., *Contemporary Issues in Theory and Research*, pp. 211–233. Westport, Conn.: Greenwood Press.

Towers, Frank. 1987. "Bernard Bailyn's *The Ideological Origins of the the American Revolution* as an Example of the Privileged Status of Events in Historical riting." Seminar paper presented at the University of California, Los Angeles.

Traugott, Mark. 1984. "Durkheim and Social Movements." *European Journal of Sociology* 25:319–326.

—— 1985. *Armies of the Poor*. Princeton: Princeton University Press.

Trevor-Roper, H. R. 1965. "Religion, the Reformation, and Social Change." *Historical Studies* 4:18–45.

Treiman, Donald. 1977. *Occupational Prestige in Comparative Perspective*. New York: Wiley and Sons.

Turner, Jonathan. 1986. "Review: 'The Theory of Structuration.'" *American Journal of Sociology* 91:969–977.

Turner, Stephen P. 1987. "Underdetermination and the Promise of Statistical Sociology." *Sociological Theory* 5 (2):172–184.

Walby, Sylvia. 1986. *Patriarchy at Work*. London: Macmillan.

Wallace, Walter L. 1983. *Principles of Scientific Sociology*. Chicago: Aldine.

Wearne, Bruce. 1985. "The Theory and Scholarship of Talcott Parsons to 1951: A Critical Commentary." Ph. D. dissertation, la Trobe University, Melbourne, Australia.

Weber, Max [1904–05] 1958. *The Protestant Ethic and the Spirit of Capitalism*. New York: Scribner's.

Whimpster, Sam, and Scott Lash, eds. 1986. *Max Weber and Rationality.* London: Allen and Unwin.

Whitehead, Alfred North. [1917] 1974. "The Organization of Thought." In Whitehead, *The Organization of Thought,* pp. 105–133. Westport, Conn.: Greenwood Press.

Wiley, Norbert, ed. 1987. *The Marx-Weber Debate.* Beverly Hills and London: Sage Publications.

Wrong, Dennis. 1961. "The Over-Socialized Conception of Man in Modern Sociology." *American Sociological Review* 26:183–193.

Zeitlin, Irving. 1968. *Ideology and the Development of Sociological Theory.* Englewood Cliffs, N.J.: Prentice-Hall.

The Dialectic of Individuation and Domination: Weber's Rationalization Theory and Beyond

Social theory not only explains the world but reflects upon it. Committed to empirical standards of truth, it is tied, as well, to the metaphysical demand for reflective equilibrium (Rawls 1981). While, more than any other modern theorist, Max Weber insisted that scientific social theory be absolved of metaphysical ambition, he was obsessed, more than any other, with the meaning of modern life. This paradox was far from accidental. We will see that it reflected Weber's understanding of the fate of meaning in a secular world. I will argue, indeed, that Weber's empirical sociology establishes the criteria—the fundamental boundary conditions—for rational reflection about the fate and possibilities of the modern age.

Social theory is, with art, the primary source of self-reflection in the modern world. The product of secularization, it responds to the problems raised by secularization in turn. As the modern world emerged, the unified cosmos which had enmeshed traditional societies broke down. God withdrew from the world, first from the world of nature, then from the worlds of society and self. In place of divine, architectonic meaning —the teleology of the great chain of being—there emerged the possibility, indeed the necessity, for thinking in terms of efficient, mechanical causes. Though in principle as determinate as God's will, and even more permeable to the human mind, such causes are by their very nature metaphysically accidental. Yet the human need to know the "meaning" of

Scott Lash, Colin Loader, and Sam Whimster made helpful comments on an earlier draft of this essay.

the world remains, even as the human mind learns that it cannot support this need in a cosmological way.

Social theory is an attempt to address the problem of meaning in a de-divinized world. It offers mechanical explanations of the facts of this world, but at the same time tries to "go beyond" these facts to establish their meaning in a more generalized and existential sense. In this way it provides a kind of self-reflection unavailable in traditional life, a "rational" way to approach metaphysical issues that even the most modern man or woman still desparately needs.

Social Theory Before the Twentieth Century

The resort to mechanical explanation, the emergence of social theory, and the de-divinization of the world appeared gradually and unevenly over the course of four centuries (see, e.g., Seidman 1983). The scientific revolution of the sixteenth century desacralized nature, but even Newton, the greatest progenitor of mechanism vis-á-vis nature, remained committed to a religious view of society and self. Only in the seventeenth and eighteenth centuries did naturalistic explanations of self and society emerge in a consistent way. Yet, though seventeenth and eighteenth century social theorists made mechanical causation the basis for their reflection about self and society, strong elements of cosmological thinking remained in their work. For one thing, they usually found a contract to be at the origins of human societies, which amounted to an imaginary device ensuring for society an "originating purpose" and a teleological goal. In the second place, most early modern and Enlightenment theorists posited some version of natural rights. With this concept they linked social organization to values which were given in a nonhuman way.

As the nineteenth century unfolded the social and cultural props for these religious remnants largely disappeared. Scientific thinking about the origins of the earth and human race—geological breakthroughs and the Darwinian revolution were clearly interconnected—made it much less possible to think in ahistorical, contractual terms about the origin of human societies. New anthropological material about the diversity of early societies made it equally difficult to posit some suprahistorical notion of natural rights. These desacralizing developments were underscored by the social developments of the day: the outbreak of organized, largely secular revolutions, the spread of urbanization, the emergence of industrialization and class struggle.

Yet if social theory in the nineteenth century largely dispensed with contract theory and natural rights, developing in its stead thoroughly mechanistic explanations of individuals and societies, it did not escape the legacy of cosmological thinking entirely. Both of the great theoretical traditions—materialism and idealism—took over significant themes from the Judeo-Christian tradition. They both manifest an overriding faith in progress, a belief that a good and cooperative world would eventually emerge. They also took over from the Western religious tradition a strong faith in the ultimate rationality of human beings, giving to the species what later thinkers would view as an incredible capacity to interpret their world in an enlightened way.

Each tradition conceptualized this faith in progress and rationality in its own particular terms. Materialist theories found mechanistic causes in science, technology, and economic interest. Organized in one kind of system or order, carried by this group or that, materalism posited that political, economic, or cognitive factors would eventually lead human societies to a good end. While idealist theory provided explanations of self and motivation *(Bildung)* that materialism lacked, it manifested the same strong faith in inevitable progress and in the human capacity for rationally evaluating the world. Hegel felt certain that the universal was about to become concrete, and he equated the coming of the concrete universal with rationality and the manifestation of God's will on earth.

For these reasons, I believe, social theory in the nineteenth century never faced the "problem of meaning" in the fullest sense of that term. Because theorists wrote with a comforting sense of the right direction of their universe, the opportunity for self-reflection they provided never compelled a final break with the cosmological underpinnings of the traditional world. In this sense, Marxism occupied an intermediate place. While Marx attacked his contemporaries' naive faith in immediate progress and "unearned" rationality, he himself manifested an unshaken confidence in the ultimate transformation of the world in a rational and progressive direction.

The Great Transformation: Social Theory
in the Twentieth Century

All this was shattered in the fin-de-siécle period. Nietzsche announced that God was dead, and the awesome and terrifying ramifications of secularization were finally recognized. By the end of the nineteenth century, moreover, many reflective people were coming to feel that the world was not turning out as social theory had promised. True, there was economic advance, but this was accompanied by conflict and exploitation on a scale which classical economics had never predicted. The political equilibrium marked by fifty years of European peace had given way to war and threats of more international wars to come. Efforts at rational control through government had become enmeshed in large and top-heavy bureaucracies. Throughout the educated classes of Europe there developed a sense of ennui, a suffocating sense of the limitedness of possibilities.

These dramatic social and cultural shifts set a new agenda for social theory. It is disillusionment rather than optimism that has characterized most great social theory in the twentieth century. Faith in progress has been almost entirely given up, confidence in the inherent rationality of human beings almost entirely abandoned. The last vestiges of cosmological thinking have dropped away, and social theory has resigned itself to explaining individual action and social order in entirely naturalistic and mechanical terms.

All of this is not to say that the metaphysical concerns of social theory disappeared. To the contrary, the developments I have described made "the problem of meaning" one of the central theoretical issues of the day. As theorists labored to develop new, thoroughly mechanistic explanations for the troublesome "facts" of the emerging century, they dedicated themselves, just as resolutely, to describing these empirical problems in culturally meaningful terms. Metaphysical, supraempirical issues were never abandoned. What had changed was the way they were addressed. When a theorist in the twentieth century offered an answer to the question of ultimate meaning, he did so in a radically secular, postcosmological way.

Max Weber embodied this transition in his own life. Like most of the other great theorists in the turn-of-the-century period, he began his intellectual life with beliefs firmly rooted in the nineteenth century. Though more bellicose in his nationalism than some, he shared the general intellectual faith in the progress that lay open for Western societies. He felt that the rational transformation of nature, and the rational organization of society, were positive developments well within man's reach; and he tied these political and economical changes to increasing freedom for modern man.

In 1897 Weber suffered a nervous breakdown. When he emerged from this period of emotional and intellectual mortification, he was not only a different person but a chastened thinker. He was prepared, in a way he had not been before, to reflect on the dark side of the twentieth century. Like others in his generation, Weber expressed such sentiments most pointedly in his reactions to the First World War, an event which seemed to sum up the prospects of the new age. "Not summer's bloom lies ahead of us," he told students in his now famous lecture on politics as a vocation, "but rather a polar night of icy darkness and hardness" (Weber 1946a:128).

Weber explicitly linked this despair about the future course of the twentieth century to his disillusionment with the social theory of the nineteenth. In his companion lecture on science as a vocation he scored "the naive optimism" according to which science "has been celebrated as the way to happiness." To interpret in this way what is, after all, a mere "technique of mastering life" is a sign of immaturity. "Who believes in this?" he asked the students rhetorically, "aside from a few big children in university chairs or editorial offices" (Weber 1946b:143).

Weber is suggesting here that a mature thinker must sever the link between cognitive explanation and existential salvation. To assume such a link belies, according to Weber, the dire predicament of the twentieth century, and, indeed, he traces the establishment of the connection back to the time when religion still dominated human thought. He had discovered an effort to establish just this kind of relationship in his work on Puritanism. Asking his students to recall Swammerdam's exhaltation, "Here I bring you the proof of God's providence in the anatomy of a louse," Weber suggested they would see in this statement "what the scientific worker, influenced (indirectly) by Protestantism and Puritanism, conceived to be his task: to show the path to God" (Weber 1946b:142). For a man of that earlier period, such a connection was understandable. It is a regressive and intellectually immature for the man of today, for it fails to come to terms with the inevitably naturalistic character of explanation in the secular age.

"An empirical explanation has to eliminate as causal factors," Weber (1946b:147) insisted, all "supernatural interventions." To accept a supernatural cause is to accept the teleological notion that natural events have occurred for some higher purpose, that their cause is neither efficient nor mechanical but derives from their ethical goal. Since modern science was first promoted by religious men, it is not surprising that in the beginning even naturalistic explanations were squeezed into this teleological frame. But once the full implications of science are understood, its effect must inevitably be exactly the opposite. "If these natural sciences lead to anything," Weber suggests, "they are apt to make the belief that there is such a thing as the 'meaning' of the universe die out at its very roots" (Weber 1946b:142). Not to understand this is, once again, to reveal a disturbing lack of inner strength. "Who—aside from certain big children who are indeed found in the natural sciences—still believes that the findings of astronomy, biology, physics, or chemistry could teach us anything about the *meaning* of the world?" (original italics).

Science, then, has contributed to the icy darkness that lies ahead. A world where the very hope for meaning has died out at its roots is not a happy or reassuring prospect. But it has for Weber another implication as well. By separating causal explanation and existential evaluation, science offers the potential for individual autonomy. Science offers a mundane technique of calculation which is available to every person. Weber describes the goal of scientific training in just this way: it is "to present scientific problems in such a manner that an untutored but receptive mind can understand them and—*what for us is alone decisive*—can come to think about them independently" (Weber 1946b:134, italics added). This second implication must not be denied if Weber's sociology is to be properly understood.*

Weber's sociology is defined, and I will suggest also limited by, the dilemma he has just described. On the one hand, there is disillusionment and an existential despair that psychological maturity and cultural integrity cannot be sustained. On the other hand, there is real evidence of the increasing autonomy and strength of the individual. These poles embody the paradox of the twentieth century. Weber spent the last fifteen years of his life trying to understand how both could be true.

How have we come to a condition of "icy darkness and hardness" which

---

*This point is made decisively by Seidman (1983), who insists that Weber does not view the postcosmological world in purely negative terms.

threatens to extinguish human life, which is at the same time a condition in which for the first time human freedom is finally possible? It is to answer this question that Weber suggested his master concept of rationalization. Rationalization is at once disenchantment, intellectualization, and rational empowerment. It has led to increased freedom and at the same time facilitated enormous domination. This ambiguity is intended. Rationalization is at once a terrible condition, the worst evil, and the only human path for liberation.

Rationalization as Individuation

Those who have seen the critical thrust of Weber's rationalization concept (e.g., Mitzman 1970) have, not surprisingly, failed to appreciate that it also implies the increasing freedom of human beings from the tyranny of forced belief.* "Increasing intellectualization and rationalization," Weber acknowledges, does not mean that there has actually been increased knowledge about the "conditions under which one lives." This would limit rationalization to a cognitive force. Weber wants to get at something else, and something more.

It means something else, namely, the knowledge or belief that if one but wished one *could* learn it at any time. Hence, it means that principally there are no mysterious incalculable forces that come into play, but rather that one can, in principle, master all things by calculation. This means that the world is disenchanted. One need no longer have recourse to magical means in order to master or implore the spirits, as did the savage, for whom such mysterious powers existed. Technical means and calculations perform the service. This above all is what intellectualization means. (Weber 1946b:139)

World mastery, or at least the potential for it, has come to man through rationalization. Humans have replaced God as the masters of their destiny. Modern people are governed, or at least would like to think of themselves as being governed, by institutions which are man-made, which have been constructed for their effectiveness in achieving human goals. In principle, leaders are held accountable for the way these institutions work.

*The only major exception is Lowith (1982), who differentiated Weber's rationalization theory from Marx's alienation theory precisely in these terms, i.e., by pointing out that Weber tied this development to the increasing existentialism of modern life (a point reiterated by Seidman 1983). For more on this existential theme, see my discussion below.

If this sounds suspiciously like the nineteenth century outlook which Weber designed his theory to replace, this is because a crucial qualification has been left out: in no sense did Weber conceive this rationality to be a natural condition of human life. The point of his life's work is to show that the very opposite is the case. He believed that intellectualization rested upon the most unnatural motivation, led to the most abstracted orientation, and inspired the most dessicated organization that the world had ever known. Far from rationality being given or inherent, it must be understood as the result of a long and complicated evolution of irrational, religious belief. The anti-religious nature of the modern world has a religious base. This appears to mark an inconsistency, but it would be considered so only for nineteenth century thought. Weber holds that only if the irrational basis of rationality is accepted can the tortuous development of rationality properly be understood and the precarious condition of individual autonomy really be appreciated.

To understand what modern rationalization entails, what it allows and what it proscribes, one must understand from what it has emerged. The religious world we have lost addressed the meaning of life in a particular way: it harnessed all the different elements of life to the ethical goal incarnated in the godhead. This single goal sits atop a cultural hierarchy. It is the telos towards which every other dimension of culture is oriented. Artistic expression, understanding of the truth, love between human beings, material success or political power—all are conceived of as serving this ethical end. Even more, all are conceived of as expressions of this ultimate goal.

Weber usually turned to Tolstoy as the modern who best articulated this anti-rationalistic spirit, and, indeed, Tolstoy's later works display just the kind of radical spiritualization that Weber is trying to describe. Tolstoy is not content to let events "simply happen" in a mechanistic way; he is bent on avoiding the naturalistic conclusions to which his literary realism would seem logically to lead. In his denouements, the humiliation of Anna Karenina and the death of Ivan Ilyich are turned into events that have meaning in a higher, metaphysical sense. Tolstoy seems to suggest that it was somehow right for these events to unfold as they did.

Though Weber is not unsympathetic to this Tolstoyan point of view, he rejects it as a defendable standpoint for modern man. In the first place, such a Tolstoyan position is wrong because, quite simply, it "presupposes that the world does have a meaning" (Weber 1946b:153). By meaning,

Weber is referring here not to the ongoing existential effort of individual interpetation but to a conception of teleological purpose in the cosmological sense. It is to this that he objects, and he does so because it depends upon an empirical acceptance of God. The religious world view presupposes "that certain 'revelations' are facts . . . and as such make possible a meaningful conduct of life." What Weber objects to, in sum, is the notion that certain presuppositions "simply must be accepted," that is, accepted without any rational argument (Weber 1946b:154). This is the "intellectual sacrifice" which religion demands as its price for providing a meaningful world.

Weber asks how we have moved from a "meaningful" world to this disenchanted one of rational choice. The answer lies in his sociology of religion. While the existential need for meaning is constant, the intellectual approach to meaning varies. Religious interpretation emerges before nature or society can be rationally explained. It is a way of explaining the "inexplicable" problems of suffering and unfairness. This origin in inexplicability is what leads religions to center on the problem of salvation. It is because empirical explanation is impossible that there is the postulate of God. God had created the world; we suffer because of him, and we will be saved insofar as we meet his demands.

Weber created the cross-cutting ideal types of his religious sociology in order to explain the approaches to salvation—the theodices—which had evolved in the course of world history. With the typologies mysticism/ asceticism and this-worldly/other-worldly Weber sought to describe the degree of emotionality as opposed to control which theodicies allowed, and the degree to which the religious organization of thought and emotion was directed toward world transformation or away from it.

Weber's aim, we must remember, is to develop a theory of the evolution of religion which can explain its self-destruction, that is, its movement toward rationality. What is at issue is whether religion forces man to become a tool of divine will rather than a vessel, an issue which will become central to understanding domination as well as individuation. Mystic religions, because they make salvation dependent upon possessing —becoming a vessel of—the spirit of god, encourage emotional expression and experience rather than self-control. Ascetic religions insist that man is a tool, that he must submit to god's will by following certain rules of good conduct. In this way asceticism encourages self-control and calculation.

Religious history present a long march away from mystical to ascetic forms of the search for meaning. For the Australian aborigines the gods were easily available, and the goal of religious life was an experience of oneness through ritual participation. With the development of monotheism, religion is simplified and abstracted. God withdraws from the world, and humans know him less through experience than through written texts. The Jews were the "people of the book"; they could not even know God's name. This thrust toward asceticism constitutes one of the fundamental causes of the rationalization of religious life. It promotes depersonalization, an outward rather than an inward orientation, and discipline of the self. Though the teleological structure of meaning remains intact, within its confines there has been significant rationalization.

The movement beyond the religious world view cannot be understood without following out the implications of Weber's second typology. Early mysticism was almost entirely this-worldly, but later mysticism, Hinduism, for example, had a strikingly other-worldly component. For their part, the great ascetic religions had been, until the Reformation, almost entirely other-worldly. They placed their great virtuosi outside the world, for example in the monasteries of Buddhist and Christian monks. In this earlier period of religious history, renunciation could only occur if ascetics were physically separated from the world. This constituted a tremendous barrier against the spread of rationality.

With the Reformation, all this changed. Ascetic religion, and the rationalizing characteristics it represented, was brought deeply into the world. To achieve salvation one had to organize the world in accord with the impersonal word of God. This required intense depersonalization and self-control. Everything in the world of nature, self, and society had now to be transformed in accordance with God's will. But for this transformation to happen, the whys and the whats would have to be strictly and accurately calculated. Feelings must be renounced in order to estimate God's will in a rational way; indeed, given the awesome abstraction of God, the Puritan could know his calculation had been rational only if the transformation of this world had actually occurred. The Puritan would be known by his works. His calling was to master the world.

The stage was now set for the transition to the modern era. This-worldly asceticism continued to permeate the world, but its religious content faded away. The great Protestant scientists—Newton, for example—did not secularize nature in a literal sense. Still, their commitment to seeing in nature the manifestation of God's will and to act upon it through calculation of its laws was but one step away. Puritan emphasis on the reason of nature and its accessibility to human calculation led directly to the notion of natural law. Nature governed by natural law allowed causality to be assessed in purely mechanical terms. True, such antimetaphysical explanation remained in the service of teleology, but it was but one short step to the idea that no force outside of nature—nothing metaphysical—could govern what was contained within it. Science, and modern rationality more generally, represent the Puritan obsession with calculation, impersonal rules, and self-discipline—without the Puritan belief in their divine origin. It is Puritan epistemology without Puritan ontology.

When a calculating and ascetic consciousness comes to dominate the world without being anchored in metaphysics, the result is a sense of meaninglessness. Once the anchor has been tossed away, human existence seems disorderly, tossed this way and that. Weber (1946b:140) writes that the post-religious understanding of life can only be "provisional, not definitive." Rational truth is still pursued, but it becomes cognitively specialized, separated from ultimate values and from other significations. For the Greeks, the exact opposite was the case. They occupied a transitional niche between religion and secular thought, much as did the Puritans. Greek science, it was widely believed at the time, could give guidance in all the essentials of life.

If one only found the right concept of the beautiful, the good, or, for instance of bravery, of the soul . . . one would also grasp its true being. And this, in turn, seemed to open the way for knowing and for teaching how to act rightly in life and, above all, how to act as a citizen of the state. (Weber 1946b:141)

But once science has become separated from metaphysics, rationality can only describe what is, not what ought to be. In this sense, it is meaningless, for it cannot answer "the only question important to us," writes Weber, quoting Tolstoy: " 'What shall we do and how shall we live?' " This is true, moreover, not only for natural science, but for every form of knowledge that seeks to be rational. Consider aesthetics. "The fact that there are works of art is given for aesthetics," Weber argues. "While it seeks to find out under what conditions this fact exists, . . . it does not raise the question whether or not the realm of art is perhaps a realm of diabolical grandeur." Aesthetics does not, in other words, ask the normative question, "should there be works or art?" (Weber 1946b:144).

Or take jurisprudence. "It establishes what is valid according to the rules of juristic thought," but it never asks "whether there should be law and whether one should establish just these rules." To do the latter would be to assume the meaningfulness of law in a teleological way. The same goes for the historical and cultural sciences. They teach us how to understand and interpret, but "they give us no answer to the question, whether the existence of these cultural phenomena have been and are worth while" (Weber 1946b:145).

This compartmentalization of rationality has fragmented the once-integrated universe. Where once there was security and direction, there is now a metaphysical disorder which gives little solace. "So long as life remains immanent and is interpreted in its own terms," he believes, "it knows only of an unceasing struggle of these gods with one another" (Weber 1946b:152). Though he senses keenly what has been lost, Weber does not wish that the cosmological world—where a single, ontologically real god ruled—could be reconstructed again. He accepts its loss as the price of freedom. This-worldly asceticism has produced a fragmented world without any metaphysical integration, but it is precisely this lack of metaphysical anchorage which throws the individual back upon himself. Once God directed man; now man chooses his gods: "You serve this god and you offend the other god when you decide to adhere to [a] position" (Weber 1946b:151).

Rationalization as Domination

Yet while Weber revered the hard-won autonomy of the modern individual, he did not see individualism as the single defining trait of the twentieth century. Metaphysical nostalgia was far from the only threat to individuality. Against the individual stood barriers of much more material shape. These were the "hard and cold" institutions of the modern world. Even while rationalization had stripped illusions from men's minds and created the possibility for active and mastering behavior, it had created the psychological and cultural basis for an extension of institutional coercion which threatened to make this potential for freedom a bitter joke. The very forces which free humans allow them to become dominated in turn. This is the ominous insight with which Weber chose to conclude his last edition of *The Protestant Ethic and the Spirit of Capitalism*. "The

Puritan wanted to work in a calling," he rued (Weber 1958:181); "we are forced to do so."*

Weber's emphasis in this famous sentence on the voluntariness of the Puritan calling could have occurred only for rhetorical effect, for his point certainly is that asceticism constitutes a form of spiritual domination which facilitates the domination by external life. Hence the sentence which follows: "For when asceticism was carried out of monastic cells into everyday life, and began to dominate worldly morality, it did its part in building the tremendous cosmos of the modern economic order" (Weber 1958:181). Demands for large-scale organization have, of course, existed from the beginning of time. Efficiency creates functional reasons for the development of such organization, and the human desire for domination creates the psychological fuel. But the culture and psychology of this-worldly asceticism have allowed such "natural developments" to be rationalized in a tremendous way.†

Theoretical problems in Weber's work (see, e.g., Alexander 1983a) made it difficult—indeed, virtually impossible—for him to carry out this "other side" of his religious evolution argument in a consistent way. For us to do so here would involve the systematic incorporation of other theoretical traditions.‡ Yet the burden of Weber's argument seems clear enough. The manner in which he constructed his historical sociology, the very nature of the categories he chose, convinces us that the outline for this other side was there—"in his head", so to speak—even if he was unable to make it explicit, much less to carry it out systematically.

---

*When one examines the passages in the final version of *The Protestant Ethic* which Weber added after its original publication—in response to criticisms and second thoughts —it seems clear that as his later writings developed he became more able to articulate the negative implications of the turn he had taken in his post-breakdown period. This should not be considered, however, a completely linear development. Relatively "optimistic" statements—e.g., those on the vocation—appeared periodically throughout his life.

†Only once did Weber allow himself seriously to consider the possibility that this-worldly asceticism could become institutionalized in a democratic way. For a discussion of this anomalous but extremely revealing effort (Weber [1906] 1985), see chapter 3, below.

‡The darker side of rationalization has, of course, been pursued by Marxism, and the specifically Weberian understanding of this development has been elaborated within the Marxist tradition by "critical theory" as, e.g., Habermas (1984) has recently shown. This tradition, however, has been unable to bring into its understanding of decline Weber's phenomenological thrust, particularly his commitment to understanding the contributions to this darker development of independently constituted symbolic systems. The traditions I have more in mind are those of Elias and Foucault. This will become more apparent in the discussion of discipline below.

Weber believed that this-worldly asceticism made it possible not only to master the world but to master other human beings. Depersonalization and self-discipline promoted autonomy in part because they allowed the actor to distance his ego from emotions that represented dependency. But this rejection of one's own dependency needs forced one to reject the needs of others as well. The capacity to make a "tool" out of oneself, therefore, also allowed one to depersonalize and objectify others. Domination could only become ruthless when the personal and idiosyncratic qualities of the other were eliminated. Just as the self became a tool for God, so would others be used for His greater glory. The God of the first great monotheistic religion—the Israeli God Yahweh—was also its God of war, and the very notion of a "just" and crusading war emerged only with Western Judeo-Christianity.

Bureaucracy is the most obvious institutional manifestation of the "other side" of this abstracted, mastering spirit. The Christian church was the world's first large-scale, successful bureaucracy. The discipline and rationality developed by the monks were important in rationalizing this bureaucracy further, and it was this form of political organization, not only the economic form of capitalism, which later became institutionalized in the world when the metaphysical content of this-worldly asceticism was removed. But economic coercion should not be neglected. Because the Puritans made themselves into tools, they were able to organize others in depersonalized struggle and work. The Puritan objectification of the spirit promoted, in this way, not only economic individualism but the subjective conditions for methodical domination in business and factory.

Politics were transformed in much the same way. Activism and individuality were certainly fundamental to democratization, and Weber himself wrote that religious "election" could be viewed as an incipient form of democracy. Yet as Weber demonstrated at great length in "Politics as a Vocation," the discipline which underlay modernity would much more likely have the effect of turning political parties, the vehicles for mass political participation, into organizations which resembled machines. To produce votes, citizens in a mass society are transformed into tools, and modern politics comes to embody the domination and depersonalized motivation left over from asceticized religious life. Even the universities and the enterprises of modern science, institutions which embody more than any other the rational promise of secularizing change, were subject, in Weber's mind, to this transvaluation of values. Chance rather than merit now governs academic advancement (Weber 1946b:131–132), and the centralization of research is proletarianizing the scientist, turning him into a mere cog in the scientific machine.

Even when he indicated this other side of religious rationalization, Weber did not entirely ignore the benefits which were promoted along the way. Economic growth and political efficiency were not to be sneezed at, nor was the most important benefit of all, namely, equality. The objectification which made men into tools of God's will made them all equally so. The domination of impersonal rules reduced all men to the same status. Citizenship was the other side of depersonalized domination. Weber demonstrated this in *The City*, but at very few places outside of this historical essay did he suggest that the cultural and psychological capacity for citizenship would lead to political activism and democratic change. He was much more concerned to show how citizenship allowed the mass organization of individuals for demogogic ends.

There is a vast discussion in Weber's work of the material causes for such dominating tendencies. In *Economy and Society,* for example, he conceptualizes the sequence from patriarchal estate to patrimonial/prebendary domination, and he outlines the economic and political exegencies which lead on from there to modern bureaucratization. The problem with this whole line of discussion, however (Alexander, 1983a, 1983b), is that Weber fails to bring into it the theory of the objectification of the spirit I have just described. That he knew such a connection existed there seems little doubt. It is only the intention to establish such a link which can explain the brief, condensed discussion of the relation between charisma and discipline in *Economy and Society.* Weberian interpretation (with the exception of Mitzman 1969) has neatly confined charisma to Weber's typology of political legitimacy and to his technical accounts of religious and political innovation. Given Weber's own ambiguity on this point, this is understandable. Still, it is not correct. There is evidence in Weber's work that he tried to use the concept of charisma in a much broader form. It was to be the opening by which Weber could outline the dark side of spiritual rationalization.

He begins this short segment of *Economy and Society* (Weber 1978:1148–1157) with a general, nonhistorical statement about charisma and discipline: "It is the fate of charisma to recede before the powers of tradition or of rational association after it has entered the permanent structures of social action (p. 1148)." This is simply a restatement of the typology of legitimation. What follows, however, shows that Weber has something very different in mind. "The waning of charisma," he writes, "generally indicates the diminishing importance of individual action." Now according to the more positive side of his rationalization theory—the side which illuminates the development of individuation—rational socialization should promote individual action, not diminish it. What can explain the dramatic change in Weber's point of view?

The answer seems to be that in this essay Weber wants to point to the ironic fact that rational ideas can work against individualism. He stresses that charisma can be the carrier of different kinds of ideas, that it must be treated in an historical way. Of all those powers that lessen the importance of individual action, he writes (p. 1148), "the most irresistible force is rational discipline." In other words, while the waning of charisma always undermines individuality, it does so variably. When it is the carrier of rationalizing ideas, it does so very forcefully indeed.

Weber goes on to connect increased discipline not only to rationalizing charisma, but to another key element of religious evolution, namely, to increased equality. Discipline "eradicates not only personal charisma," he writes (ibid.), "but also stratification by status groups." And in the sentence which follows he makes the link between subjugation and rationalization as explicit as it could possibly be: "The content of discipline is nothing but the consistently rationalized, methodically prepared and exact execution of the received order, in which all personal criticism is unconditionally suspended and the actor is unswervingly and exclusively set for carrying out the command."

Weber can now discuss the darker side of Puritan development, for he can show how the religious rationalization it entailed led to increased discipline and not just greater autonomy. "Insofar as discipline appeals to firm ethical motives," Weber suggests (pp. 1149–50), "it presupposes a sense of duty and conscientiousness," and in a parenthetical aside he contrasts " 'men of conscience' " and " 'men of honor', in Cromwell's terms." Rather than entrepreneurial activity, Weber makes war the secular outgrowth of the Protestant ethic. He writes that it was "the sober and rational Puritan discipline [that] made Cromwell's victories possible," and he goes on to elaborate the contrasting military styles in technical terms. When Weber talks about routinization in this discussion he is referring not to the economic patterns that result from active religious commitment but to the discipline that remains. What is left after the charismatic phase of Puritanism is the habit of strict obedience.

Weber has added, then, a fundamentally new and quite different twist to his famous Protestant Ethic thesis about the relation between religious development and modern society. Yet there are strong indications in this essay that he intended to go much further. He refers, for example, to the "disciplinary aspect" of every sphere and every historical period, without specifically tying this aspect to the development of this-worldly asceticism. He talks about "the varying impact of discipline on the conduct of war" and argues that it has had "even greater effects upon the political and social order."

Discipline, as the basis of warfare, gave birth to patriarchal kingship among the Zulus . . . Similarly, discipline gave birth to the Hellenic *polis* with its *gymnasia* . . . Military discipline was also the basis of Swiss democracy. (Weber 1978:1152)

In other words, key elements in ancient, pre-Judeo-Christian societies and modern post-Reformation ones alike can be causally linked to charismatically generated subjection: "Military discipline was also instrumental in establishing the rule of the Roman patriciate and, finally, the bureaucratic states of Egypt, Assyria and modern Europe." Weber (1153) goes on pointedly to suggest that the "warrior is the perfect counterpart to the monk." He is not referring here to the causal power of religion. He wishes to suggest, rather, that the disciplinary dimension of cultural evolution promoted monasteries just as it promoted war. The "garrisoned and communistic life in the monastery," Weber writes, "serves the purpose of disciplining [the monk] in the service of his other-worldly master (ibid)." Just in case his point is not yet understood, Weber adds that a direct result of such service might well be subjection of the monk to "his this-worldly master" as well.

The cultural development of discipline is presented here as an independent variable in human history, a cultural push just as important as the evolution toward individuation. Weber writes, for example, that "the emancipation of the warrior community from the unlimited power of the overlord—as evidenced in Sparta through the institution of the Ephors —proceeds only so far as the interest in discipline permits (1154)." This essay, indeed, marks the only point in Weber's entire corpus where he explicitly develops a subjective side for his explanation of bureaucracy. He calls bureaucracy the "most rational offspring" of discipline.

Weber emphasizes not only that cultural discipline—the "other side" of religious rationalization—creates the desire for voluntary subjection, but that it provides a tool for domination over others as well. While the existence of discipline certainly precedes any particular leader's drive for power, its existence clearly helps a power-hungry leader to achieve his ends. Would-be demagogues seize on discipline and learn how to turn it to their particular purpose; they can make good use of "the rationally calculated optimum of the physical and psychic preparedness of the uniformly conditioned masses." Acknowledging that enthusiasm and voluntary devotion continue to mediate even the most disciplined subjection, Weber (p. 1150) insists that "the sociologically decisive points" in such relationships must be connected to the historical rise of discipline and the way it facilitates external domination rather than voluntary legitimation. First, the rise of disciplined domination means that "these seemingly imponderable and irrational emotional factors," i.e., enthusiasm and devotion, are "in principle, at least, calculated in the same manner as one calculates the yield of coal and iron deposits" (ibid). Second, the followers' enthusiasm assumes a rationalized form which makes them much more open to discipline: "Devotion is normally impersonal, oriented toward a purpose, a common cause, a rationally intended goal, not a person as such, however personally tinged devotion may be in the case of a fascinating leader (ibid)."

When Weber writes (p. 1156) that "discipline inexorably takes over ever larger areas as the satisfaction of political and economic needs is increasingly rationalized," and that "this universal phenomenon more and more restricts the importance of charisma and of individually differentiated conduct," his intention could not be more clear. He is arguing that rationalization results not only in increased autonomy but in the spread of impersonal domination through every sphere of life. The increased capacity for this-worldly calculation sustains individuation, it is true. But it simultaneously facilitates subjection and domination. Weber invented the concept of rationalization to explain the seemingly irreconcilable qualities of the twentieth century. Once he succeeded in developing his theory of the paradox of rationalization, he had accomplished his goal. It is not simply the technical growth of military and industrial power, Weber now understands, which explains the horrors of our time. This depressing situation is also the outcome, quite simply, of the increasing inhumanity of man to man. This inhumanity is a subjective capacity that has developed alongside the capacity for objectification. It is the capacity for depersonalization of the self and other. It promotes discipline and subjection, on the one hand, and mastery and autonomy on the other. With this new understanding Weber has translated his personal meditation on the human condition into a profound sociology of modern life.*

Flights From Rationalization

Not surprisingly, Weber is not content with the simple demonstration that this paradoxical structure exists.† He launched his later theory as a means of reflecting on the meaning of modern life. He is not just interested in explanations of life, but in approaching, as closely as any modern science can, the question "How should we live?" This commitment leads him to concretize the paradox of rationalization in terms of the agonizing options of existence that every modern individual confronts. Like Sartre's analysis in *Being and Nothingness,* Weber's account derives its pathos from the fact that he starts with an individual who has the capacity for freedom, though for Weber this capacity results from historical conditions, not ontology. Outside of his self, Sartre's individual faces an inert

---

*This discussion of discipline demonstrates that there are fundamental connections between one tendency in Weber's sociology, at least, and the theory of modernity produced by Foucault (e.g., most directly, Foucault 1977). Yet while Foucault certainly draws out the nature and ramifications of anti-individualistic discipline to an extent Weber might only have imagined, he also does it in a manner that Weber would not have entirely approved. In the first place, Foucault focused only on one side of the dialectic of domination and individuation: he did not see that the expanding domination he described was intimately tied up with the extension of individuality. In the second place, Foucault is, compared with Weber, quite antihistorical in his explanation for disciplinary expansion, both in his insistence on a relatively recent "epistemological break" as its source and in his failure to develop a comparative understanding of this phenomenon in non-Western civilizations. For both of these reasons, Foucault is able to appreciate neither the fact of the continuing—if not continuous—vitality of human responsibility in the modern world nor its sociological foundations. Much the same can be said for many other leading contemporary cultural critics, for example MacIntyre (1981) and Bell (1976).

†While Schluchter (1979) certainly advanced the discussion by emphasizing that Weber described the "paradoxes of rationalization," this leaves modernity in a more "liberal" and optimistic position than Weber intended. Weber's sensibility was more Gothic and brooding. His soteriology of flight rests on a vision of moral agony, not simple paradox.

world; internally, the self faces its own cravings for objectification and cowardice. These internally and externally generated dangers threaten to turn the "existing" individual into a thing, to convert the self-consciousness that allows freedom and action into the self-objectification that converts contingency into determinism and consciousness into being.

Weber's understanding is remarkably similar. His actor, of course, is already objectified. Weber sees this as the basis of freedom; his historical understanding allowed him to see that individuality is sociology not just ontology. Yet the structures that exist outside Weber's "self" are just as inert—they form the iron cage of depersonalized domination. And the dangers that exist inside of Weber's "self" are just as real. The ego that Weber describes as the proud product of rationalization must contend, he insists, with its own capacity for self-mortification and its puerile desire to submit to discipline. For Weber, too, this dangerous situation marks the existential condition of the modern world.

What can an individual do? Like Sartre, Weber precedes this question with another: what is the individual likely to do? Sartre believes that the pressures of existence push the individual toward some "mode of flight." One way or another, most people find ways to deny their freedom. They may give up the anguish of being a free person for the horror of viewing themselves as a determined one, constituting their selves as enslaved to external, inhuman force. Or they engage in a kind of play-acting which wraps them in a sentimental fantasy and denies the threatening qualities of the world. Both responses are acts of bad faith; both are escapes from freedom. Weber, too, explores "flights from the world" at great length, though he characterizes them more historically than ontologically, as escapes peculiar to a modern society. He, too, characterizes such flights in terms of whether they refer to pressures from without or within.

On the one hand, Weber describes the constant tendency for cynical adaptation to the demands of the day. Here is the bureaucrat who obediently follows his orders, the practical politician who pleads his helplessness before the demands of interest groups and the pressures of the moment, the scientist who becomes a cog in the research machine. In this mode of flight the individual becomes a mere tool of the disciplined spirit; he is no more than a means for some other determinate power or end. On the other hand, flight from the world can take an internal form. Rather than accepting the "reality" of his objectified position, the individual tries to recreate some sense of oneness with the world, the cosmological experience of premodern man. This internal flight can take two forms. It might involve the attempt to redivinize the world. In this situation the individual tries to replace the warring gods with a single, all-powerful one which can provide a firm, all-encompassing meaning for the world. Here is the idealistic, reality-denying politician of "conviction"; the professor who pretends that science can discover the meaning of life and manipulates his position of scientific authority to impart this meaning to his students; the believer who thinks he has heard the clarion call of modern day prophecy.

Yet the recreation of oneness need not take on this kind of metaphysical hue. It can find expression completely on the psychological level, as a commitment to what might be called experientialism (see, e.g., Weber 1946c:340–358). The person aims here to deny the status of "tool" bequeathed by asceticism and to recover the status of "vessel" allowed by mysticism. Eroticism is one major escape of this kind. Sex is pursued for the sake of physical gratification alone, and sexual satisfaction becomes the principal meaning of life. Aestheticism is another mystical form of escape, in which the experience of art is pursued for itself, for its form, quite separated from the ethical or intellectual meaning that marks its content.

Sartre's analysis of flight was abstract and philosophical. Weber's is historical and concrete. With it he typified the most terrible and unrelenting pathologies of modern times, from the destructive addictions and fantasies of private life to the totalitarian temptations and murderous dictatorships which have marked the public world. Weber is not simply describing "social problems." He has developed a typology of the horrors of the twentieth century which is systematically related to a vast reconstruction of its institutional and cultural archeology. Few have appreciated this achievement.

But this is not where Weber wants to leave us, any more than Sartre wishes to portray bad faith as ontological rather than simply epidemic. There is an alternative to flight from the world. For Sartre one must accept the anguish of freedom. Weber's answer is not different, just more sociological: one must find a vocation.

Existential Courage and "Vocation"

With the notion of vocation, elaborated primarily in the two essays bearing that title written toward the end of his life, Weber recalls a central theme from his analysis of cultural development in the presecular age. It was Luther who first emphasized the *Beruf,* and the Puritans who first made the "calling" central to religious salvation. The Puritans' vocation represented the first and most important result of the turn toward this-worldly asceticism, the religious movement that so decisively supported the movement toward rationality and individuation even while it ushered in the forces that threatened to overwhelm them in turn. The fact that the Puritans could still practice a vocation meant that they had not yet been overwhelmed by these institutional forces, forces which proceeded from the Puritans' own objectification of the religious spirit.

To practice a vocation as the Puritans did means to be disciplined by a moral spirit that facilitates the realization of the self. In the first place, therefore, it is to avoid the mystical experientialism that represents a major flight from reality in the modern world. Vocational commitment also prevents the cynical adaptation to external conditions that self-objectification and material domination are likely to beget. Finally, the Puritan vocation, while definitely a conviction, was not an idealistic commitment in the utopian sense of world-flight. Vocational conviction accepts the limits of the division of labor and institutional rationalization, in the sense that its moral discipline is narrowed to the requirements of a specific task.

In all these ways the ancient vocation of the Puritans and the contemporary vocation of moderns are the same. Yet there is an enormous difference as well.* The Puritan maintained his vocation in the service of God, his conviction and his work serving to maintain the fabric of cosmological meaning. In Weber's view, the modern vocation cannot allow this intellectual sacrifice. The fruits of rationalization must be maintained. Once this-worldly asceticism escaped from the cosmological net, it allowed a radically new form of autonomy and self-control. This-worldly asceticism created the first opportunity for vocation, but only in postreligious, secular society can the vocational commitment achieve its

---

*Here, my interpretation departs from the "neoreligious" tack taken by Shils (1975) and other conservative Weberians, who use Weber to oppose a strong secularization thesis.

highest result. Indeed, Weber believes that only with vocational morality can the modern person maintain his or her autonomy in the face of the objective pressures of the iron cage.

The language Weber uses to describe vocation in contemporary society make this link between Puritan and modern vocation clear, for it seems intended to demonstrate that secular vocations can allow some of the same psychological and cultural satisfactions as religious life. Science, he writes, can become an *"inward* calling" (Weber 1946b:134, original italics) whose significance for the practitioner touches the most profound issues of existence: "Whoever lacks the capacity to . . . come up to the idea that the fate of his soul depends upon whether or not he makes the correct conjecture at this passage of this manuscript may as well stay away from science" (Weber 1946b:135). Vocations, then, are concerned with salvation in the deepest sense of the word. What they have done is to connect the "soul" of modern man—which, evidently, Weber thinks still exists—to rationalized tasks in the modern world. The experience of a vocation can even be mystical in a thoroughly secular way, though the passion it inspires and the "strange intoxication" it affords may be "ridiculed by outsiders." Vocational commitment allows, for example, the experience of perfection associated with being a vessel of God: "The individual can acquire the sure consciousness of achieving something truly perfect in the field of science" (Weber 1946b:134). To have such a calling is to realize the great humanistic ideals, "for nothing is worthy of man as man unless he can pursue it with passionate devotion" (Weber 1946b:135).

The same possibility for maintaining "rational religion" is held out in Weber's politics essay. Here, too, Weber wants to suggest that the result of this-worldly asceticism need not be self-mortification and the crushing discipline of external force. Here, too, he presents this argument by using religious language in a secular way. Politics, of course, is intimately associated with violence. At first this association was mitigated by the degree to which politicians could live "for" politics, maintaining, thereby, some sense of individual responsibility and control. But with mass democracy, the need develops to organize and discipline the masses, and the mass politician learns to live "off" politics. The ideal-type of this new politician, the man without a vocation for politics, is the boss, the "absolutely sober man" (Weber 1946a:109) who embodies the flight from rationalization typified as cynical adaptation to the demands of the day.

It is the rudderless man without the calling for politics that produces the "soullessness" of modern politics. But this situation is not inevitable. There remains the possibility for "innerly 'called' " leaders (Weber 1946a:79). To have a calling the politician must subject himself to the discipline of a moral cause—"the serving of a cause must not be absent if action is to have inner strength" (Weber 1946a:117). The exact nature of the cause is a matter of individual choice, but "some kind of faith must always exist." But commitment to a cause must remain "secular"; it must not reflect the search for redivinization that represents another kind of flight from the world. If the politician were to submit to such an essentially religious point of view he would be committed not to a vocation but to an ethic of ultimate ends, to the "politics of conviction." What Weber advocates instead is the "ethic of responsibility."

Responsible, vocational political ethics can be achieved only if moral commitment is disciplined by rational assessment of the realistic possibilities for gaining one's ideals. "One has to give an account for the foreseeable results of one's action" (Weber 1946a:120). Faith, then, need not be eliminated from modern politics, but it must be disciplined by rationality. "It takes both passion and perspective," Weber writes (Weber 1946a:128). "What is decisive," he insists, is not only idealistic commitment but "the trained relentlessness in viewing the realities of life" (Weber 1946a:126–27). Adding such scientific realism to faith, of course, is precisely what pushes this-worldly asceticism to individuation rather than cosmology, and it is this demand for "rational accounting" that makes the pressure on the postcosmological individual so much more intense. What becomes decisive in achieving individuation is "the ability to face such realities and to measure up to them inwardly" (Weber 1946a:127). Only if this strength is achieved can a person have a calling for politics. Anyone "who is not spiritually dead" must realize that such a possibility does exist.

It is certainly not correct, then, to say, as so many of Weber's interpreters have, that Weber saw no escape from the iron cage other than the pursuit of irrational, charismatic politics. It is no more correct, indeed, than to describe Weber's sociology, as have so many others, as a paean to the realization of individuality in its various forms.* Rationalization is a

---

*Mitzman (1970) is not the only interpreter to make the former charge, viz., that Weber saw irrational, charismatic politics as the only way out. Loewenstein (1966) and Mommsen (1974), e.g., have made much the same point. Parsons and Bendix, of course, are the major figures associated with the identification of Weber as a progressive liberal who saw freedom

movement toward individuation, but it provides only for the conditions of individuality rather than individuality as such. Rationalization also creates the psychological needs and the cultural codes which sustain anti-individualistic institutional coercion. Faced with such destructive, depersonalizing forces, the individual either flees from them, giving up his or her independence, or confronts them and maintains it.

Weber presents this confrontation as an existential choice, with all the arbitrariness that such a position implies. Sartre is quite right to insist that there is nothing that can explain or predict whether an actor has the courage to accept the anguish of freedom. Weber expresses exactly the same sentiment when he suggests that vocational commitment depends on "the ability to face these realities and to measure up to them inwardly." Sartre is convinced that such courage is rarely to be found. Weber entirely agrees. In the emendations to *The Protestant Ethic* which he added during the period he was writing his vocation essays, Weber emphasizes just how unlikely vocational behavior in the modern world will be. "The idea of duty in one's calling," he writes, "prowls about in our lives like the ghost of dead religious beliefs" (Weber 1958:182). When occupational behavior is disconnected from religious direction or direct economic necessity, he suggests—he is clearly referring to conditions which develop in the twentieth century—it will rarely be elevated to a calling: "Where the fulfilment of the calling cannot directly be related to the highest spiritual and cultural values, or when, on the other hand, it need not be felt simply as economic compulsion, the individual generally abandons the attempt to justify it at all."

---

as the emerging product of world history. Though Schluchter's interpretation of Weber is more nuanced (1981), he has likewise seriously underplayed the apocalyptic, darker side of Weber's work. In general, Habermas (1984) agrees with these three liberal interpreters, though he is much more critical of Weber's failure to spell out the prerequisites even of a liberal and democratic society (a criticism which I will echo below). Yet Habermas also differs from Parsons, Bendix, and Schluchter by trying to focus on the negative side of the dialectic. As I mentioned earlier, however, he ultimately fails to illuminate this side of Weber's work because he conflates it with the anti-normative instrumentalism of critical theory.

Beyond Rationalization Theory: Toward a Fuller Dialectic

This sociology of modern life leaves us in a rather uncomfortable position. Weber has described an extraordinary dialectic of individuality and domination, and he has shown how, from this crucible, there emerge the flights from reality and the courageous assertions of freedom that are so characteristic of our time. Secularization has made freedom a possibility open to the exercise of personal courage; from the standpoint of any particular individual actor, however, it is impossible to predict whether individuality in this sense will ever be realized. Depersonalization is just as much an undeniable, yet profoundly disturbing modern fact. The topography of the twentieth century is strewn with societies wrecked by technological domination, totalitarian discipline, and existential flight.

Yet for all its breathtaking illumination—and Weber achieved more clarity about the dangers of modernity than any theorist before or since—this theory does not seem entirely satisfactory. It has identified certain crucial features of modern societies, but it has not identified them all. Weber has ignored, or at least seriously underplayed, the features that can help to sustain individuality and mitigate modern society's coercive and destructive features. His analysis is incomplete; as a result, his pessimism, while salutary, is to an important degree overdrawn.*

The course of modernity has indeed been marked by dreadful self-enslavement, but it has also been the site of extraordinary breakthroughs in the rational understanding of mental life and the democratic support of individual rights, breakthroughs that in turn† have bolstered the self. Institutional destruction has been unprecedented in our time; there have also been institutional developments that have increased human control of social processes on an unprecedented scale. Every society has been

---

*Weber's extremism in this regard has inspired social theorists who, ignoring the subtleties of his argument, describe the modern condition as a choice between chaotic freedom and conservative regulation. Thus, drawing on Weber, MacIntyre (1981) claims one must choose between Nietzche and Aristotle, and he chooses the teleological, hierarchical value framework of the latter. Neoconservatives like Bell (1976) pose a similar choice and reject the fragmentation of modernity for religious revival. In doing so, such theorists are succumbing to what I earlier called "metaphysical nostalgia," which is one intellectual form of world flight.

†See Levine (1981) for a strong argument that Weber failed to develop the kind of motivational theory which could account for such significant "rational" movements in modernity as psychotherapy.

undermined by individual and group flights from reality and crippled in significant ways by hierarchical domination; yet several critically important societies have managed acute crises and chronic strains in such a way as to sustain reasonable patterns of life. Finally, even societies that have succumbed to the modern horrors that Weber described—Nazi Germany, prewar Japan, Stalinist Russia—contained movements and institutions of a more rational and responsive character. The new forms of organization that often emerge from the destruction of such societies, moreover, demonstrate that "rational learning" can take place on a societal scale.[1]

Weber's sociology allows us to see what such positive moments in modernity have had to overcome, but it does not allow us to explain how it is that such experiences have been able to occur. They have not been random, and they have not depended simply upon the exercise of individual courage. They have occurred for structural reasons that can be sociologically explained.

It is true that most of the great theorists of the twentieth century have been extraordinarily pessimistic. There have been a few, however, who in considering the future have offered more grounds for hope. Parsons is certainly the most significant example, and it is not an accident that among the great social theorists he is the only American.* But there have been Europeans as well—Durkheim to an important degree, Keynes in significant ways, Piaget, and Habermas as well. In critical respects these more optimistic theorists often seriously underestimated the perils of their day.† Yet, if we are to understand how individual and social vitality can

---

*In the remarkable concluding chapter to their reconsideration of Parsonian sociology, Holton and Turner (1986) emphasize Parsons' distance from the "metaphysical nostalgia" that lingered in the work of classical sociologists, despite their commitment to the norms of democracy. They, too, link this to the American origins of Parsons' thought: "For Parsons, the preoccupation of European sociological thought with questions like the fate of capitalism and the politics of class interest represents a concern with transitional features of the great transformation, rather than with modern society itself" (P. 219). It should be noted that Habermas (1984) draws extensively on Parsons' framework to criticize the instrumentalism of Weber's account of modernization, though he does not explicitly acknowledge the debt. For a similar account of the relation of Parsons to Weber, see Munch (1982).

†Marcel Mauss remarked in the 1930s that he and Durkheim had never imagined that their anthropological concept of symbolic "mana" could ever become a vehicle for something as ideologically primitive as Nazism. The naivete retrospectively acknowledged by this forthright admission shows that in crucial respects Durkheimian thought did not fully come to grips with the great transformation of the twentieth century. For a general discussion of these problems and similar limitations in Parsons' work, see Alexander 1988.

be sustained in modern times, it is to these theorists that we must turn. It is they who have explained how rationality, control, and community actually can be institutionalized in a modern world.

Durkheim stressed the anomic and egotistical in modernity, and in critical respects he never fully accepted its postcosmological state. He denounced the "moral cold" of contemporary societies and complained that "the old gods are growing old or already dead, and others are not yet born" [1912] 1965:475). At the same time, his work provides an ambitious if not fully developed account of how solidarity, cultural meaning, and individuality can be maintained in a secular way.*

While Weber argued that scientific rationality and ethical values can in principle coexist, he did not identify the conditions under which this might be achieved. Durkheim did, most importantly by making a broad and systematic argument for the continuing "religious" needs of human beings (Alexander, ed., 1988). He analyzed the social processes by which such needs could be met, suggesting the importance of symbol systems that did not embrace a supranatural telos. Durkheim knew that existential courage was not enough to overcome the minimalism of scientific rationality. He agreed that modern people were bound to be dissatisfied, and he considered it inevitable that rational knowledge would be experienced as radically incomplete. The search for meaning that results, however, did not have to be pursued in an entirely individualistic way. Naturalistic processes support meaningful belief systems by sustaining social solidarity. This group experience can, moreover, have a substantively rational form. Not only flights from reality but attempts to confront it ethically can be sustained by sources outside the individual. Even science, Durkheim came to believe, can be viewed in such solidaristic terms, as an ideal that holds moral and idealistic sway.†

Keynes also recognized the endemic instability of Western economic systems. Indeed, he replaced the instrumental approach to economic calculation with a theory that made capitalist investment dependent on irrational psychology and the vagaries of public confidence (Keynes [1936] 1965:e.g., 147–52, 315–20). While recognizing and explaining irrationality, however, Keynes was confident that twentieth-century civilizations

*See chapters 4–6 below.

†Prager (1981) draws a powerful contrast between Durkheim's and Weber's political sociologies, arguing that only Durkheim took the possibility of contemporary public morality seriously.

did not have to succumb to it. He insisted that scientific knowledge about society could control these irrational tendencies [1926] (1963). Public symbols of trust could be developed by professional, scientifically trained officials working in the context of a democratic government. Such democracies could overcome market instability and humanize economic life on a far-reaching scale (Keynes [1930] 1963). Agreeing with Weber that cultural life had undergone a profound differentiation, he insisted (Keynes [1938] 1972) on the independence of beauty from truth, moral commitments, and especially from economic life. Aestheticism need not, however, represent moral flight. As the economy became increasingly regulated, modern individuals would be free to pursue the sublimity of aesthetic ideals.

Parsons drew upon Keynes and Durkheim, but also upon Weber, Freud, and Piaget. While he acknowledged, particularly in his early work, that modernization might lead to aggression and polarization, he devoted most of his life to developing a theory of how this reaction could be avoided. Freud and Piaget allowed him to transform socialization theory from an account of social indoctrination to an explanation of how modern childhood can create reservoirs of individual strength and rationality. The separation of psyche from social and cultural givens need not create pain and world flight. If individuals are sustained by their initial socialization, this differentiation encourages creative independence and responsibility. Parsons argued that depersonalization can lead to more inclusive communities and more tolerant binding values. Secularization should be understood as the differentiation of guiding values, not their elimination. Generalized postreligious values can produce personal flexibility and social adaptiveness rather than discipline and rigid control.

Given this context of psychological and cultural change, rationalized economies and polities need not be seen as exploitative and materialistic (cf. Holton and Turner 1986). Parsons saw economies as hedged in by normative constraints, from professional obligations to cultural tastes, and polities as bound by the legal and moral ties of citizenship. Inclusion, not discipline, is the catchword for Parsons' modern state. Social systems institutionalize values. Critical rationality should be seen, not as a destructive commitment set apart from society, but as integral to the structures of modern societies and the belief systems of their members. If modern social systems are flexible enough, irrationality will continually be challenged by social movements that embody rational and emancipatory values. Domination will be confronted by differentiated structures and processes that aim to institutionalize individual autonomy.*

It is Habermas, of course, who has introduced the very concept of "rational learning" into the discourse of contemporary social science. Because he emerged from the critical tradition of Marx, Habermas never loses sight of the dark side of Weber's dialectic.† Yet he has incorporated the main thrust of Parsons' theorizing and emphasized even more than Parsons the developmental tradition of Piaget. The movement toward autonomy, rationality, and responsibility, he has suggested, is immanent in human societies. Throughout history, moral evolution has been intertwined with economic and political rationalization. Social systems do contain deep contradictions, but the crises that result are not necessarily destructive. They present opportunities for social learning and movement to a new stage.

I am not suggesting that Weber denied entirely the possibility that these kinds of positive developments might exist. It was he, after all, who wrote about vocational, professional commitments. He acknowledged that the profession of law might allow some politicians to live for politics rather than off it. In an important early essay Weber even suggested that participatory democracy could be maintained in nations that had experienced sect rather than church religion (see chapter 3, below). Weber outlined a theory of citizenship for the early modern period, and he acknowledged that the formal abstractions of modern law could be abrogated by oppressed groups seeking substantive rationality.

What I am suggesting is that theoretical weaknesses in Weber's work, on the one hand, and his ideological sensibility, on the other, made it impossible for him to convert these insights into systematic sociological theory. Weber saw that religious evolution had freed the individual in modern societies, but he described this modern individual as isolated and culturally abandoned. Weber described how depersonalization had changed

---

* In their argument for Parsons' "anti-nostalgia," Holton and Turner describe his thought in much the same way. "Compared with the sociologists of the classical period, Parsons is far less ambivalent about the modern world. The evaluative yardstick of 'community' does not appear in a strong form—whether as utopia or social ontology—as a moral foil to such modern developments as instrumental rationality, or individual achievement-orientation. Parsons is neither equivocal with respect to the operation of the market economy, political democracy and the rule of law, nor tortured by pessimistic doubts as to the possibility of a future world based on humanitarian values" (1986:216).

† I will suggest in chapter 7, however, that the residues of Marxian critical theory leave Habermas vulnerable to some of the same kinds of difficulties that mar Weber's own work.

institutional structures in a positive way, but he viewed the institutional residue of the twentieth century as coercive and the socialized motivation attached to it as dependent and authoritarian.

I have argued that these insights represent the strengths of Weber's sociology as surely as they represent its limits. As this great and terrible century draws to a close, we must reclaim Weber's dialectic of individuation and domination as our theoretical legacy. We must compell ourselves to go beyond it as well.

NOTE

1. Johnson's (1983) devastating synoptic history of the twentieth century is weakened by his refusal to acknowledge the existence of such positive strands. His attack on the subjective and internal focus of psychological and social theory in the twentieth century as leading to moral relativism is superficial. It fails to recognize that nineteenth-century liberal "moral absolutism," while providing an ostensibly powerful support for rationality and freedom, operated with such a limited understanding of motive and social integration that it could not understand the threats to freedom in an accurate way. "Relativism" has its obvious disadvantages, but it is also central to democratic tolerance and inclusion. Moreover, the more profound understanding of the nonrational aspects of motive in this century has opened up mental and spiritual life to the possibility of rational insight and control. Johnson also wildly exaggerates the "success" of nineteenth-century market systems. On this faulty basis he condemns the modern democratic welfare state as guilty of the same kind of "social engineering" that underlay communist and fascist societies. His inability to appreciate the extension of citizenship as one of the distinct triumphs of this century, or to explain it as anything other than unintended offshoot of market expansion, is a fundamental blind spot in this book.

REFERENCES

Alexander, Jeffrey C. 1983a. *The Classical Attempt at Theoretical Synthesis: Max Weber*. Vol. 3 of *Theoretical Logic in Sociology*. Berkeley and Los Angeles: University of California Press.

—— 1983b. "Max Weber, la théorie de la rationalization et le marxisme." *Sociologie et Sociétés* 14(2):33–43.

—— 1983c. *The Modern Reconstruction of Classical Thought: Talcott Parsons*. Vol. 4 of *Theoretical Logic in Sociology*. Berkeley and Los Angeles: University of California Press.

—— 1985. "Habermas' New Critical Theory: Problems and Prospects." *American Journal of Sociology* 91:400–424.

—— 1988. "Durkheim's Problem and Differentiation Theory Today." In Alexander, *Action and Its Environments: Toward a New Synthesis*, pp. 49–76. New York: Columbia University Press.

Alexander, Jeffrey C., ed. 1988. *Durkheimian Sociology: Cultural Studies*. New York: Cambridge University Press.

Alexander, Jeffrey C., and Colin Loader. 1985. "Max Weber on Churches and Sects in North America: An Alternative Path Toward Rationalization." *Sociological Theory* 3(1):1–13.

Bell, Daniel. 1976. *The Cultural Contradictions of Capitalism*. New York: Basic Books.

Durkheim, Emile. [1912] 1965. *The Elementary Forms of Religious Life*. New York: Free Press.

Foucault, Michel. 1977. *Discipline and Punish: The Birth of the Prison*. New York: Random House.

Habermas, Jurgen. 1984. *Reason and the Rationalization of Society*. Vol. 1 of *Theory of Communicative Action*. Boston: Beacon.

Holton, Robert J, and Bryan S. Turner. 1986. *Talcott Parsons on Economy and Society*. London and New York: Routledge and Kegan Paul.

Johnson, Paul. 1983. *Modern Times: The World from the Twenties to the Eighties*. New York: Harper and Row.

Keynes, John Maynard. [1926] 1963. "The End of Laissez-Faire." In Keynes, *Essays in Persuasion*, pp. 312–322. New York: Norton.

—— [1930] 1963. "Economic Possibilities for our Grandchildren." In Keynes, *Essays in Persuasion*, pp. 358–373.

—— [1936] 1965. *General Theory of Employment, Interest, and Money*. New York: Harcourt Brace Jovanovich.

—— [1938] 1972. "My Early Beliefs." In Donald Moggridge, ed., *The Collected Writings of John Maynard Keynes*, 10:433–450. Cambridge, England: St. Martin's Press.

Levine, Donald N. 1981. "Rationality and Freedom: Weber and Beyond." *Sociological Inquiry* 51:5–25.

Loewenstein, Karl. 1966. *Max Weber's Political Ideas in the Perspective of Our Time*. Amherst, MA: University of Massachusetts Press.

Lowith, Karl. 1982. *Max Weber and Karl Marx*. London: Allen and Unwin.

MacIntyre, Alisdaire. 1981. *After Virtue*. South Bend, Ind.: Notre Dame University Press.

Mitzman, Arthur. 1970. *The Iron Cage*. New York: Grosset and Dunlap.

Mommsen, Wolfgang. 1974. *The Age of Bureaucracy*. New York: Harper and Row.

Münch, Richard. 1982. "Talcott Parsons and the Theory of Action, II: The Continuity of the Development." *American Journal of Sociology* 87:771–826.

Prager, Jeffrey. 1981. "Moral Integration and Political Inclusion: A Comparison of Durkheim's and Weber's Theories of Democracy." *Social Forces* 59:918–950.

Rawls, John. 1971. *A Theory of Justice*. Cambridge: Harvard University Press.

Schluchter, Wolfgang. 1979. "The Paradoxes of Rationalization." In Guenther Roth and Wolfgang Schluchter, *Max Weber's Vision of History*, pp. 11–64. Berkeley and Los Angeles: University of California Press.

—— 1981. *The Rise of Western Rationalism: Max Weber's Developmental History*. Berkeley and Los Angeles: University of Calfornia Press.

Seidman, Steven. 1983. "Modernity, Meaning, and Cultural Pessimism in Max Weber." *Sociological Analysis* 44:267–278.

Shils, Edward. 1975. "Charisma, Order, and Status." In Shils, *Center and Periphery: Essays in Macro-Sociology*, pp. 256–275. Chicago: University of Chicago Press.

Weber, Max. [1906] 1985. "Church and Sect in North America," *Sociological Theory*, vol. 3(1): 7–13.

—— 1946a. "Politics as a Vocation." In Hans Gerth and C. Wright Mills, eds., *From Max Weber*, pp. 77–128. New York: Oxford University Press.

—— 1946b. "Science as a Vocation." In Hans Gerth and C. Wright Mills, eds., *From Max Weber*, pp. 129–156.

—— 1946c. "Religious Rejections of the World and Their Directions." In Hans Gerth and C. Wright Mills, eds., *From Max Weber*, pp. 323–359.

—— 1958. *The Protestant Ethic and the Spirit of Capitalism*. New York: Scribner.

—— 1978. *Economy and Society*. Berkeley and Los Angeles: University of California Press.

THREE

The Cultural Grounds of Rationalization: Sect Democracy Versus the Iron Cage

Western liberals, from Parsons and Bendix to Aron and Schluchter, have viewed Max Weber as exploring the foundations of freedom in modern society. Marxists, like Marcuse, have seen him as rationalizing the end of freedom with his notion of modernity as an iron cage. Both sides, of course, have a point. While Weber remained committed to defending the individual against all the forces of domination, his very theory of modern development made this onslaught seem like a force against which—for all but the most heroic—it would be impossible to fight.

This, at least, is the clear perspective of Weber's later, postbreakdown work. Hidden inside the Weberian corpus, however, one can find an important essay which, while systematically related to the historical and comparative concerns of mature Weberian theory, departs from its most pessimistic and unidimensional conclusions in profoundly illuminating ways. It does so by placing the cultural ground of rationalization into a comparative context, developing a novel contrast not just between Protestant and Catholic countries but between different kinds of Protestant nations themselves. We have recently published a translation of this long-neglected work (Weber [1906] 1985). In what follows we explore the potentially far-reaching implications of this early work for the study of contemporary society.

Shortly after returning from an extended trip to America in 1904, Max Weber wrote a reflection on what he had learned entitled " 'Churches' and

This essay was written with Colin Loader.

'Sects' in North America: An Ecclesiastical, Socio-Political Sketch." Published by Weber first in the *Frankfurter Zeitung* and later in a slightly amplified version in *Christliche Welt* (Weber 1906), the essay did not appear in English until 1985. Given the manifest relevance of its subject matter, it is curious that this work, by one of the great founding figures of modern sociology, had to wait eighty years to make its English-language debut.

The reason for this extraordinary oversight seems to be a fateful misunderstanding of the relation between "Churches and Sects" and later, revised versions of the essay, especially "The Protestant Sects and the Spirit of Capitalism" (Weber [1920] 1946).* The latter piece, which was, in fact, among the first of Weber's essays to be translated, is described by the leading historical interpretor of Weber's work (Mommsen 1974:80) as "the attempt to give a more comprehensive scope to [Weber's] empirical observations [in "Churches and Sects"] and to give them a scientific underpinning." The implication of Mommsen's statement is clear. The later version is more comprehensive and sophisticated, the original superfluous as a result. This view is echoed throughout Weberian scholarship. Beetham (1974:214), who has written the most comprehensive account of Weber's political sociology, calls "The Protestant Sects" essay a "later reworking" of "Churches and Sects," and Roth (in Weber 1978:1211), the editor of the authoritative edition of Weber's *Economy and Society,* dismisses the 1906 essay as merely an "earlier and shorter version" of the later work. Berger (1971:489), the only writer who has ever devoted an entire article to Weber's sect theory, claims that "the later analysis of the Protestant sects is a clearer and subtler continuation of [the] earlier work."

We strongly disagree with this received view, believing that the original is remarkable in a number of ways, and even, in certain important respects, far superior.† First, the essay sheds new light on Weber's intellec-

---

*A third treatment of this topic is the very short segment entitled "Church, Sect, and Democracy" (Weber 1978:1204–1211) which concludes Weber's chapter on "Political and Hierocratic Domination" in *Economy and Society.* While segments like these are difficult to date, it was probably composed between 1913 and 1920.

†The grounds for this comparative judgement will be elaborated below, but the following points can briefly be made. The *Economy and Society* segment is much briefer than "Churches and Sects." Moreover, while it has the advantage of placing the issue into the systematic conceptualization of Weber's later work, it speaks mainly of the political implications of sect life and makes little reference to American society as such. It also pushes the

tual biography and the contours of his scientific development. Second, it has significant implications for the interpretive debates which rage around the Weber corpus. Finally, and most important of all, it retains contemporary empirical and theoretical significance in its own right.*

I

Weber's trip to America in 1904 came at an important time in his life, just as he began to emerge from the debilitating mental illness that had forced him to withdraw from a promising academic career. In the year before his trip, he had written four major essays—two on methodology, one which continued his agrarian studies from the 1890s, and the first part (unpublished before the trip) of *The Protestant Ethic and the Spirit of Capitalism* —all of which moved him further away from the academic mainstream in which his career had begun. Yet, while these studies declared his independence from the old order, Weber at this point had no positive alternative. In the fifteen years which remained to him, Weber did, of course, develop an original and provocative theory of world-historical scope. This theory described the universal rationalization of the Western world. While this rationalization was initially conceived as liberating and certainly as indispensible for modernization, it was linked in this later theory to the

---

effects of the sect phenomenon much more into the past than does "Churches and Sects." In the 1920 "Protestant Sects," by contrast, America becomes the exclusive focus, but the essay deals almost entirely with economic implications and places the effects of the sect phenomenon almost completely in the past. Neither of the other two treatments of the issue, therefore—and this is perhaps the most important difference—achieves the kind of generalized meditation on modernity which would seem to be the most distinctive quality of "Churches and Sects."

*In light of these considerations, it is a surprising fact that, with the exception of the works by Berger, Beetham, and Mommsen cited above, Weber's theory of sect-life and its relationship to modern social structure has received virtually no attention. Beetham refers to the topic only in a summary of Weber's work on Russia and never discusses it on its own. Mommsen discusses the importance of the sect to America, but does not develop its implications either in his article or in his more comprehensive works. Berger discusses the sects merely as the insitutional form of the Protestant Ethic, emphasizing only their role in the destruction of a "tenacious" traditional society. In taking this tack he fails not only to add anything new to the Protestant Ethic debate, but also to see the fundamental role of sect-life for posttraditional society. Even so close a student of Weber's work as Kalberg (1987) has entirely neglected the sect-versus-church contrast in his comparison of German and American religio-cultural values.

eventual closing out of democratic and emancipatory possibilities throughout the Western world.*

When Weber made his American trip, however, this theory was not yet laid out, though there were clear premonitions to be sure. Indeed, it is our belief that a quite different conception of modernization—or at least the clear potential for one—crystallized for Weber on his American trip and that the residue of this crucial experience was formalized in "Churches and Sects."

Certainly in Marianne Weber's (1975:279–304) account of the trip one can see that it marked an important shift in Weber's personal outlook. She records how the other German intellectuals accompanying the Webers were repulsed by the cold, impersonal products of the new world's "capitalistic spirit," which they contrasted to German "congeniality" *(Gemütlichkeit)*. Weber, on the other hand, enthralled by the new, held out for a more considered opinion. During the four months of his stay, he sought out ordinary Americans in all walks of life and almost every section of the country. The fruit of this activity, according to Marianne, was his discovery of the "moral kernel" beneath America's objectified shell. "Weber eagerly absorbed all this," she writes (1975:299). "He was stimulated to give effortlessly of his own resources what was able to delight these simple people, and thus unearthed in them the treasures of the experiences of a lifetime." Weber himself wrote that the trip had widened his scholarly horizons as well as improved his health. However, he acknowledged (Marianne Weber 1975:304) that "its fruits in this respect can, of course, not be seen for some time." Despite the fact that it has been virtually forgotten since its appearance, "Churches and Sects," published just sixteen months after Weber's return, turns out to have been a very important intellectual fruit indeed.

What did Weber see in America that stimulated him so? We believe that it was a glimmer of a way out of the "iron cage" of reified modern society, the very same oppressive environment which he himself would later portray as an inevitable characteristic of modern life. It was not only Weber's later work but the mainstream of German intellectual life which portrayed modernity in this way. Throughout the German university system (Ringer 1969), modernity was depicted in dualistic terms similar

---

*See my argument in chapter 2, "The Dialectic of Individuation and Domination."

to Ferdinand Tönnies's famous set of types, *Gemeinschaft* and *Gesellschaft*. The *Gemeinschaft* represented the traditional, pre-industrial "community," which was seen as an organic totality in which an elite governed in the name of values common to the entire group. The *Gesellschaft*, on the contrary, represented modern, industrial "society," a mechanistic grouping of individuals who felt no common will or values, sharing only a set of instrumental ends. The epitome of the *Gesellschaft* to most German academics was mass democratic society. Most importantly, the *Gesellschaft* was seen as something essentially negative (König 1955)—as the decay of the *Gemeinschaft*, as the dissolution of the organic unity into an atomistic "sandpile" in which material interests became independent of the meaningful ideal realm. The process of modernization from *Gemeinschaft* to *Gesellschaft* was viewed, then, as a tragic one in which something was irretrievably lost.* It was to resist this trend that mainstream academics sought to reinforce the traditional elites, which included, along with themselves, the nobility and the bureaucracy (Dahrendorf 1969).

This is not to say that Weber ever identified with this traditional position. The very forces which most academics saw as the antidote to the *Gesellschaft*—Protestant religious ideals, academic learning, the bureaucratic establishment and even the nobility—were described by him as contributors to the modernization process. He sharply rejected the academic mandarins' reactionary sentimentality.† In "Churches and Sects,"

---

*Many German academics did not actually use the terminology of Tönnies's 1887 book until shortly before World War I, although Weber himself does use the terms in his 1906 essay. We have simplified the use of terms in order to emphasize the essence of what was at issue. An important sub-theme in the German discussion was the role of "society" as distinct from the typologized *Gesellschaft*. Many academics saw society as a level properly subordinated to the ideal realm of values, which was embodied in the spheres of culture and/or the state. Society, to them, consisted basically of material interests and the relationships resulting from those interests. When such forces escaped from their subordination to the ideal spheres of culture and the state, they ceased to be simply society and became instead the *Gesellschaft*, a negative alternative to the ideal, organic sphere. For discussions of different aspects of this issue, see Lindenlaub (1967), Loader (1976), Lenk (1972), and Kalberg (1987).

†Our argument, then, differs fundamentally from the one put forward by Mitzman (1970), which holds that Weber's efforts to escape form the "iron cage" of contemporary Germany were directed in an entirely anti-ascetic direction. Mitzman believes, moreover, that it was this kind of proto-mystical attack on the Protestant ethic which inspired Weber in the immediate postbreakdown period after 1903. "Churches and Sects" reveals, to the

for example, he describes the established, Lutheran church of Germany as indifferent to values, as rigidly institutionalized and overly abstract when compared to the highly committed sects of the American type. In placing a rather mystical ceremonial element beside an ambition for secular power, the established church is seen by Weber as inherently hypocritical. Further, the church is identified with both the state bureaucracy and the German tradition of learning *(Bildung)*, the basic components of the old German elite.

At the same time, however, Weber was attracted throughout much of his work to the same dichotomizing ideological and philosophical framework as his traditional colleagues, and to the same vision of decline. Insofar as these powerful sympathies ruled his later work, he ascribed only instrumental motives to modern actors and groups, for he believed that values in modern society had become dissolved into reified forms. The treatment of modern society in Weber's later work, in other words, conforms to the *Gemeinschaft/Gesellschaft* dichotomy. Unlike most other German academics, however, Weber did not believe that the acceptance of this dichotomy allowed retreat into some imagined organic *Gemeinschaft,* in either a reactionary or a radical form. Any attempt to combine an organic unity with modernity, he believed, represented the same inherent hypocrisy which he saw in the established German church. Weber insisted that the repressive and mechanistic *Gesellschaft* had to be faced directly, even if only a few heroic individuals would be able to do so without fear or flight (see Chapter 2).

In "Churches and Sects," however, one finds a more multidimensional view of modernity, one strand of which stands quite fully at odds with that of Weber's traditional colleagues. In this line of his thinking, which virtually disappears from the later versions of the essay, Weber conceives of the possibility, not of a few individuals breaking through the iron cage, but of whole societies escaping it altogether. He envisioned the possibility

---

contrary, that it was Weber's very enthusiasm for one form of ascetic Protestantism which provided such inspiration, and that Weber certainly glimpsed at least one significant way to escape from the iron cage which did not involve rejecting this tradition. In terms of the conceptualization of Weber's later writings, Mitzman is correct that Weber sought some way of reinjecting charisma into routinized modern life, but, in the line of his thought that we are concerned with here, he conceived of this as follows: a national tradition of sect-organization reinvigorates and democratically redefines the "office charisma" upon which modern rational-legal authority rests. See especially, in this regard, Weber 1978:1204–1211.

of a new type of *Gesellschaft* based on a complex form of rational conduct, a form which combined purposive rational action with adherence to values.* Such a possibility was acknowledged only rarely in Weber's subsequent work. Only at the end of his life, in "Politics as a Vocation" ([1919] 1946), did he write about it once more in a systematic way, but this time in a more political than sociological form (see section IV below).

II

Weber begins "Churches and Sects" with a surprising new concept, an historical apprehension, and a pithy ethnographic observation.

The considerable development of ecclesiastical communal life in the United States is a phenomenon which strikes all but the most superficial visitor. Nevertheless, today rapid Europeanization is repressing everywhere the total ecclesiastical permeation of life that characterized authentic "Americana." One can observe the singular compromises in which this repression expresses itself, for example, the following statutory regulations at one of the two Chicago universities: attendance at chapel, which is compulsory for students by penalty of expulsion, (1) can be "discharged" by registering for certain courses beyond the required minimum number, (2) and when one's chapel record (sic!) has clearly exceeded the semester's requirements, either *in natura* or by substitution, the accumulated *opera supererogationis* can be *credited* toward subsequent semesters. (Weber [1906] 1985:7)

The historical apprehension and observation are real enough, but the gist of the essay that follows qualifies them in substantial ways. What is never taken back is Weber's concept of "Europeanization." Weber invents the term to describe a form of secularization from which, he hopes, America may be immune. When secularization takes a European form, social life escapes entirely from the ethical effects of earlier religious life, not only from the direct control of religion itself. Europeanization implies, in other words, an indifference to substantive moral commitments in favor of merely formal compliance.

It is just this formality and "absolute indifference" (Weber [1906] 1985:12) that characterizes the church as a form of religious organization. Weber convicts churches of a "deep inner insincerity" about the religious

* It is in this sense that virtually Weber's entire corpus can be seen as a critical response to German mandarin ideology. Thus, one concept missing from Weber's work which can be found throughout much of the traditional academic literature is "Manchesterism," with its implication that modern industrial society was a foreign thing invading Germany.

commitments of laity, and he believes that this insincerity lays the foundation for "customary and expedient" behavior among citizens of nations guided by churchly religion. To this phenomenon he contrasts the American form of secularization that emanates from religious sects. Where the church breeds indifference and formalism, the sect fosters fierce commitment and an almost fanatical concern for substantive obedience to the spirit of the law. The passion that sects demand in the religious life of the laity, moreover, fosters principled and radical forms of political participation.

Europeanization, then, means not simply secularization but rather the encroachment of the "church" model of social organization upon a more sect-like one. Weber is not talking, in other words, about the *Gesellschaft* encroaching upon the *Gemeinschaft,* for he believed that America had no real organic traditional entity, but about the encroachment of one form of *Gesellschaft* upon another. For Weber, sect-like religion is not traditional, i.e., not *gemeinschaftlich,* a denial that is consistent with his assignment of its origins to the Reformation. "Modernization," Europeanization, and "secularization" must be distinguished. While the three may be coterminous, they are not necessarily synonymous.

Because these concepts are not identical for Weber, he believes that in modern societies the functions of religion—the social patterns first established by religious organization—can be maintained even while the scope of religious institutions is diminished. While worried about the possible Europeanization of America, he believes that the "ecclesiastical character" of America remains, even in the early twentieth century, "one of the most powerful components of conduct as a whole" (Weber [1906] 1985:7). Indeed, it is this essay's central contention that ecclesiastic patterns can be carried on by secular groups whose role is largely defined by the nature of the religious community from which they grew. "Today," Weber reports about an America which is increasingly secular, "large numbers of 'orders' and clubs of all sorts have begun to assume in part the functions of the religious community." Noting that "almost every small businessman who thinks something of himself wears some kind of badge in his lapel," he immediately reminds his readers that "the archetype of this form which *all* use to guarantee the 'honorableness' of the individual, is indeed the ecclesiastical community" (Weber [1906] 1985:8, original italics). Shortly after this discussion, Weber describes how sect membership "sanitizes" members who have bad debts by restoring their reputations.

"This practice is in decline among the sects today," he notes in parentheses (Weber [1906] 1985:8), "but can be found in numerous 'orders.' " Near the end of the essay, Weber ([1906] 1985:10–11) asserts that, insofar as Europeanization has not occurred, "the old 'sect spirit' holds sway with relentless effect" throughout American clubs and associations, "be it a football team or a political party."

Historically prior religious communities, then, establish the dominant cultural code or schema, and succeeding secular forms embody this initial impulse. "The tremendous flood of social structures which penetrates every nook and cranny of American life," Weber writes (1985:10), "is constituted in accordance with the schema of the 'sect.' " The ethical and moral identity of contemporary American institutions, particularly voluntary organizations, is determined by the moral and psychological qualities of these earlier Protestant groups. No wonder Weber insists that "the sects' importance extends beyond the religious sphere" ([1906] 1985:10).*

This insistence on historical specificity—and the accompanying emphasis on the continuity between religious and moral commitments and their possible centrality in contemporary societies—opens up links between Weber and other theoretical traditions which have usually been considered antagonistic. Tocqueville, too, found the roots of American democracy in America's "voluntaristic religion." Durkheim emphasized the religious foundations of modernity, and Parsons, with his notion of cultural specification, very much followed suit.† This emphasis in Weber's work, moreover, opens up a clear line to the fertile field of "American Studies," whose research on the religious grounding of American democratic institutions has flourished from Perry Miller's pathbreaking studies (e.g., Miller 1956, 1965) to the present day (e.g., Bloch 1985).

At least as important for the history of sociology, however, is the conflict which this alternative understanding establishes inside of Weber's sociological theory itself. The contrast between Europeanization and secularization leads to a decisive critique of the univocal rationalization thesis. If contemporary institutions do, indeed, inherit a society's initial religious impulses in a more secular form, then rationalization, or mod-

*This emphasis should not be taken to imply an exclusively cultural explanation of American democracy. At several points in "Churches and Sects," Weber shows he is thoroughly aware of other variables. His point is that sect organization is the key variable differentiating Europe and America in terms of the development of democracy.

†See my argument about Durkheim in chapter 4–6, below. For 'specification' in Parsons's cultural theory, see Alexander 1988 and chapter 6, below.

ernization, cannot be seen simply as an objective development that possesses a purely universal, cross-national character. Rather, modernization, would have to be seen, in Weber's words, as occurring within historically given "modes of life." Weber himself seemed aware of the provocative challenge this line of thinking implied. "We modern, religiously 'unattuned' people," he warned his German readers, "are hard pressed to conceptualize or even simply to *believe* what a powerful role these religious factors had in those periods when the characters of the modern national cultures were being stamped ([1906] 1985:11, original italics).

Yet while these reflections on modernization reflect the far-reaching implications of "Churches and Sects," Weber's concern in this essay is less with such general questions than with the particular contrast between America and Germany. "It is and remains the fate of us Germans," he writes ([1906] 1985:11), "that, due to numerous historical causes, the religious revolution at that time [i.e., the Reformation] meant a development that favored not the energy of the individual but the prestige of the 'office.' " The result was that "the religious community withheld from itself the development of that community-forming energy which the school of the 'sects' . . . had imparted to an Anglo-Saxon world so completely different in these respects from the German" (p. 11).* By contrast, it is the American history of sectarian religion which gives to "American democracy its own flexible structure and its individualistic stamp" (p. 10).

III

So much for the general significance of religious forms. It is time to consider what Weber means by the sect/church distinction in more detail. In one long passage Weber offers a succinct comparison.

A church sees itself as an "institution *[Anstalt],* a kind of divinely endowed foundation *[Fideikomisstiftung]* for the salvation of individual souls who are *born into it* and are the *object* of its efforts, which are bound to the "office" in principle. Conversely, a "sect" . . . is a voluntary community of individuals purely on the basis of their religious *qualification.* The individual is *admitted* by virtue of a voluntary resolution by both parties. (Weber [1906] 1985:9, original italics)

---

*In 1906 Weber wrote to Adolf von Harnack: "It is an inherently difficult and typical situation that none of us [Germans] can be a sect-person, Quaker, Baptist, etc. Each of us must notice at first glance the dominance of, basically, the institutional church measured by non-ethical and non-religious values" (Mommsen 1974:83–84).

Weber concentrates here on the relation between individuals and organizations and on the crucial mediation of entrance criteria—what he calls "the concept of 'membership' " (p. 7). In authoritarian groupings, individuals are objectified by the organizational structure; they are conceived as serving the organization's interests. In democratic organizations, by contrast, the apparatus is conceived of as serving the ends of individuals themselves. How is this affected by the particular membership criteria of a sect as compared to a church?

Weber stresses that sect religion is not individualistic. It organizes individuals into powerful groups. "The entire social existence of the borrower," Weber writes in reference to the credit mechanism in sect communities, "rests on his membership in that community" (p. 8). The membership concept in a sect is, however, in itself radically individualistic. Entrance is based on voluntary decision. This is most obvious in the sect's emphasis on conversion rather than birth as the condition for religious election. "Whereas the baptismal ceremony itself, exclusively on the basis of the voluntary resolution of *adult* followers, was the adequate symbol for the 'sect-like' character of the Baptist community," Weber writes (p. 9), "the intrinsic falsity of the 'confirmation' [in a church] demonstrates the intrinsic contradiction of the avowal, which is only formally 'spontaneous.' " Sect membership, moreover, usually involves intensive individual scrutiny as well. Weber emphasizes, for example, "the *on-going inquiries* about moral and business conduct which precede acceptance" into the Baptist congregation (p. 8, original italics).

The emphasis on voluntary entrance is responsible for the famous exclusivity of sect religion. Because they are choosey, they are particularistic. "The 'purity' of its membership," Weber acknowledges (p. 8), "is a vital question for the genuine 'sect.' " The church, by contrast, is in principle inclusive and tolerant: "The 'universalism' of the 'churches' allows their light to shine on both the righteous and the unrighteous" (p. 8). In Weber's view, however, its very intolerance ironically signals the sect's fundamental contribution to democracy in the society at large. Sect membership is exclusive because individuals must demonstrate that they have been called by God himself. Universalism in church membership, by contrast, is based on a requirement to abide by institutional requirements and earthly religious authority.

It is for this reason, Weber believes, that only with sect development does the democratic impulse in the Western religious tradition finally emerge: "The principle that 'one must obey God above men,' whose various interpretations and explanations in a certain sense incorporate the whole cultural mission of Western European Christianity, acquires here its specific anti-authoritarian character" (p. 10). Only the commitment to religious exclusivity, Weber insists, can undermine the authoritarianism of the feudal past. "The exclusive appraisal of a person purely in terms of the religious qualities evidenced in his conduct," he writes (p. 10), "necessarily prunes feudal and dynastic romanticism from its roots." Because it is God who sets membership rules rather than man, sect religion seeks to institutionalize individual freedom against the state. Thus Weber (p. 10) attributes to sect development "the unconditional rejection of all . . . demands that the state recognize 'freedom of conscience' as the inalienable right of the individual." It is not a vague tolerance but a fierce commitment to the individual which, Weber concludes, makes freedom possible: "The autonomy of the individual, then, is anchored not to indifference but to religious positions; and the struggle against all types of 'authoritarian' arbitrariness is elevated to the level of a religious duty" (p. 10).

Voluntary membership and exclusivity also entail a continuous emphasis on achievement rather than ascription as the basis for distributing social rewards. "Life-long sober diligence in one's 'calling,' " Weber writes "appears as the specific, indeed really the *only,* form by which one can demonstrate his qualification as a Christian and therewith his moral legitimation" (p. 8, original italics). To remain a sect member one cannot rest on one's laurels, one must always be "proving oneself in life" (p. 8). There are no fixed or rigid rewards upon which the member of a sect can rely. "Not objectivized contracts and traditions," Weber writes, "but rather the religiously qualified individual is seen as the bearer of revelation which continues without ever being completed." Thus, while the individual is, in fact, enmeshed in a powerful form of social organization, the effect of that form is to create a situation in which the individual must be treated and evaluated as an individual alone.

The idea that the religious qualifications bestowed on the individual by God are alone decisive for his salvation, that no form of sacramental magic is of use to him here, that only his practical conduct, his 'probation,' can be taken by him as a *symptom* that he is on his way to salvation, places the individual absolutely on his own in the matter most important to him (p. 10, original italics).

The social milieu remains extraordinarily important, but it is a milieu designed to create and sustain individual prowess.* Thus, while Weber insists on "the individual's need to constantly attend to his self-affirmation," he argues that "this task of *'proving' himself* is present more than ever within the group, in the circle of his associates" (p. 11, original italics). This emphasis on the possibility for an individual-centered group life, we will suggest below, distinctively marks off Weber's position from the traditionalist/academic approach to modern culture.

It seems clear that what Weber has tried to outline here is a form of social organization which can sustain integration in a differentiated, individualistic, and democratic society. This form ensures that even in the most modern society there will be "on-going inquiries about moral and social conduct" (p. 8). Such inquiries guarantee that the individuals with whom one interacts have the proper *"social* qualities" (p. 8)—i.e., qualities linked to achievement. Organizations set standards for membership that are geared to specific types of action, not to qualities generated by birth. Membership, then, is open, and it is such membership, or "achieved quality," that guarantees the honorableness of the individuals with whom one interacts. "The old 'sect spirit' holds sway with relentless effect in the intrinsic nature of such associations," Weber writes (p. 11), for the sect was the first mass organization to combine individual and social in this way.

In the sect, the religious qualifications bestowed on the individual by God could be evidenced only by this-worldly action. In sect society, grace is an achievement by individuals, an achievement, ironically, that guarantees sociability. Sect-like organization, therefore, is the only way to ensure trust in a differentiated and mobile society. Societies whose culture

---

*It is for this reason, Weber suggests, that small size has usually been considered a prerequisite of sect activity, in contrast to the great populations often encompassed by the church. "The canonical limitation of the size of the unity, the congregation, to such dimensions that all members personally know one another and, therefore, can judge and supervise their "probation" reciprocally has always been a fundamental Baptist principle. A form of this principle was also found in genuine Methodism in the cultivation of the so-called class meetings in which members practiced (originally weekly) a kind of reciprocal examination through confessions, just as it was in the small communities (ecclediolae) of Pietism. One needs only to see the Berlin Cathedral to know that the most consequential form of the Protestant "spirit" is alive not in this caesaro-papist state hall but rather in the small chapels of the Quakers and the Baptists which lack such mystical ornamentation" (p. 9). Yet while size is significant, Weber insists that membership criteria alone define sects as opposed to churches.

is not rooted in sect religion, Weber suggests, may never be able to allow trust to be produced through such autonomous, individual-centered, voluntaristic procedures. Yet is is upon the ability to produce just such a fluid and responsive reservoir of trust that contemporary democracy depends.*

IV

In reflecting on the light which Weber's sect theory throws on the relation between his work and the traditional German mandarin critique of modern society, it is important to note that in assigning the sect to one of Tönnies's institutional ideal types, Weber chooses the *Gesellschaft* rather than the *Gemeinschaft*. He writes:

The individual [sect member] seeks to maintain *his own* position by becoming a member of a social group. . . . The social association to which the individual belongs is for him never something "organic," never a mystical total essence which floats over him and envelops him. Rather, he is always completely conscious of it as a mechanism for his own material and ideal *ends (Zwecke)*. ([1906] 1985:11)

It is precisely this conceptual choice that allows Weber to emphasize the rational individualism fostered by American sects. A description he offers of a baptismal ceremony in North Carolina is a case in point.

On a cold Sunday morning in October, I attended a Baptist baptism in the forelands of the Blue Ridge Mountains in North Carolina. Approximately ten people of both sexes in their Sunday-best entered the icy water of a mountain

---

*It is in this sect theory of democracy, then, that Weber's understanding of contemporary society converges with Parson's notion (e.g., 1967:297–382) that differentiated societies depend upon the ability to communicate and coordinate actions through "generalized media of exchange." In Parsons's view, these media all depend on trust, but at the same time they are acceptable to institutions and individuals only if they are drawn upon systems which perform in effective ways. Typically, Parsons couched this theory in systemic, general, and universalistic terms, scarcely referring to the historical and comparative issues to which Weber—in this singular section of his work—paid such close attention. In other parts of his work, however, Parsons was himself extremely sensitive to the long-term consequences of what might be called religious foundations. The particular distinction he made, however, was between denomination and church (Parsons 1967:385–421), and he was more interested in tolerance than in the promotion of individualistic motivation and self-control. Nor did Parsons connect this comparative discussion to his theory of the generalized media. It does not seem farfetched to suggest, however, that this exploration of individually centered, credit-creating processes could only have occurred to a theorist immersed in a political culture formed by sect-religion.

stream one after another and after voluminous declarations of allegiance bent their knees, leaned back into the arms of a black-clothed reverend (who stood waist-deep in the water during the entire procedure) until their faces disappeared under the water, climbed out sneezing and shivering, were congratulated by the farmers who had come in large numbers by horse and wagon, and quickly made for home (which in some cases was hours away). Faith protects one from catching cold, the saying goes. One of my cousins, who had escorted me from his farm and who scorned the procedure by spitting irreverently (he abstained from joining a church as a sign of his German descent), showed a certain interest as an intelligent-looking young man submersed himself. "Oh see, Mr. X. I told you so!" Pressed to explain, he responded at first only that Mr. X intended to open a bank in Mt. Airy and needed significant credit. From further discussion I learned that admittance into the Baptist congregation was primarily of decisive importance not on account of his Baptist customers but much more for the non-Baptist ones, because the *on-going inquiries* about moral and business conduct which precede acceptance [into the Baptist congregation] are considered by far the strongest and most reliable. ([1906] 1985:8)

Mr. X was not born into a religious group in which he felt some kind of organic oneness with the other members. Rather, whatever his motives —commercial, religious, or a mixture of the two—he made a conscious decision to join the sect and uphold its ethical standards. While he will reap certain advantages from his position, he will also accept the responsibility to constantly "prove" his worthiness. Should he fail to meet these individual responsibilities, the contract is broken and he is excluded. His conduct reflects "cool objectivity" *(Sachlichkeit)* and "purposive activity" *(Zwecktätigkeit)*. The sect itself, then, is not an institution that is somehow greater than the sum of its parts. Rather it is a collection of individuals who engage in reciprocal acts of "probation" for the sake of certain individual ideal and material ends. In this sense it is a classic *Gesellschaft.*

Yet, the sect differs from the mainstream German academic conception of *Gesellschaft* in that it is not barren of values.* While the conduct of the

---

* Ironically, Mitzman (1970:194–201) uses Weber's classification of the sect as a *Gesellschaft* to support his argument that Weber became increasingly taken with acosmic mysticism. He cites Weber's discussion of a presentation by Troeltsch at the German Sociological Convention of 1910 in which Weber places mysticism at the opposite pole from sect-rationality (cf. Mitzman 1973). However, here Weber does not advocate one pole over the other, but simply elaborates on Troeltsch's typology. Mitzman's error would seem to be a faulty syllogism: the *Gesellschaft* is an iron cage; the Protestant sect is a *Gesellschaft;* therefore, the Protestant sect is an iron cage. The acosmic mystic *Gemeinschaft* stands opposed to this *Gesellschaft* and thus represents the alternative to the reified iron cage. While Mitzman points to the existence of more than one form of *Gemeinschaft* in Weber's

sect members is rational, it is also strongly tied to values. The best example Weber provides is that of the Quakers, for whom "the struggle against all types of 'authoritarian' arbitrariness is elevated to a religious duty" ([1906] 1985:9). This vision of a modern actor whose very rationality is rooted deeply in value standards allows us to understand a nonutilitarian aspect in Weber's later discussions of rationality. In much of Weber's later writings, rational action takes on antivaluative tones (Alexander 1983: ch. 3–5), just as terms like "objectivity" *(Sachlichkeit)* take on an aura of reification. But even in his later writings there is another vision of modern life which competes with this prophecy of the iron cage. The antithetical notion is articulated by the concept of complex rationality, which embodies a substantive moral definition of rational action. Not until "Politics as a Vocation" can one gain the insight into this conception of rational conduct provided by "Churches and Sects."*

Our connection of these two essays goes beyond the fact that both talk about rationality in a more complex way. The paradox of "Politics as a Vocation," it seems to us, is that, while Weber advocates an ethic of

---

thought, he seems unwilling to do the same for *Gesellschaft.* The result of this lack of appreciation for complex rationality is that Mitzman is forced to treat the "ethic of responsibility" almost as an anomaly. We, to the contrary, will describe it below as one of the most significant concepts in Weber's later work.

*It is difficult to relate exactly this type of "complex rationality" to the formal conceptual distinctions among the types of rational action that Weber introduced in the first part of *Economy and Society,* in part because of the very problem we are pointing to here: it was much less conspicuous in Weber's theorizing and empirical work during the years between 1906 and the postwar period. This complex rationality could be considered a form of "value-rationality" *(Wertrationalität),* though Weber generally conceived of this term as relating to rationalized forms of religion, like Puritanism, that were precursors of truly "modern" rational action. On the other hand, this complex rationality might be considered a form of "purposive-rationality" *(Zweckrationalität).* Yet, while Weber certainly intended that the latter form refer to contemporary rational action, he tended to define this as instrumental rationality in a utilitarian sense.

The very ambiguity of these two types reflects the difficulty Weber had in conceptualizing a complex rationality that was both informed by values and disciplined by the universalistic, contingent, and empirical commitments of the secular age. Levine (1981) and Kalberg (1980) both have recently provided extensive accounts of the "multivalent" character of Weber's conception of rationality. Neither account, however, appreciates the profound ambiguity that permeates Weber's treatment and the contradictory characterizations of rationality that result. Both miss the historicist aspect of Weber's characterization, and the way in which his anxiety about modern rationality creates difficulties in his conceptualization. For an account which emphasizes the shifting quality of Weber's rationality definition, see Alexander 1983.

responsibility, the political organizations he ascribes to modern societies would make morally responsible participation in politics on any widespread basis all but impossible.* For it is in that important essay that Weber lays out the unenviable choice between the crassness of American political machines and the charismatic domination of plebiscitarian leaders, which is not really democratic at all (Alexander 1983:98–127). In "Churches and Sects," by contrast, Weber sharply criticizes the mass-society image upon which such a theory of machine democracy rests. Rather than embracing the notion himself—as he seems to in the later essay—he decries atomization as produced by the fears of German romantics and by the policies of the bureaucratic state.

Whoever represents "democracy" as a mass fragmented into atoms, as our romantics prefer to do, is fundamentally mistaken so far as the American democracy is concerned. "Atomization" is usually a consequence not of democracy but of bureaucratic rationalism and, therefore, it cannot be eliminated through the favored imposition of an "organizational structure" from above. ([1906] 1985:10)

Here again one sees Weber turning the tables on mainstream academicians by attributing the reified type of *Gesellschaft* to a bureaucratic structure (as in Germany) rather than to a democratic one. In the essay's only footnote (1985:12–13), he refutes his friend Troeltsch's attempt to equate "aristocracy," i.e., an exclusivity based on certain standards, with traditional institutions, that is, with political conservatism. Rather, he implies, there is a traditional form of exclusivity, based on ascribed status, and a modern one, based on "personal qualities and achievements." The latter he sees as characteristic of American democracy.

Indeed, as Weber knows from his recent experience in America and the insight into sect society that he has derived from it, American democracy is itself filled with exclusivities of every kind. It is this very membership in particular groups which promotes high individual standards and responsibilities.

The genuine American society—and here we include especially the "middle" and "lower" strata of the population—was never . . . a sandpile. Nor was it a building where everyone who entered without exception found open doors. It was and is permeated with "exclusivities" of every kind [and] the latter are always "artifacts"

---

* Yet, while a paradox, this is not a contradiction. I have explained in the essay preceding how Weber insists the responsibility in the modern world can be conceived only in a radically individualistic way.

of "societies" *[Gesellschaften]* and not "communities" *[Gemeinschaften]*, to use the terminology of Ferdinand Tönnies ([1906] 1985:10).

Because in democracies individuals are constantly confronting situations for which there is no authoritative interpretation and new individuals with whom there is no ascribed relation, new forms of control are needed which are neither top-down nor rigid, but real and constraining nonetheless. Democracy must allow for the possibility of face-to-face organization in a differentiated society. Only the sect form provides control mechanisms that allow this possibility to be realized. Only sects, moreover, were able to instill this capacity for democracy in broad masses of people. Ironically, it is the very radicalism of the sect that allows democratic behavior—a critical and antiauthoritarian character—to be positively incorporated into established communities. Church-organized polities, by contrast, allow traditional elites to monopolize grace. The result for these societies has been "to force all individual striving for emancipation from 'authority,' all 'liberalism' in the broadest sense of the word, along the path of hostility to the religious communities" (1985:11). In these church-founded situations, antiauthoritarian and critical sentiments must be expressed outside the social and political mainstream, in radical social movements. Only the sects, Weber argues, "have achieved the combination of positive religiosity and political radicalism" ([1906] 1985:10). They can do so because they allow mainstream social and political life to itself assume a democratic and antiauthoritarian form. "On the basis of Protestant religiosity and political radicalism," Weber maintains, sects "alone . . . have been able to instill in the broad masses, and especially in modern workers, an intensity for ecclesiastical interests which is elsewhere to be found only in the bigoted fanaticism of backward peasants."

In this essay, then, in contrast to "Politics as a Vocation," Weber sees democratic morality permeating the masses of people. Yet it cannot be gainsaid that American democracy in Weber's time was still a political process dominated by big city machines. Is it possible to reconcile this phenomenon with Weber's early sect theory? We believe that it is and that Weber himself actually makes a subtle attempt to do so.

The key to reconciliation is to understand that sects do not themselves become directly involved in politics. In fact, they are purposely apolitical, refusing to grant any divine legitimation to the political structure or to court favor from the secular authorities. Weber (Mommson 1974:76) sees the sects' demand for a constitutional guarantee of freedom of conscience as one of their great contributions to modernity. He realized that such a position could allow for machine politics, which was governed by *zweck-rational* efficiency and was as devoid of values as the bureaucracy which Germans contrasted with it. Yet, what comes through much more clearly in this essay than in his later treatments is that Weber did not perceive the American political machine as dangerous to individual responsibility. Why not? Because this aspect of political life could not be "consecrated" by an idealist system of values. Noting the " 'lack of respect' typical of modern Americans" vis-à-vis even "the highest social bodies," Weber makes the following observation.

Discounting bills of exchange is a business, as is the introduction of dispositions into government records, and the latter cannot be distinguished from the former by some sort of "consecration." Unsuspecting German officials very often concede with great astonishment, "it works that way as well!" when they come to know the excellent work accomplished by American officials which takes place hidden from our eyes under a heavy blanket of big city corruption, party manuevers and bluff. ([1906]1985:11)

It is the German established church, Weber notes here, not the political machine, that subordinates individual values to the bureaucratic state. It did so by granting the state legitimation in return for certain privileges. The German bureaucracy was a reified system disguised as a moral one. The city machine, on the other hand, has no such pretensions; devoid of moral legitimation, it does not represent the same threat to the ethical conduct of the individual.

American sect organization produced at least two important qualities that Weber saw as crucial for the political rejuvenation of Germany: a strong individualism and a tendency to form cohesive social groups open to all social strata. The sect, for Weber, was a mass organization whose cohesiveness was based neither on an organic spiritual unity nor on a materialistically organized interest; rather it was based on individual achievement and responsibility. When, at the end of his career, Weber returned to the critical study of comparative political morality, this sect-inspired quality emerges as the now famous "ethic of responsibility"—the only substantively rational norm that can guide the modern political vocation. Sect-like qualities were necessary if democratic political institutions characterized by a union of moral commitment and rational perspective were to emerge in Germany. For this to happen, the existing bureaucratic system—the iron cage—would have to be dismantled, a task Weber now assigned to charismatic political leadership. Weber's theoretical ambivalence, and the applied, programmatic nature of this later work led him to discuss the sources of democratic change in this purely political, acultural way. Yet it seems clear that one lineage of his "ethic of responsibility" goes back to his earlier emphasis on the role of sects. The weakness of his later theory of plebiscitary democracy, in fact, may be connected to Weber's inability make this link explicit and distinct.*

The reasons for the eventual attenuation of Weber's sect-church dualism can be linked to the predicament Weber faced in 1906. Despite his admiration for sect-democracy and American political life, Weber saw no way of transforming the socio-religious conduct of Germany in a similar way. His optimism about the American *Gesellschaft* is matched by his pessimism about the German one. At the same time, Weber saw the American sect-like institutions being threatened by "Europeanization," a fear that became greater toward the end of his life (Weber [1918] 1980:197). This tension between sect democracy and Europeanization, was, unfortunately, a dialectic that Weber never explored further, for in his later work he dropped the moral side of the antinomy altogether. If he had explored it, his theory of modern society might have been able to point to the possibilities for escaping the iron cage in a more sociological and less existentialist way. That he did not develop this aspect of his theory indicates, of course, as much about Weber's own time as it does about Weber himself.†

In the American religious sect Weber had discovered a unique creature which, despite its importance, faced possible extinction from the form of modernization represented by Europe. Weber's earliest hope seem to have been to find a home for that creature in Germany—indeed, to use his

---

* It is the failure to see the relatively submerged theme of sect-democracy that mars David Beetham's fine study of Weber's "applied" political theory. Beetham argues (e.g., 1974:201) that in the writings Weber dedicated explicitly to topical political issues—in contrast to his scholarly and systematic writings on politics—he emphasized the relation between politics and class forces to the exclusion of the "importance of ideas." Yet, Beetham (1974:205) acknowledges that Weber, in his major discussion of the Russian revolution of 1905, listed the failure of sect-religion as one of the three major reasons for the failure of Russian democracy. It is true, of course, that Weber's approach to these issues was usually the instrumental one of *Realpolitik*. Nonetheless, "Churches and Sects" demonstrates quite clearly that Weber's thinking about reform did contain another element, albeit one that became increasingly submerged.

† For a discussion of some of these possibilities, see the last section in chapter 2, above.

knowledge of the true underpinnings of American democracy to transform Europe itself. This hope lay dormant until the turmoil at the end of the First World War. Ironically it was at this later time that the revised version of "Churches and Sects" appeared. In this later essay, some of the most important elements we have discussed were omitted, and the main effects of the sect phenomenon were placed distinctly in the past.

REFERENCES

Alexander, Jeffrey C. 1983. *Max Weber: The Classical Attempt at Synthesis.* Vol. 3 of *Theoretical Logic in Sociology.* Berkeley and Los Angeles: University of California Press.

—— 1988. "Three Models of Culture and Society Relation: Toward an Analysis of Watergate." In Alexander, *Action and Its Environments,* pp. 152–174. New York: Columbia University Press.

Beetham, David. 1974. *Max Weber and the Theory of Modern Politics.* London: Allen and Unwin.

Berger, Stephen. 1971. "The Sects and the Breakthrough into the Modern World: On the Centrality of the Sects in Weber's Protestant Ethic Thesis." *The Sociological Quarterly* 12:456–499.

Bloch, Ruth. 1985. *Visionary Republic: Millenial Themes in American Thought, 1756–1800.* New York: Cambridge University Press.

Dahrendorf, Ralf. 1969. *Society and Democracy in Germany.* Garden City, N.Y.: Doubleday.

Kalberg, Steven. 1980. "Max Weber's Types of Rationality: Cornerstones for the Analysis of Rationalization Processes in History." *American Journal of Sociology* 85:1145–1179.

—— 1987. "The Origin and Expansion of *Kulturpessimismus.*" *Sociological Theory* 5 (2):150–164.

König, Renig. 1955. "Die Begriffe Gemeinschaft und Gesellschaft bei Ferdinand Tönnies." *Kölner Zeitschrift für Soziologie und Sozial-psychologie* 7:348–420.

Lenk, Kurt. 1972. *Marx in der Wissenssoziologie.* Neuwied: Luchterhand.

Levine, Donald N. 1981. "Rationality and Freedom: Weber and Beyond." *Sociological Inquiry* 51:5–26.

Lindenlaub, Dieter. 19676. *Richtungskämpfe im Verein für Sozialpolitik.* Wiesbaden: Franz Steiner.

Loader, Colin. 1976. "German Historicism and Its Crisis." *Journal of Modern History* 48:85–119. On-demand supplement.

Miller, Perry. 1956. *Errand Into the Wilderness.* New York: Harper and Row.

—— 1965. *The Life of the Mind in America.* New York: Harcourt, Brace and World.

Mitzman, Arthur. 1970. *The Iron Cage: An Historical Interpretation of Max Weber.* New York: Knopf.

—— 1973. "Max Weber on Church, Sect, and Mysticism." *Sociological Analysis* 34:140–149.

Mommsen, Wolfgang. 1974. *Max Weber: Gesellschaft, Politik und Geschichte.* Frankfurt: Suhrkamp.

Parsons, Talcott. 1967. *Sociological Theory and Modern Society.* New York: Free Press.

Ringer, Fritz. 1969. *The Decline of the German Mandarins.* Cambridge: Harvard University Press.

Weber, Marianne. 1975. *Max Weber: A Biography.*

Weber, Max. 1906. " 'Kirchen' und 'Sekten.' " *Frankfurter Zeitung* 50 (102/104).

—— [1906] 1985. " 'Churches' and 'Sects' in North America: An Ecclesiastical Socio-Political Sketch." (Translation by Colin Loader). *Sociological Theory* 3(1)7–13.

—— [1918] 1980. "Socialism." In J. E. T. Eldridge, ed. *Max Weber: The Interpretation of Social Reality.* London: Joseph.

—— [1919] 1946. "Politics as a Vocation." In Hans Gerth and C. Wright Mills, eds. *From Max Weber.* New York: Oxford University Press.

—— [1920] 1946. "The Protestant Sects and the Spirit of Capitalism." In Gerth and Mills, eds. *From Max Weber.*

—— 1978. *Economy and Society.* Berkeley and Los Angeles: University of California Press.

Rethinking Durkheim's Intellectual Development: On the Complex Origins of a Cultural Sociology

Readings of great theorists are geared to the times. Just as Marx has recently been decisively reinterpreted, so has Durkheim. On one thing most of Durkheim's readers, past and present, have always agreed: he, like Marx, emphasizes social structure. Durkheim helped to create classical sociology because he located social forces outside of the individual actor. But at this point the serious theoretical problems only really begin. The problem for Durkheim, as for Marx, is what does structure mean? How does structure hold individuals within its limits? Of what are these limits composed? If structure exists, somehow, outside of the individual, can it act only in opposition to freedom? The problematics of Durkheim interpretation, then, are precisely the ones around which Marxist inquiry has also revolved. The fundamental question has always been how Durkheim stipulates the relation between determinism and free action. People keep reading Durkheim, and arguing about him, to find out whether the determinateness of social structures must involve the sacrifice of voluntary control and, conversely, whether the postulate of individual control can be purchased only at the price of denying the realities of external force. How generations have understood Durkheim has fundamentally shaped the pattern of their sociological discourse. The debates over Durkheim's work are, inevitably, arguments about the most basic directions of sociological thought.

Yet Durkheim has become the resource for such theorizing in fundamentally different ways and at fundamentally different levels of analysis. Theorists have argued for and against the "Durkheimian solution" in ways that, ironically, have eliminated properly theoretical analysis altogether. Merton (1967:59–60) and Stinchcombe (1968:25) insist that Durkheim's greatness lies in the power of his empirical generalizations, an insistance which would remove from our consideration of Durkheim the power of his theoretical reflection as such. The mirror image of this argument is that, far from being observational and scientific, Durkheim's work must be viewed as the immediate product of his social environment. For Zeitlin (1968:235) and Kagan (1938:243), if Durkheim's conception of social structure leads in one direction or another, it is for ideological reasons, not for merely empirical ones.

The present essay insists, to the contrary, that Durkheim's understanding of the critical relation between individual and society cannot be reduced to either of these anti-theoretical extremes. It involves, rather, reference to *sui generis* analytic issues that are neither simply ideological nor completely empirical, issues that revolve around the "problem of order" in a strictly delineated sense. This analytical problem of order has been seriously misunderstood in the recent history of sociological debate. In the first place, it has been falsely conflated with theoretical issues of a much more specific kind. For Coser (1960), Nizan (1932:191–92), Rex (1961:105–108), and Kagan (1938), "order" means simply assumptions about the empirical frequency of conflict or equilibrium, and on these grounds they find Durkheim's insistence on a modicum of social stability to be seriously deficient. In Kagan's words, Durkheim "is the anti-revolutionary par excellence in the sense that he is profoundly attached to tradition" (1938:243). Yet those who defend Durkheim frequently make the same theoretical mistake. Nisbet (1965:28) claims that Durkheim's acceptance of social harmony and obedience constitutes "a massive attack on the philosophical foundations of liberalism," and for this attack he applauds and embraces him. Following the same narrow definition of the order problem but rejecting Nisbet's reading of where Durkheim stood in relation to it, Giddens (1972b:41) claims that because of Durkheim's concern with change and historicity "it can perfectly well be said that it [the problem of order] was not a problem for Durkheim at all" (cf. Giddens 1972a:358–361). Much of this confusion, of course, can be traced back to Parsons' influential interpretation in *The Structure of Social Action* (1937:313, 346–347), for while Parsons sharply differentiated the concern with empirical stability from any necessary ideological orientation, he often linked Durkheim's analytical solution to the order problem—which Parsons himself did so much to illuminate—with Durkheim's perception of empirical equilibrium.

In terms of the present essay, the "problem of order" involves two distinctive theoretical issues, each of which concerns the fundamental nature of social relationships. First, the order problem involves a decision about the random versus structured quality of human events, about whether the sources of individual interaction are individualistic or collective and supra-individual. This question, which involves the sociological reformulation of the nominalism/realism debate, must be crosscut by assumptions about the nature of human action. Whether or not individuals act simply in an instrumentally efficient and purely calculating way or whether every act involves reference to a nonrational and ideal standard vitally affects the nature of the individual or collective order that a theorist describes. It is as a result of such decisions about the nature of action that individualistic order is portrayed as an "exchange" (e.g., Homans 1961) or a "symbolic interaction" (e.g., Blumer 1969), and that collective orders are described as external and coercive (e.g., Marx [1847] 1962) or internal and voluntaristic (e.g., Parsons 1937).*

The conflict between Marxism and Durkheimian sociology, I contend, revolves precisely around this latter issue. Various theorists, of course, have contended that this conflict does not exist, that Durkheim, like Marx, is a "structuralist" who emphasizes social organization and external control. But the notion of "structure," as I insisted above, is where sociological theory begins, not where it ends. The most critical issues in theoretical logic are lost if Durkheim's and Marx's common collectivism is taken to exhaust their theoretical relationship. While Marx and Durkheim agreed that social science must focus on supra-individual social

---

*In so defining the "problem of order" as concerned with instrumental versus nonrational action and with the problem of individualism versus collective structuration, I am following a long tradition of epistemological and ontological debate in social thought, a debate which for present purposes may be said to have begun with Marx's "Theses on Feuerbach" ([1845] 1965) and the most important contemporary articulations of which have been presented by Parsons (1937) and Habermas (1973). The problem of action involves conflicts over idealism (e.g., purely normative action) and materialism (purely efficient, amoral action). The problem of individualism versus collectivism centers on the problem of whether order is simply negotiated by individual interaction or whether it has *sui generis,* emergent properties. For an important treatment of this latter problem in terms of the split between nominalist and realist tendencies in the Chicago school of sociology, see Lewis and Smith (1980). I have discussed these "presuppositional" issues at much greater length in Alexander Alexander (1982c, 1988:222-257), and in Alexander and Giesen 1988.

structure, they disagreed profoundly about the nature of action upon which such structures are based.

This profound disagreement with the Marxist understanding of order was, at least, the position at which Durkheim arrived by the time of his fully mature theoretical work. What has not been understood is that, on the way to this latter position, Durkheim seriously considered a variety of theoretical alternatives. Indeed, in the process of his early theoretical development he came, in his own view, precariously close to the position of Marx himself. It is on the nature of this early development, and on the rationales for Durkheim's changes in theoretical position, that this essay will focus. In so reconstructing the dialectic between Durkheim and the shadow of Marx, the following argument seeks to illuminate not just the central dilemmas of classical sociology, but those of contemporary thought as well. It will also refer to some of the most basic controversies in contemporary studies of science and knowledge production in a more general sense.

Durkheim's Early Writings: Ideological Consistency and Theoretical Change

Durkheim came to maturity in the late 1870s and 1880s, in the crucible of the formation of the Third Republic in France. From the very beginning of his identification as a sociologist—which Mauss dates from 1881—he linked his intellectual vocation to certain normative or ideological goals: first, French society must be changed so that it could become stable; second, this stability could be achieved only if there were justice, particularly justice in economic distribution; third, the increased state organization necessary to create justice should never occur at the expense of individual freedom. Durkheim described these goals as socialism, but he insisted, to use contemporary terms, that this be socialism with a voluntaristic or human face. This ideological dimension of order remained constant throughout the course of his life. The problem, for Durkheim, was the translation of these goals into a theoretical and empirical perspective. It is precisely here that the changes in Durkheim's sociology occurred.

From the beginning, Durkheim was convinced that the achievement of democratic socialism depended upon avoiding the kind of instrumentally rationalistic theory of collective order that was proposed by the English utilitarians and by Marxist socialists. Such a reductionist and instrumental understanding of the issue, Durkheim believed, could describe the reformist state only as an external and coercive force vis-à-vis individual will (Durkheim [1888] 1975:379). Quoting approvingly from Schaeffle, the German socialist of the chair, Durkheim (1886:77) insists that the concept of socialism "could be unburdened of all contradictions" only if "the fundamental principles of Marx's theory are renounced" (cf. Durkheim [1888] 1975:387).*

Yet in the years between the publication of Durkheim's first essay reviews, in 1885, and the appearance of his first mature work, *The Division of Labor in Society,* in 1893, Durkheim proved unable to transform this general analytic conviction into a viable and precise theory. Although the full story of Durkheim's earliest writings cannot be recounted here, the fundamental lines of his frustrating early development can briefly be presented. In the eight-year period that defines Durkheim's early writings —a period that covers sixteen essays and two major monographs—one can discern an ambivalent yet nonetheless distinctive theoretical evolution away from his ideological goal of combining collective order with individual freedom. In the earliest of these writings, Durkheim emphasized the importance of "sympathetic instincts" inherent in every human being. Since these natural sentiments led to associations, Durkheim (e.g., 1886:309) thought he had discovered a way that moral order could be social and individual at the same time. Yet eventually he rejected this solution as too precarious. Such independently motivated individuals, he came to believe, would develop no sense of the social whole outside of their own selves. Even if they were enmeshed in society, they would not be conscious of any subjective connection (e.g., Durkheim 1885:453, [1885] 1978:114). As an alternative to this vision, Durkheim considered the position that morality was in some way external to the individual and could, therefore, more powerfully control him. Yet even as he elaborated

---

*It is an undecided historical questions whether or not Durkheim actually knew Marx's own work. Although there is some evidence that he did, he was surely responding more immediately to the mechanical Marxism of the German and French "Marxists" of the First International. Whether his criticism, therefore, can be considered a valid response to Marx's original theory depends on what one considers the relation to be between Marx and his immediate followers. In my view, Durkheim's understanding of Marxism as a mechanistic theory was essentially correct, although this judgment is not relevant to the argument of the present essay, which concerns only Durkheim's *understanding* of Marx and Marxism. For an extensive comparison of Marx's actual theory with Durkheim's, see Alexander 1982a.

this new position, he worried about the status of the individual in such a scheme, and to resolve this worry he postulated that such a moral order could grow out of the individual action itself. Following Wundt, he portrayed the individual as permeable and "anti-substantialist," so order could be internal and external at the same time (Durkheim 1887b:128). Yet this flirtation with Wundt turned out to be brief, for, once again, Durkheim (1886:76) concluded that if individual volition were involved, social order was bound to be unstable.*

Because he did not yet understand the process by which social order could be outside the isolated individual and still be subjective, or "inside," at the same time, Durkheim was compelled at this early point to turn to the notion that order could be stable only if it were external in an ontological sense. He turned, in other words, back to an instrumental, quasi-materialist position. Even in his earlier work he had often evoked, in a hesitant and ambivalent way, a model of the actor as an adaptive and rationalizing force (e.g., Durkheim 1886:60–69). This model now became explicit: the adaptive actor was endowed with egoistic motives and portrayed as responding primarily to external conditions. What has happened, ironically, is that Durkheim has retreated to the very instrumental position he had, at the very beginning of his career, so criticized in Marx. He has laid the groundwork for a vision of state and society which was as mechanical and coercive as what he has supposed to be Marx's own.

What is extraordinary is that Durkheim himself seemed to feel that exactly the opposite was true. In his opening lectures at Bordeaux in 1888 and 1889, during which he first developed this more instrumentalist perspective, and in his 1892 Latin dissertation when he first systematized it, Durkheim asserted that this instrumental transformation would, in fact, allow him finally to reconcile individual freedom and social order. The trick was his empirical focus on the division of labor. Like the classical economists whom he had earlier criticized, at this point in his

---

*It is interesting to recall that Wundt also had a profound influence on the social behaviorism of George Herbert Mead. Mead took over the same "anti-substantialist" understanding of the individual that so attracted Durkheim, and for the same reason: only with this conception could order be both collective and "voluntary" at the same time. The subsequent misrepresentation of Mead's thought as a form of "substantialist" individualism —by Blumer and others—has obscured this commonality between the two thinkers, as has the reading of Durkheim that concentrates only on such semi-materialist works as *The Division of Labor* ([1893] 1964). Yet although Durkheim rejected Wundt's understanding in these early writings, he returned to it, in a more sophisticated way, in the later work I will discuss below.

development Durkheim ([1888] 1978:207) believed that the division of labor was a device for reconciling free choice with the collective ordering of individual interests. With this new understanding of modern life, he announced in the preface to The Division of Labor ([1893] 1964:37), the "apparent antinomy" between individual autonomy and social determinism had been resolved: social solidarity would be transformed in a manner beneficial to both individual and society, and this would occur because of "the steadily growing development of the division of labor." *

In fact, of course, these hopes were illusory. Durkheim's earliest premonitions were correct: He could not maintain voluntarism if order was to be given a purely external and material cast. In Book 1 of Division, Durkheim (1864 [1893], p. 127) begins by eulogizing labor division in an extremely individualistic way. "It is in the nature of special tasks," he writes, "to escape the action of the collective conscience." The contract itself, according to this logic, becomes the prototypical form of cooperation and aggregation. Since "society is made up of a system of differentiated parts which mutually complement each other" (p. 151, translation altered), it is only natural to assume that "the involvement of one party results either from the involvement assumed by the other, or from some service already rendered by the latter" (p. 124, translation altered). But as Durkheim's argument develops, he very quickly sees through the individualistic quality of such reasoning. As he does so, he emphasizes the noncontractual, supra-individual controls which are necessary if the freedom inherent in labor division is to be balanced by stability and collective control. In the course of the remainder of Book 1, Durkheim vascillates between describing these collective elements as normative and nonrational, or as state-directed and instrumentally coercive. Durkheim's normative version of noncontractual social control is best known, and the notion of the diffusion of the collective conscience in modern society is certainly a significant point in Durkheim's fifth chapter (pp. 147–73). What is much less widely recognized, however, is that alongside this

---

*The preceding analysis of the gradual but nonetheless distinctive shift from moral individualism to moral collectivism and, finally, to instrumental collectivism in the course of Durkheim's early writings suggests that earlier interpreters have been wrong to stress the internal consistency of this period and its continuity with the rest of Durkheim's work (e.g., Giddens 1970; Wallwork 1972:27–46; Filloux 1977:23–34). Such an insistance on the continuity of Durkheim's early writings makes it virtually impossible to understand his emerging perspective on the importance of the division of labor and, even more importantly, his eventual dissatisfaction with this position.

exposition of the normative dimension there also exists in Durkheim's first book a strongly instrumentalist approach to social order. The restitutive law that creates the noncontractual regulation of contract is portrayed by Durkheim (p. 11) as "only a means" *(C'est seulement un moyen)*, and he insists (p. 112) that "these prescriptions do not correspond to any sentiment in us." Modern law becomes a purely rational and coercive vehicle, and the modern regulating state merely "the essential cog in the machine" (p. 113).

In the second Book of *Division,* this instrumental perspective on collective order emerges with full force: labor division becomes the product not of free and rational choice or the normatively regulated pursuit of interest, but the result of "the struggle for existence"—*"la lutte pour la vie"* (Durkheim [1893] 1964:226)—a struggle that is itself determined by changes in ecological volume and density and, ultimately, by unequal control over scarce resources. By Book 3, the results of this shifting theoretical logic are clear: Durkheim is forced to recognize, and eventually to give causal primacy to, unequal material conditions and to the purely coercive state. Because of the "great inequality of the external conditions of the struggle *[la lutte]"* (p. 370 n. 26), the modern worker is subject to the "forced division of labor," an order that operates with unstoppable mechanical force. If Durkheim had begun the *Division of Labor* with an empirical emphasis on individualism that belied his emerging—if somewhat anomalous—theoretical determinism, he had concluded it with an explanation of order that seemed emphatically to confirm it.

If one class of society is obliged, in order to live, to take any price for its services, while another can abstain from such action thanks to resources at its disposal which, however, are not necessarily due to any social superiority, the second has an unjust advantage over the first at law. (Durkheim [1893] 1964:384).

Durkheim's Middle Period: Dissatisfaction, Misinterpretation, and Radical Revision

Despite the fact that Durkheim trumpeted the results of *Division of Labor* as demonstrating the empirical power of his new science, there is good reason to believe that, consciously or unconsciously, he felt enormous dissatisfaction with what he had wrought in his first great work. First, of course, there is the great discrepancy between his theoretical development in *Division of Labor* and the goals he had set out eight years before. He had started out to provide an alternative to the Marxian understanding of socialist industrial society; he had concluded, in the third Book of *Division,* offering a model of capitalism that differed from Marx only in its inability to describe fully the class origins of the material inequality it described (see, e.g., O'Connor 1980).[1] Second, there is evidence for this dissatisfaction in the ambiguous and contradictory quality of *Division* itself. If Durkheim had concluded with an instrumental and coercive understanding of modern social order, he had certainly given ample evidence elsewhere in the work, particularly in the individualistic and normative passages in Book 1, that he still valued more voluntaristic understandings even if he could not successfully articulate them.

Still more powerful evidence of Durkheim's theoretical dissatisfaction can be found in two little-known essays that he published in 1893, in the very shadow of *The Division of Labor.* In the first, a review of Gaston Richard's *Essai sur l'origine de l'idée de droit,* Durkheim argues against the notion that the simple calculus of interest, structured by a powerful state, can teach humanity to follow a more just path. It is, he writes (1893b:292), only "completely interior sentiments" that can be relied on, for "it is inside the conscience and not outside, it is in the sympathetic and altruistic disposition and not in the sentiments of interest that it is necessary to go look for the solution." Later that year, in his "Note sur la définition du socialisme," Durkheim makes this challenge to the latter Books of *Division* even more forcefully. The problem of capitalism, he writes (1893a:510), does *not* derive from its failure to provide "material contiguity." That it did, of course, had been a central argument in *Division* (Book 3). Durkheim acknowledges that businesses may well have material relations with one another, "acting and reacting" among themselves. Workers, too, may pursue their interests alongside of their fellows. He now argues, however, that problems of industrial society arise because such material contiguities do not, in and of themselves, guarantee that businesses or workers "have ends which are common to them," do not ensure that they can actually form among themselves any "moral community." It is the moral community, he now insists, that must be the object of socialist change, not the economic redistribution and reorganization he had identified in *Division.* One must understand, he insists, that "a revolution could not occur without a profound moral transformation," and that the famous "social question" of Marxist socialism is not economic but moral.

These essays, in fact, presaged long-term shifts in Durkheim's theory of order, shifts that Durkheim himself (with a single brief exception to be discussed below) never admitted as having occurred at all. In the following year, in an essay that would become the first chapter of *Rules,* Durkheim (1938 [1895]) laid out an affective and normative understanding of the roots of social life that systematically called into question the instrumental theory of interaction, volume, and density that had informed Book 2 of *Division of Labor.**

Durkheim begins innocuously enough, claiming in his preface ([1895] 1938:ix) that he wishes only "to expound the results of our work in applied sociology," yet in the very first paragraph he reveals that this is hardly the case. "When I execute my contracts," Durkheim writes (p. 1), "I perform duties which . . . conform to my own sentiments and I feel their reality subjectively." The social order that contracts represent, apparently, need not be based primarily on the external sanctions of state supported law. Durkheim proceeds in the following pages to define sociological facts in a startlingly subjective way. They are, he writes (p. 2), "ways of acting, thinking, and feeling," a phrase that he often reduces (p. 9) to the short-hand "beliefs and practices" *(les croyances et les pratiques).* Durkheim still insists that social facts be grounded in a substratum, but he (p. 3) now defines this organizational base as "religious denominations, political, literary, and occupational associations." The "actions and reactions" that create social organization—and which in Book 2 of *Division* were ecological and economic—are here completely emotionalized. They refer to the "special energy" that is created when individual consciences interact, and their product is "collective sentiment" (p. 9). Collective facts, Durkheim now insists, consist only of more or less crystallized emotion. In periods of pure association, this emotion is still close to the primordial "liquid" form, and the significant collective facts are volatile phenomena like "transitory outbursts" and "great movements of enthusiasm" (p. 4). Eventually, however, emotion acquires a certain "rigidity"; it develops "a body, a tangible form" that is more sharply differentiated from the individual psyches that first produced it

---

*The essays that became *Rules* were first published in 1894 in the *Revue philosophique.*

(p. 7). Social order, in sum, is simply "currents of opinion" more or less solidified, currents that reflect the state of the collective "soul" or "spirit" *(l'âme collective)* at different times (p. 8).*

In his lectures on socialism in 1895–96, Durkheim used his new perspective to elaborate his remarks in the 1894 *"Note"* about socialism as a voluntary moral system. He now insists ([1895–99] 1958:204) that the crucial reforms suggested in Book 3 of *Division,* political reorganization and economic redistribution, will be ineffective unless the "state of our morality" is also reformed. The problem of order is posed here as one of renewed symbolic or moral authority.

What is needed if social order is to reign is that the mass of men be content with their lot. But what is needed for them to be content, is not that they have more or less but that they be convinced that they have no right to more. And for this, it is absolutely essential that there be an authority whose superiority they acknowledge and which tells them what is right. ([1895–96] 1958:200)

In *Suicide,* written the following year, this new insistence on solidarity and affectivity as the source of collective order is applied to a wide range of modern social institutions. If the object of *Suicide* is the social fact which Durkheim calls "suicidogenic currents," the status of this supra-individual fact is the inverse of the economic or political "facts" that Durkheim had early emphasized. Durkheim ([1897] 1951:299) defines suicidogenic currents as composed of a "collective force of a definite amount of energy." They reflect a social substratum which is itself composed of "beliefs and practices" ([1897] 1951:170) and they form a society that Durkheim ([1897] 1951:310) describes as only in the last analysis having "a physical existence."

In the same year that *Suicide* was written—indeed, by the time that monograph had appeared in print—Durkheim was embarked on a radically new, more explicitly spiritualized elaboration of this subjective mode of theorizing. I will discuss this later development in the final section of this essay. Before doing so, the extratheoretical sources of Durkheim's intellectual shift must be closely examined, for it is only in this fuller context that the true ramifications of Durkheim's development can clearly be understood.

I have insisted on "theoretical" dissatisfaction as the trigger to this

---

* *"L'âme"* is translated as "mind" through *Rules*—and in Durkheim's other work as well —but it seems more appropriate in light of the emerging direction of Durkheim's theorizing to translate it more literally as "soul" or "spirit."

upheaval in Durkheim's work. Indeed, no major social or personal event could have created such a rapid disavowal, for the intellectual changes began almost simultaneously with the publication of *Division* itself. What I would like to suggest, however, is that Durkheim's profound intellectual misgivings made him particularly sensitive to change in his social and cultural environment. France was changing in a way that could only have hastened the theoretical evolution Durkheim was experiencing.

The early 1890s marked the renewal of Marxism in French society. This was stimulated in part by increased class conflict in the political and economic realms, as indicated, for example, by the election in 1893 of fifty socialists—by no means all of the Marxian variety—to the French parliament and by the great upsurge in strikes and worker protests that characterized this period.* These social developments were certainly not primarily stimulated by Marxian ideology, but they constituted, nonetheless, important reasons for the growing attention that French intellectuals paid to Marxist theory.† Leading journals like the *Revue de métaphysique et de morale* and the *Revue philosophique,* where Durkheim had published most of his important early work, now published ongoing discussions of socialist theory and reviewed numerous works by Marx and Engels and their followers. The first exclusively sociological journal in France, the *Revue internationale de sociologie,* also devoted considerable space to articles on socialism and Marx, and in the first issue of the *Annales de l'institut international de sociologie,* historical materialism became the focus of a number of the authors. This new enthusiasm for Marxism spread even to Durkheim's inner circle. "Some of the most brilliant among his own students," writes Durkheim's nephew and collaborator, Marcel Mauss ([1928] 1958:2–3), "were converted to socialism, especially Marxism." Mauss adds that "in one 'Social Study' circle some examined *Capital* as they elsewhere considered Spinoza".

This contextual knowledge helps us to reconstruct—hypothetically, to be sure—Durkheim's predicament in the early 1890s. He had just concluded his first major work, a treatment that evidently he had already begun to regret and apparently had already begun to revise. Moreover, he

---

*For an excellent discussion of this political development and its relation to new and more normative developments in Durkheim's work, see Tiryakian (1978:233–234).

†This portrait of the impact of Marxian and socialist ideas on French intellectual circles draws upon Vogt (1976) and Llobera (1978), although I disagree substantially with the interpretations these authors give.

was in the midst of the revival in popularity of a system of thought—
Marxism—that seemed closely to resemble the one he had just publicly
proclaimed, not only in its ideological commitment to socialism and
science but, more importantly, in its analytical theory and its empirical
analysis of modern society. One might imagine that Durkheim wished
very badly to distinguish his new ideas from those of Marxism. At the
same time, he would not wish to indicate that these new ideas differed in
any way from those he had previously held. We will shortly see, in fact,
that this was precisely the course Durkheim took. First, we must examine
Durkheim's situation in more detail; we will discover that Durkheim's
"predicament" was far from being purely an imagined one.

In the very midst of Durkheim's theoretical shift away from the instrumentalism of *Division,* he was confronted with what could only have been
an enormously frustrating realization: his French audience viewed him as
a confirmed materialist very much in the Marxist mode, if not a Marxist
himself! Almost without exception, the reviews that Durkheim received
in the four years following publication of *Division* presented his subsequent writing—as he himself had asked for it to be read—merely as the
extension of that first work.* The reviewers were in universal agreement,
32reover, that *Division* had itself been one-sidedly materialist in its orientation. In the first and probably most important review, Brunschvicg
and Halévy (1894) wrote that even if Durkheim refused to accept all the
consequences of his position, the *Division of Labor* was, in the last
analysis, "mechanical and material" in its causal analysis. Reading *Division* into the later *Rules,* they argued (1894:565–67) in the face of Durkheim's very explicit theorizing that his proposed method excluded all
psychological elements from society. And in a series of concluding arguments that must have been especially grating to Durkheim, they offered
suggestions that Durkheim had actually already taken up. Social laws,
they write (1894:571), should be studied in terms of the spontaneous
interaction of the individuals whose spirit gives them life. Only in this

---

*The sole exception that I have been able to locate to these negative reviews is an essay
written by Paul Lapie (1895:309–310), "L'Année sociologique, 1894." Lapie saw very
clearly the subjective, normative basis that Durkheim gave to social facts in the essays that
became *Rules,* and he applauded him for it. Later, as director of primary education in
France, Lapie introduced Durkheimian sociology into the required national curriculum.
This movement toward subjectivity may have pleased Lapie because he shared Durkheim's
opinion that scientifically based Republican ethics were essential to the survival of French
democracy.

way could these so-called laws be seen for what they really are, namely, common ideas and sentiments.

The same perspective on Durkheim's sociology is expressed in the 1896 issue of the same review. Charles Andler finds the determinism and fatalism of Durkheim's sociological analysis to be antithetical to the democratic culture he is trying to create. In concluding, he accuses Durkheim of the "Marxist error."

The 'conditions of economic production' are an example where Durkheim's theory could no doubt be better applied [than to society as a whole], without, however, still being completely relevant. Monsieur Durkheim generalizes the economic *thingism [le choisisme]* of Marx while making from it a *thingism* that is specifically sociological. In doing so, he generalizes the marxist error. (1896:252 n. 1).

And in a review published in Germany in 1897 by Paul Barth, a follower of Dilthey, Durkheim had evidence that this materialist misinterpretation had spread beyond the border of France alone. Barth's *Die Philosophie der Geschichte als Soziologie* discusses Durkheim's work in his chapter entitled "The Economic Conception of History." He attacks Durkheim for being, like Spencer, "an almost superstitious worshiper of the contract" and he argues (Barth [1897] 1922:612) that, in his early works at least, Durkheim views morality as a "hindrance to economic progress" and as "unfavorable to the autonomy of the individual."

As if to confirm this materialist evaluation by his non-Marxist critics, Durkheim was hailed in 1895 by Sorel, the major Marxist intellectual in France, as a kindred spirit. In the lead article of the first issue of the Marxist journal, *Le Devenir,* Sorel (1895:16–17) applauds *Rules* for its antipsychological emphasis on coercion and constraint. Neatly summing up the prevailing perspective on *Rules* as in complete continuity with *Division,* he notes (1895:1) that Durkheim had "just brought together in a small volume of very modest style, what is essential in his doctrine." As for the earlier *Division,* Sorel (1895:23) calls it an exposition of "great beauty" and makes a direct parallel between it and the theory of Marx. "With Durkheim," he writes, "we are placed on the ground of real science, and we see the importance of struggle *[la lutte]*." But Durkheim seems to hesitate, Sorel regretfully notes, before taking the final step toward a fully materialist history. In order to define the conditions of existence more specifically, "he would have to place himself on the ground of Marxist philosophy" (1895:177). If Durkheim could borrow from Marxism the conception of classes, "I would be the first," Sorel affirms

(1895:180), "to acclaim him my master," for he is the "only French sociologist who possesses a sufficient philosophical preparation and well developed critical spirit to be able to perceive in historical change scientific laws and the material conditions of becoming." Durkheim could only have read Sorel's essay with alarm.

Insofar as they referred to Durkheim's *Division of Labor,* these reviews must be read as fully legitimate criticisms of key elements of his work, and they must have brought home to Durkheim with unassailable force certain vital implications of his first theoretical work. As such, they could only have reinforced his growing conviction that radical theoretical renovation was necessary. The intensity of Durkheim's feelings on this issue are revealed, ironically perhaps, by the vehemence with which he rejected these critical claims. Durkheim protests too much: he never acknowledged even their partial validity. Indeed, he carried a bitter resentment against these criticisms throughout the rest of his life. In his preface to the first edition of *Rules,* in 1895, he ([1895] 1938:xxxiv) protests against "what critics have called our 'positivism,'" objecting that although his method "will perhaps be judged crude and will possibly be termed 'materialistic,' it is actually nothing of the kind." In 1896, he (1896) responded to Andler's review by writing to the editor that "I regret absolutely the ideas that are attributed to me." He (1896) insists Andler "has been able to attribute them to me only by taking advantage of several isolated words, while I had myself taken greater care to put the reader on guard against such an abuse." In a private letter the following year that refers to the German review by Barth, he writes to his follower Célèstin Bouglé that he had "never dreamt of saying that one could do sociology without any psychological background, or that sociology is anything other than a form of psychology" (Lukes 1972:234 n. 35).

Durkheim's frustration could only have been increased by the realization that this critical response to his work failed completely to recognize the enormous changes that he himself had introduced in *Rules*—changes that were intended to circumvent the very errors of which he stood accused. But Durkheim himself had never acknowledged that a break existed. Is it any wonder that his reviewers simply took him at his word? They saw in *Rules* only the formalization of the method of *Division.* "On the very points on which we had expressed ourselves most explicitly," Durkheim ([1895]1938: xli) writes in exasperation in his preface to the second edition of *Rules* in 1901, "views were freely attributed to us which had nothing in common with our own; and opponents held that they were refuting us in refuting these mistaken ideas." The critics, he wrote ([1895]1938:liii), "claimed that we are explaining social phenomena by constraint." But this, he insists rather lamely, "was far from our intention —in fact, it had never even occurred to us that it could have been so interpreted, so much is it contrary to our entire method."

Such disingenuousness can be explained only if we understand the true quandary in which Durkheim found himself. He had realized, consciously or not, that the theory that informed so much of *Division* was a drastic mistake. Yet his positivist faith that scientific objectivity would reveal the very consistency of social life, his intellectual pride in the integrity of his theorizing, and perhaps also his lack of critical self-consciousness—all of these factors prevented Durkheim from acknowledging in the mid-1890s that he was, in fact, embarked upon a drastic theoretical revision. To his understandable but, nonetheless, illegitimate indignation, no one seemed aware of this fateful turn—neither his antagonistic critics nor his faithful students. If his new path were to be recognized—if his divergence from the theory of Marxian socialism were ever to be recognized for what it was—his innovation would have to be asserted in a much more emphatic and radical way.

The Transition: "Revelation" and Anti-Materialist Reconstruction

At a later and more secure point in his intellectual career, Durkheim talked about the "revelation" that had allowed him to resolve this quandary. "It was not until 1895," he wrote in the 1907 letter (Durkheim 1907) that protested a polemical review of his oeuvre, "that I achieved a clear sense of the essential role played by religion in social life."

It was in that year that, for the first time, I found the means of tackling the study of religion sociologically. This was a revelation to me. That course of 1895 marks a dividing line in the development of my thought, to such an extent that all my previous researches had to be taken up afresh in order to be made to harmonize with these new insights. . . . [This reorientation] was entirely due to the studies of religious history which I have just undertaken, and notably to the reading of the works of Robertson Smith and his school. (1907:612–14).*

---

*I have made a few alterations here from Lukes' translation (1972:237), the most important of which is that in the original Durkheim employs the verb *marquer* (to mark) in the

Durkheim refers here to the course on religion that he first offered at Bordeaux in the school year 1894–95, a course in which he encountered the new historical approach to religion. Smith's work was revolutionary because it linked the theological ideas of the great religions to religious practice and ritual association, and it argued that this interaction is what gave to symbols their sacred power.* Knowledge of Smith's work was crucial for Durkheim, because it allowed him to transform the scheme of affective and moral interaction of his middle period work into a more comprehensive understanding that linked the power of solidarity to the sacred ideational forces he called collective representations.

Few analysts have been aware of this formative break in Durkheim's development, and those who have noted it have almost always taken this encounter with Smith as being revolutionary in itself, as constituting an "epistemological break" *sui generis.*† In view of the preceding discussion, however, it is clear that this encounter must be seen in the context of Durkheim's ongoing development: it offered him an escape from the quandary he faced. Durkheim felt compelled to find a way of making his subjectification of social order at once more explicit and more refined. It was only within this context that he gave his course on religion and encountered the new anthropological writings of Smith and his followers.

Durkheim could have been so attracted to Smith only because he

---

present tense, whereas Lukes translates it in the past tense, as "marked." The literal translation gives a more vivid sense of the fact that Durkheim feels as if the "revelation" about the role of religion which he is recounting some ten years subsequent to the event is still, in fact, occurring.

*The work that had the most impact on Durkheim was Smith's *Lectures on the Religion of the Semites,* written in 1887.

†Those who emphasize the continuity of Durkheim's work, of course, ignore the break (see n. 1 above). As for those who make the opposite mistake—taking the encounter with Smith's work as constituting, in itself, an epistemological break—see, for example, Beidelman (1974), who overemphasizes Smith's effect on Durkheim primarily because he is not aware of the movement of Durkheim's thought before he encountered Smith's work. Lukes (1972:238–239) is guilty of the same exaggeration when he tries to demonstrate the impact of Smith simply by comparing his religious theory with Durkheim's earlier writing on the narrow topic of religion itself, igoring the considerable shifts that had taken place in Durkheim's general social theory in the immediately preceding years. While Filloux's (1977:91–92) assessment is more cautious on this point, he moves too far over to the other side by claiming that Durkheim knew "in principle that all is religious" as early as 1886 and 1887, and that Smith merely gave him a better understanding of how this social permeation of religion could come about. Filloux, in other words, inverts an interpretation like Giddens', asserting that Durkheim's work consistently emphasizes religion from beginning to end.

himself had already embarked on a similar path. Moreover, while Smith shared with Durkheim an emphasis on the human practice, or association, that underlined any commitment to ideal beliefs, Smith applied this thinking about the relation between beliefs and practices only to religious activity, not to social action itself. Why, then, does Durkheim's public statement insist that his encounter with Smith initiated a much more radical break, one that forced him completely to rethink all his previous work? Because, quite simply, Durkheim had never publicly admitted, and may himself never consciously have been aware, that his own writing had already taken a dramatic turn with the earlier publication of *Rules*. Nonetheless, Durkheim did not, in fact, really abandon all of his pre-1895 sociology. Indeed, it was the momentum created by his earlier shift that led him to find in the anthropology of religion the more voluntaristic vocabulary he so urgently sought. The subjective model of association was already in place in early 1894. When he encounters religion later that year, or in 1895, there is more of a convergence than a radical break. Rather than a call to start anew, Durkheim must have seen in Smith's writing on religion a means of finally completing a renewal already well underway. He read this theory of religion in a way that meshed perfectly with his own developing theory of association.

The result was a theory that, no matter how flawed by an idealist strain, allowed Durkheim to solve the theoretical problems that had always prevented him from achieving his fundamental theoretical and ideological goals. He now understood how society could be determinate, organized, and voluntary at the same time: collective order would be accepted because it was held to be sacred. It would be revered and sanctified in the very same moment that it would be obeyed. Although Durkheim's systematic understanding of the religious nature of society did not appear until 1897, he had already begun to express this intuition in 1896, and in the final Book of *Suicide* we find him arguing that legal and moral precepts are the "sacrosanct" form of living sentiments. After making this point, in fact, he makes a footnoted assertion that strikingly reveals the polemical animus that is behind this new religious reference:

We do not expect to be reproached further, after this explanation, with wishing to substitute the exterior for the interior in sociology. We start from the exterior because it alone is immediately given, but only to reach the interior. Doubtless the procedure is complicated; but there is no other unless one would risk having his research apply to his personal feeling concerning the order of facts under investigation, instead of to this factual order itself. ([1897] 1951:315 n. 12)

Two years later, in the conclusion to his first attempt to describe religious representations as the center of secular order, he makes precisely the same point. "Nothing is wider of the mark," he writes, "than the accusation of materialism which has been levelled against us." Quite the contrary, he argues ([1898] 1974:34; italics in original), "from the point of view of our position, if one is to call the distinctive property of the individual representational life *spirituality,* one should say that social life is defined by its hyperspirituality." And perhaps most revealing, in the 1902 preface to the second edition of *Division of Labor,* he announced ([1893] 1964:4) that his earlier explanation had been "incomplete." "If it is true," he writes, "that social functions spontaneously seek to adapt themselves to one another, provided they are regularly in relationship, nevertheless this mode of adaptation becomes a rule of conduct only if the group consecrates it with its authority." The strain of mechanistic functionalism in *Division* has here been publically disavowed.

With the spiritualization of his understanding of order, Durkheim could, therefore, finally fulfill his thwarted theoretical and ideological ambition. In doing so, moreover, he meets head on the threat of misinterpretation produced by the increasingly polarized intellectual and political climate of the day. It seems only fitting that, as soon as his new understanding has been articulated, Durkheim should return to the problem of instrumental Marxism, the theoretical tradition against which he had tried initially to direct his work and with which he felt he had so mistakenly been identified. In the very first year that his first explicitly "religious" sociology appeared, Durkheim initiated debate with two of the leading Marxists of the day.

One of these, Paul Lafargue, the son-in-law of Marx himself, was engaged only indirectly (see Vogt 1976). Lafargue had reviewed a book on Marxist socialism by Gaston Richard, at the time a member of Durkheim's circle and the author of the book on law that had earlier been the occasion of Durkheim's first break with the *Division of Labor.* Lafargue denounced Richard's work on socialism as anti-Marxist and idealist. Durkheim chose to reply to Lafargue with a review of his own. For the most part, this review consisted of a complimentary summary of Richard's sharp rejection of Marx's ideas. Toward the end of the review, however,

Durkheim took Lafargue directly to task. "We . . . find at once surprising and regrettable," he wrote ([1897] 1978b:135), "the attacks to which he [Richard] has been subject on the part of the authorized representatives of socialist doctrine." After this rebuke, Durkheim stresses that his own position on socialism is similar to Richard's. Socialism has no validity as a scientific theory, he writes. It must, rather, be viewed as a collective representation: "Socialism is, above all, the way in which certain strata of society which have been tested by collective suffering represent the latter to themselves" ([1897] 1978b:137)." The popularity or persuasiveness of socialism must not be viewed, in other words, as evidence for the validity of Marx's theory about the coercive and external nature of social order. To the contrary, socialism itself was a "religious" force; its power, therefore, only demonstrated the representational character of social life. Socialism could be understood, Durkheim concludes, only by penetrating the underlying moral reality that produced it. It was Durkheim's new ability to define socialism specifically as a "representation" that evidently gave him the confidence to make the challenge to Marx much more direct.

More important, however, is Durkheim's challenge to Antonio Labriola in a review that directly engages Marxism as a theoretical system. Labriola's *Essay on the Materialist Conception of History* had just been translated into French, and George Sorel, in an introduction to the work, had hailed its publication as a "landmark in the history of socialism" (Labriola 1897:19). Labriola was one of the premier Marxist philosophers of his time, and he presented his master's theory in anything but a vulgar light. In making his review, therefore, Durkheim could publicly confront the major alternative to the nascent sociological theory of his middle-period work. He could finally respond to the gauntlet Sorel had thrown down two years before.

Durkheim organized his response to illuminate the differences between his theory and Marx's at the most general level. After a balanced presentation of Labriola's argument, he approvingly discusses the anti-individualist position of historical materialism. Rather than focusing on pure ideas, or on isolated individuals, historical materialism focuses on a much more fundamental level, on "the artificial milieu which the work of associated men has created of whole cloth and then superimposed on nature" (Durkheim [1897] 1978a:126). Durkheim insists (p. 127), however, that this kind of collective emphasis is not exclusive to Marx. What is peculiar is that Marx's collectivist theory emphasizes the primacy of material factors. "Just as it seems true to us," Durkheim writes (p. 128), "that causes of social phenomena must be sought outside individual representations, it seems to that same degree false that they can be reduced, in the final analysis, to the state of industrial technology, and that the economic factor is the mainspring of progress." Durkheim then demonstrates this Marxist error by discussing his own newly discovered view of the importance of religion. In opposition to historical materialism, he claims that "historians tend more and more to meet in the confirmation that religion is the most primitive of all social phenomena." "Everything," he insists (pp. 129–130), "is religious in principle." Is it not probable, he asks, "that the economy depends on religion much more than the second on the first?"

Durkheim's interpreters have often mistakenly read his religious theory as a kind of deracinated materialism. Others, when they have recognized the seriousness of the break, usually insist on seeing in the theory that results from it an alternative that subsumes Marx's by being much more multidimensional in scope. This 1897 confrontation with Marxism demonstrates that both views are incorrect.[2]

The Spiritual Program
of Durkheim's Later Writings

The vast implications of Durkheim's religious revelation have never been fully appreciated. It is scarcely realized that after 1896 he systematically revised every piece of his sociological writings, and every one of his sets of lectures as well, to make them reflect his new understanding of the role that ritual, sacred authority, and representation played in secular life. Durkheim's society became a hierarchy of institutions that were composed of crystallized emotions, not material forms. At the top were sacred symbols of culture, the themes of individualism that provided the most universalistic imperatives of modern social life. At the bottom were two spheres of particularist spirit, the family and occupational group. The state and legal orders mediated between these institutions and general culture through representations that had a more transcendent nature. Education was another institution that provided a universalizing spiritual force; as such, it provided the background for any effective functioning of law and government policies. In this scheme, the coercive aspects of order are eliminated. Economics, for example, was either moralized as a form of cultural particularism or relegated to the position of a residual category—an instrumental, individualist, and profane fact that simply could not be explained.

At the heart of this later religious sociology was Durkheim's journal, *L'Année sociologique*. It is important to connect this act of professional entrepreneurialism to a theoretical program. Durkheim created the journal as an intellectual vehicle only after he had achieved his symbolic breakthrough in the years 1895-97. Although many of his students implicitly demurred, he himself fully intended to make *L'Année* into a statement of his religious model of social order. "This year, as well as last," he wrote ([1899] 1960:350) in his important Preface to the *L'Année*'s second issue, "our analyses are headed by those concerning the sociology of religion." He acknowledges that "the according of the first rank to this sort of phenomenon has produced some astonishment," but he defends this decision on grounds that clearly derive from his recent theoretical insights.* "It is these [religious] phenomena," he writes (p. 350), "which are the germ from which all others—or at least almost all others—are derived."

> Religion contains in itself from the very beginning, even if an indistinct state, all the elements which in dissociating themselves from it, articulating themselves, and combining with one another in a thousand ways, have given rise to the various manifestations of collective life . . . One cannot understand our perception of the world, our philosophical conceptions of the soul, or immortality, or life, if one does not know the religious beliefs which are their primordial forms." (Pp, 350-51)

L'Année would concentrate on demonstrating exactly these historical connections and, by implication, Durkheim's analytic points as well. Durkheim concludes this defense of his organizational format by emphasizing that religion is important not only from an historical perspective; it is equally crucial in terms of the general theoretical framework it provides. "A great number of problems change their aspects completely," he writes, "as soon as their connections with the sociology of religion are recognized." He concludes by insisting that "our efforts must therefore be aimed at tracing these connections."

---

*Evidently, this "astonishment" was not limited to Durkheim's critics. Paul Lapie, the reviewer turned follower who had earlier applauded the subjective turn of Durkheim' *Rules*, complained in an 1897 letter to Célèstin Bouglé, one of Durkheim's collaborators on the *L'Année*, that "Durkheim explains everything, at this time, by religion; the interdiction against marriages between relatives is a religious affair, the punishment is a religious phenomenon, all is religious" (quoted in Lacroix 1976:213 n. 2).

With the single exception of the brief reply to a critic which I have noted above, Durkheim never admitted the extent to which his encounter with religion had transformed his sociology. Indeed, he never admitted to any radical break in his work at all. He never disclaimed the instrumental presuppositions of *Division of Labor,* nor did he ever acknowledge that *Rules* was not a codification of the theory employed in that earlier work but, instead, a blueprint of things to come. Nor, needless to say, was the religious encounter that transformed his later writing ever accorded its due. This silence about the true inner development of his work is perhaps the major reason for the gross misinterpretation to which Durkheim's work has been subject, not just among contemporary critics but among observers in his own time and even among his own students. Like all great sociological theorists, Durkheim desperately wanted to present his work as a consistent whole. To do anything else, to acknowledge, for example, that an encounter with religion could cause major theoretical upheaval, would imply that his towering oeuvre was not completely "scientific," that it was not, in other words, derived simply from acute insight into the structures of the empirical world. "What caused the failure of Saint-Simonianism," he wrote in his lectures on socialism ([1895-96] 1958:240), was that "Saint-Simon and his disciples wanted to get the most from the least, the superior from the inferior, moral rule from economic matter." Only too late had Saint-Simon realized that self-interest "was no longer enough," that "without charity, mutual obligation, and philanthropy, the social order—and still more the human order—was impossible" (p. 185). Durkheim was determined that this mistake would not happen to him. What Saint-Simon had realized only at the end of his life, Durkheim had been able to understand while there was still enough time left to change his theoretical direction in a drastic and fundamental way. Durkheim had learned that to create social order without sacrificing voluntarism, men must "feel a positive bond among them" (p. 185), and the model of this bond, he had discovered, must be the communion of religious life.

From his first day as a sociologist, it had been one of Durkheim's principal ambitions to create an alternative to instrumental Marxism. Only after his breakthrough to symbolic religious order, however, did he feel ready to create a theoretical alternative to Marxism that could match its generality and scope. This new theory, he insisted, was just as collective and structural as Marxism, but because it was also resolutely anti-instrumental it would avoid the problem of coercion that seemed to correspond to the Marxist understanding of social control. Durkheim finally had differentiated his own theory from Marx's in a conclusive way. That in doing so he had created a theory whose voluntarism was as exaggerated as the determinism he despised did not, apparently, occur to him. He was in flight from *The Division of Labor,* with all the intellectual and social consequences it had implied.

Like Marx's critique of Hegelian idealism, Durkheim's attempt to counteract the exaggerations of an antagonistic theory—Marxist materialism—became paradigmatic of an approach to social structure that denied to this theoretical emphasis any status at all. It is for this reason that, from the time of its initial conception to the present day, Durkheim's subjective structuralism has represented for sociological thought the theoretical antithesis to the objective structuralism of Marx.

Conclusion

The argument in this essay has been made at three levels. First, I have made an argument about the course of Durkheim's theoretical career. Most interpreters have seen this career as continuous, yet even those who have appreciated its discontinuity have viewed the movement in Durkheim's thought in positive, progressive and developmental terms. I have argued, by contrast, for a distinctive circularity. Durkheim went over the same intellectual problems again and again. The period between 1885 and 1893 constitutes one "full time through" these constitutive problems of Durkheim's life. This first time through was a failure, and *The Division of Labor in Society,* far from being his crowning achievement, is emblematic of this early difficulty. Durkheim began his "second time through" immediately after *Division*'s completion. This second time was a success, but it was so only partly because of Durkheim's theoretical growth. He had also narrowed his ambition in a significant way. Interpreters who have insisted on the weaknesses of Durkheim's idealist project have failed to appreciate the precisely delimited framework of his later work, and the enormous intellectual growth he evidenced within it. Those who have seen his career simply as a success have failed to see this framework's limitations, and the personal and restrictive definition of growth it produced.

This first argument, about the nature of Durkheim's theoretical career, has implied at every point a second one—an argument about the nature of sociological theory per se. I suggested at the beginning of this essay that sociologists keep returning to Durkheim in order to think through problems that remain unresolved. While arguing about Durkheim, we are really arguing about contemporary ideas, indeed about contemporary society. Some interpreters have seen in Durkheim's career a marvellous vindication of historical materialism; others have testified that its course indicates a rapprochement with interactionism; still others see in it the affirmation of a purely normative sociology. In part because my own theoretical interests and commitments are none of the above, I have been drawn to understand Durkheim's development in a very different way.

Durkheim's sociology, I have argued, is about the meaning of structure. He rejected individualism, yet he also rejected theories that postulated the external determination of individuals. To understand why Durkheim rejected these alternatives is to understand something vital about sociological theory today. In the last two decades, individualistic theories have permeated contemporary sociology: antistructuralist hermeneutic, phenomenological and action theories, symbolic interactionism, ethnomethodology, and models of rational choice. To describe Durkheim's development in the way I have is to see, through Durkheim's eyes, why such individualism is inadequate.* Though they illuminate the voluntary qualities of action, these theories underestimate the problem of order. Each posits either a natural identity of interests (an inherent social stability) or a latent social structure (a residual patterning).

Now, in rejecting such individualism, it is tempting to move, as Durkheim did in *Division*, to a so-called structural solution, that is, to its antithesis. Such objectivisit structuralism also is omnipresent in contemporary thought: in Althusserianism, in political theories like Skocpol's and Tilly's, in stratification theories like Treiman's, in development theories like Moore's. Yet the logical quandaries and personal anxieties produced by Durkheim's own experiment with such structuralism allow us to see a continuing truth. The very impersonality that is structuralism's "scientific" achievement is its existential undoing, for in explaining order, structuralism negates order's individual base (see Alexander 1988:11-45).

The theoretical step we must take today is the same as Durkheim took long ago: we must recognize that questions of order are separated from

*For a more systematic, analytic approach to the inadequacies of theoretical individualism, see Alexander (1987):156–329; and (1988b):193–333.

questions of action. Structure can be based on normative and affectual, as well as instrumental, motives. If contemporary arguments wish to preserve both order *and* volition, they must evolve in the same way as Durkheim's thought. Volition must be seen as a social act, and structure must be seen as involving individual actions in turn. The social must be given some power—sacred or otherwise—to structure by virtue of its subjective attraction, and the individual must be given some capacity for ordering that comes out of his or her personal wish (Alexander 1988:222-257). This, I have argued, is precisely what Durkheim set out to do in his later work. He described "representation" as just such a social and individual process. It is because Durkheim faced the very same quandaries that sociology is experiencing today that the story of his personal development resonates so deeply. We need not follow him into idealism to appreciate his achievement, or indeed, to make it part of our own (Alexander, ed. 1988, and chapters 5 and 6 below).

The third level of my argument concerns the sociology of knowledge, more specifically the sociology of science. To understand the nature of Durkheim's development and the issues it involved is to see the error of the positivist view that sociology is a science whose theories proceed only through accumulation and falsification. Durkheim was one of the greatest founding scientists of our discipline, but such empiricist criteria had little to do with the growth of his work. For more appropriate criteria we must consider issues raised by post-positivist philosophy and history of science, issues central to the sociology of knowledge more broadly defined.

Kuhn's work, and the controversy it has generated (see, e.g., Alexander 1982b) have raised in an acute form an issue that has dogged the sociology of knowledge since Mannheim: what is the relationship between the internal development of scientific thought and its external environment? In response to the limits of earlier empiricism, contemporary science studies have shifted to environmental and group explanations; in this emphasis, of course, they resemble most Mannheimian exercises in the sociology of knowledge. The dangers of this shift are familiar. Just as the sociology of knowledge has too often led to a dangerous relativism, so have contemporary "externalist" studies in science. These dangers spark defenses of scientific realism that are often too internalist in turn.

The account I have presented of Durkheim's development responds to these issues in two ways. I have, of course, relativized Durkheim's science by showing that it continually responded to the social and cultural contexts of his time; as these contexts changed, so did his work. Yet this externalism has not produced a complete relativism. I have sought to maintain a reconstructed realism by insisting that there were elements internal to Durkheim's theorizing that were relatively autonomous vis-à-vis external events. These elements derive not from the empirical logic of internal observation or inductive generalization but from a "theoretical logic" that proceeds from generalized understandings about action and order that are of a more metaphysical scope. Only by maintaining an analytical framework that encompasses such independent, generalized concerns can we fairly evaluate the success of Durkheim's theory in terms of some relatively specific criterion of truth.*

Historians of social thought once believed that Marxism mattered little to Durkheim. It is now beginning to be understood that the origins and growth of Marxism and socialism in France had enormous repercussions. Yet these repercussions did not, as vulgar Mannheimian or orthodox Marxist interpretations would have it (e.g., Llobera 1978), unfold in purely ideological and class-related ways. I have shown that while political developments were vital for Durkheim, they were so only as they were mediated by his scholarly milieu and by the internal logic of his work. A theorist's responsiveness to external factors depends upon the anxieties and sensibilities generated by developments in his scientific work. After he had experienced the travails of *Division,* for example, Durkheim became particularly sensitive to the challenge of Marxism. Yet external factors are actually twice mediated: political, economic, and "social" events are filtered through a scientist's more immediate and personal intellectual environment. For Durkheim, this milieu was constituted, in part, by the reviews he received. Social developments, combined with the theoretical problems of *Division,* put Durkheim into an objectively vulnerable position; still, only changes in an environment toward which he was personally cathected could make him *feel* that vulnerability. By accusing him of materialism, these reviews "spoke" Durkheim's doubts. Science is a communicative situation where information is exchanged for recognition (Hagstrom 1965). If recognition is denied, or indeed, if it is wrongly imputed, scientific information may be withdrawn or reformulated.

The reformulation of scientific theories, then, cannot be understood in

*In terms of my argument in chapter 1, above, the discursive arguments in the present essay have been conducted in relation to explicit, rather than immanent, truth criteria. In this way, the truth criteria themselves can become objects of debate.

purely cognitive and rational ways. Theorists present themselves, of course, as guided by purely rational considerations, for not only do they themselves accept the official norms of science but their audiences do as well. The impact of external and internal developments, however, can be understood only if a more complex social psychology is maintained. Denial, self-deception, and deceit are the favored defense mechanisms of social theorists, as they are of other mortal men and women. The careers of great theorists, therefore, must be understood as psychological gestalts and not just as intellectual ones. Each of their ideas has for them an emotionally laden and highly personal meaning; it is for this reason that the stakes of intellectual combat are so enormous, that the interpretive and critical debates over their work often resonate so deeply. Their own theories have emerged from hidden, and sometimes not so hidden, oppositions, oppositions that often take the form of systematic misunderstandings of their predecessors' works (Bloom, 1973).

What could be more frustrating for a great theorist, then, and more provocative of further theoretical change, than the anxiety of being misunderstood?

NOTES

1. The changing and contradictory nature of Durkheim's argument in *Division* has not been recognized by most of his interpreters. This has occurred in part because of an understandable yet unfortunate tendency to defer to Durkheim's own perspective on the work's contents. In discussing Book 2, for example, critics have accepted Durkheim's claim that he is measuring not simply demographic but also moral density. Pope (1973), for example, views Durkheim's emphasis on population expansion and exchange as simply another example of the "social realist" approach to morality that dominates the entire work. This perspective, however, collapses the problem of individualist-versus-collectivist reasoning with the problem of action, failing to distinguish the radically different approaches to the "social" that are possible even when a collectivist, social realist position is accepted. Though much more nuanced and generally more accurate than Pope's account, Lukes' (1972:154, 169) discussion similarly fails to distinguish the tremendous differences between moral and material density in Book 2. In his discussion, Lukes (1972:168–72) too often simply reproduces the vagueness and the contradictory quality of the Durkheimian original. While he accuses Durkheim of technological determinism and of being inconclusive about the basic details of the social change he describes (1972:164), these charges are never systematically documented. One reason for this failure is Lukes' argument for the close continu-

ity of *Division* with Durkheim's earlier writings. In fact, Lukes views the whole sequence of Durkheim's writings from 1885 to 1893 as clarification and specification rather than as involving the development of contradictory theoretical logics. Filloux (1977:74–78) adopts much the same sanguine posture. Giddens has gone so far as to argue not only for the internal continuity of *Division* but for its centrality in Durkheim's corpus as a whole. The work provided, Giddens writes (1971:190), "a definitive perspective upon the emergence of the modern form of society which Durkheim never abandoned and which constitutes the lasting ground of all his later works."

Even the critics who have emphasized discontinuity in *Division* have insisted that there exists within this work a developmental and logically coherent movement toward "better theory." Nisbet (1965:36–47), for example, argues that a normative perspective on social order gradually overshadows an earlier instrumental one. Earlier, Parsons (1937:308–324) had argued for much the same position, claiming that Book 1, chapter 7—the chapter I have identified as a point where Durkheim turned toward a troublesome instrumentalism—represented the emergence of a more satisfactory normative perspective.

While Durkheim's French interpreters have been much more willing to recognize the economistic and even Marxist elements of *Division* (e.g., Aimard 1962:217–218; Cuvillier 1948:83; Kagan 1938, passim), they have, almost without exception, merely turned the error of English and American critics on its head: the instrumental perspective on order, they have argued, was consistent and continuous throughout Durkheim's 1893 work.

2. Perhaps the major failure of interpretation of this crucial phase in Durkheim's theoretical development rests with the widespread inclination of writers to describe the issue he was grappling with as exactly parallel to the Marxian concern with base versus superstructure. Thus, Emile Benoît-Smullyan (1948:511) writes about the crucial relationship for Durkheim of "material substratum" and "collective representation." Pope (1973) talks about whether or not "material foundations" still play a significant role. Giddens (1977:290) tries to indicate the continuing impact, and therefore anti-idealist reference, of social institutions on ideas in Durkheim's sociology of religion. This same dichotomy is the principal organizing rubric for Lukes' (1972:237–244, 450–484) thinking about the shift in Durkheim's theory initiated by religion, as it is for La Capra (1972:245–291), Marks (1974), Gouldner (1958), and Aron (1970, pp. 53–79). These interpreters take different positions on whether or not a shift did occur, but the error is the same no matter what their conclusion. For the issue in this confrontation with religion is not whether or not the material base will be dominant. This issue had already been decided by Durkheim in 1894. The issue rather is what will be the nature of the normative order to which Durkheim is already committed.

Many interpreters, of course, have simply failed to appreciate the significance of this early encounter with religion altogether. In his influential earlier work on Durkheim, Parsons (1937:409), for example, viewed Durkheim's religious understanding as coming into play only with the publication of *Elementary Forms*. (It is an extraordinary testimony to the sensitivity of this early interpretation that Parsons was able to describe the transition to subjectivity in Durkheim's middle writings despite the fact that he was not aware of the early significance of religion.)

Yet, even among those who have seen the importance of this encounter, none have adequately assessed its enormous impact on Durkheim's later theory of society. Lukes (1972), for example, who is much more aware of this crucial biographical fact than most, basically considers this religious breakthrough as a separate line of analysis culminating in *Elementary Forms,* and he integrates it hardly at all with Durkheim's writing on education, politics, and other institutions. The only important exceptions, to my knowledge, are Gianfranco Poggi (1971:252–254, and passim), and the important dissertation by Lacroix (1976). Poggi's analysis, however, is mainly programmatic, failing to link the new importance of religion to any decisive break in Durkheim's work. Lacroix's excellent work has two problems, from my perspective. First, although he firmly exposed *"la coupure"* that Durkheim's religious revelation created in his theoretical development, he tries to tie this religion-inspired shift too closely to the middle-period work. Any definitive resolution of this question, of course, must await firmer historical evidence, but at this point it seems evident that Durkheim's theory underwent two shifts after the publication of *Division of Labor,* not one. The first, which begins even as the latter work is published—in the 1893 "Note" and socialism review cited above—reorganizes his schema in a subjective manner without any particular reference to collective representations or religion. The second phase, which is barely visible in the lectures of 1895 and which does not become explicit until 1897, brings "spiritual" considerations into the center of this newly subjectified theory. Only the second development, it would seem, can be linked to the "revelation" of 1895. The second problem is that Lacroix's analysis, valuable as it is, does not expose the "religious dimension" of Durkheim's later institutional theory in a systematic way. Bellah's interpretation (1974) takes some initial steps in the direction in which such an analysis would have to go. For a full exploration of the manner in which Durkheim's entire body of post-1896 writing is reorganized around the religious model, see Alexander 1982a.

REFERENCES

Aimard, Guy. 1962. *Durkheim et la science économique.* Paris: Presses Universitaires de France.
Alexander, Jeffrey C. 1982a. *The Antinomies of Classical Thought: Marx and Durkheim.* Berkeley and Los Angeles: University of California Press.
—— 1982b. "Kuhn's Unsuccessful Revisionism: A Reply to Selby." *Canadian Journal of Sociology* 7:66–71.
—— 1982c. *Positivism, Presuppositions, and Current Controversies:* Vol. 1 of *Theoretical Logic in Sociology.* Berkeley and Los Angeles: University of California Press.

—— 1987. *Twenty Lectures: Sociological Theory Since World War II.* New York: Columbia University Press.

—— 1988. *Action and Its Environments:* New York: Columbia University Press.

Alexander, Jeffrey C., ed. 1988. *Durkheimian Sociology: Cultural Studies.* New York: Cambridge University Press.

Alexander, Jeffrey C. and Bernard Giesen. 1988. "From Reduction to Linkage: The Long View of the Micro-Macro Debate." in Alexander (1988):257-258.

Andler, Charles. 1896. "Sociologie et démocratie." *Revue de métaaphysique et morale* 4:243-256.

Aron, Raymond. 1970. *Main Currents of Sociological Thought.* Vol. 2. New York: Doubleday Anchor.

Barth, P. [1897] 1922. *Die Philosophie der Geschichte als Soziologie.* Leipzig: O.R. Reisland.

Beidelman, T. O. 1974. *W. Robertson Smith and the Sociological Study of Religion.* Chicago: University of Chicago Press.

Bellah, Robert N. 1974. Introduction to *Emile Durkheim on Morality and Society,* ed. by Bellah. Chicago: University of Chicago.

Benoît-Smullyan, Emile. 1948. "The Sociologism of Durkheim and His School." In H.E. Barnes, ed, *An Introduction to the History of Sociology,* p. 499–537. Chicago: University of Chicago Press.

Bloom, Harold. 1973 *The Anxiety of Influence.* N.Y: Oxford University Press.

Blumer, Herbert. 1969. *Symbolic Interactionism.* Englewood Cliffs, N.J.: Prentice-Hall.

Brunschvicg, L. and E. Halévy. 1894. "L'Année philosophique, 1893." *Revue de metaphysique et de morale* 2:564-590.

Durkheim, Emile. 1885. "A Fouillée, *La Propriété sociale et la démocratie.*" *Revue philosophique* 19:446-453.

—— [1885]. "Review of Schaeflle, *Bau und Leben des Sozialen Korpers:* Erster Band." In Traugott, ed. (1978): 93-114. 3.

——[1886]. "Les Etudes de science sociale." *Revue philosophique* 22:61-80.

—— 1887a. "Guyau, *L'Irréligion de l'avenir: Etude de sociologie.*" *Revue philosophique* 23:299-311.

—— 1887b. "La Science positive de la morale en Allemagne." Part 3. *Revue philosophique* 24:113-142.

—— [1888] 1978. "Introduction to the Sociology of the Family." In Traugott, ed. (1978): 205-228.

—— [1888] 1975. "Le Programme économique de M. Schaeffle. In *Emile Durkheim: Textes,* pp. 3-7. Paris: Les Editions de Minuit.

—— [1893] 1964. *The Division of Labor in Society.* New York: Free Press.

—— [1893a] "Note sur la definition du socialisme." *Revue philosophique* 34:506-512.

—— [1893b]. "Richard, G., *Essai sur l'origine de l'idée de droit. Revue philosophique* 34:290-296.

—— [1895] 1938. *Rules of Sociological Method.* New York: Free Press.

—— [1895–1896] 1958. *Socialism and Saint-Simon.* Yellow Springs, Ohio: Antioch.

—— 1896. Letter to the Editor. *Revue de metaphysique et de morale* 4:20. (Special supplement of July 4.)

—— [1897] 1978a. "Review of Antonio Labriola, *Essai sur la conception materialiste de l'histoire.*" In Traugott, ed. (1978):123–130.

—— [1897] 1978b. "Review of Gaston Richard, Le Socialisme et la science sociale." In Traugott, ed. (1978):131–138.

—— [1897] 1951. *Suicide.* New York: Free Press.

—— [1898] 1974. "Individual and Collective Representations." In *Sociology and Philosophy.* New York: Free Press.

—— [1899] 1960. "Preface to *L'année sociologique* 2." In Kurt Wolff, ed. *Emile Durkheim et al. on Sociology and Philosophy,* pp. 347–352. New York: Harper and Row.

—— 1907. Letter to the Director. *Revue néo-scolastique* 14:612–614.

Filloux, Jean-Claude. 1977. *Durkheim et le socialisme.* Geneva: Librairie Droz.

Giddens, Anthony. 1970. "Durkheim as a Review Critic." *Sociological Review* 18:171–196.

—— 1971. *Capitalism and Modern Social Theory.* London: Cambridge Unversity Press.

—— 1972a. "Four Myths in the History of Social Thought." *Economy and Society* 1:357–385.

—— 1972b. Introduction to Anthony Giddens, ed., *Emile Durkheim: Selected Writings,* p. 1–50. London: Cambridge University Press.

—— 1977. "The Individual in the Writing of Emile Durkheim." In Giddens, *Studies in Social and Political Theory,* p. 273–291. New York: Basic.

Gouldner, Alvin W. 1958. Introduction to Gouldner, ed., *Socialism and Saint-Simon: Emile Durkheim.* Yellow Springs, Ohio: Antioch.

Habermas, Jurgen. 1973. *Knowledge and Human Interests.* Boston: Beacon.

Hagstrom, Warren. 1965. *The Scientific Community.* New York: Basic Books.

Homans, George C. 1961. *Social Behavior: Its Elementary Forms.* New York: Harcourt, Brace and World.

Kagan, George. 1938. "Durkheim et Marx." *Revue d'histoire économique et sociale* 24:233–244.

Labriola, Antonio. 1897. *Essai sur la conception matérialiste de l'histoire.* Paris: V. Giard and E. Brière.

La Capra, Dominick. 1972. *Emile Durkheim: Sociologist and Philosopher.* Ithaca, N.Y.: Cornell University Press.

Lacroix, Bernard. 1976. "Durkheim et la question politique." Ph.D. dissertation. University of Paris.

Lapie, Paul. 1895. "L'Année sociologique, 1894." *Revue de métaphysique et morale* 3:309–339.

Lewis, J. David, and Richard L. Smith. 1980. *American Sociology and Pragmatism.* Chicago: University of Chicago Press.

Llobera, Joseph R. 1978. "Durkheim, The Durkheimians, and their Collective Misrepresentation of Marx." Paper presented at the Ninth World Congress of Sociology, Uppsala, Sweden.

Lukes, Steven. 1972. *Emile Durkheim: His Life and Work.* New York: Harper and Row.

Marks, Stephen R. 1974. "Durkheim's Theory of Anomie." *American Journal of Sociology* 80:329–363.

Marx, Karl. [1845] 1965. "Theses on Feuerbach." p. 23–26. In Nathan Rotenstreich, *Key Problems in Marx's Philosophy.* Indianapolis: Bobbs-Merrill.

—— [1847] 1962. *The Communist Manifesto.* In *Marx-Engels Selected Writings,* 1:34–65. Moscow: Foreign Language Press.

Mauss, Marcel [1928] 1958. "Introduction to the First Edition." In Durkheim ([1895–1896] 1958):1–4.

Merton, Robert K. 1961. *On Theoretical Sociology.* New York: Free Press.

Nisbet, Robert A. 1965. Introduction to Nisbet, ed., *Emile Durkheim,* pp. 1–102. Englewood Cliffs, N.J.: Prentice-Hall.

Nizan, Paul. 1932. *Les Chiens de garde.* Paris: Rieder.

O'Connor, James. 1980. "The Division of Labor in Society." *The Insurgent Sociologist* 10:60–68.

Parsons, Talcott. 1937. *The Structure of Social Action.* New York: Free Press.

Poggi, Gianfranco. 1971. "The Place of Religion in Durkheim's Theory of Institutions." *European Journal of Sociology* 12:229–260.

Pope, Whitney. 1973. "Classic on Classic: Parsons' Interpretation of Durkheim." *American Sociological Review* 38:399–415.

Rex, John. 1961. *Key Problems of Sociological Theory.* London: Routledge.

Sorel, George. 1895. "Les Théories de M. Durkheim." *Le Devenir* 1:1–25, 148–180.

Stinchcombe, Arthur L. 1968. *Constructing Social Theories.* Baltimore: Johns Hopkins University Press.

Tiryakian, Edward A. 1978. "Emile Durkheim." In T.B. Bottomore and Robert A. Nisbet, eds., *A History of Sociological Analysis,* New York: Basic Books.

Traugott, Mark, ed. 1978. *Emile Durkheim on Institutional Analysis.* Chicago: University of Chicago Press.

Vogt, W. Paul. 1976. "The Confrontation of Socialists and Sociologists in Pre-War France, 1890–1914." *Proceedings of the Western Society for French History* 4: 313–320.

Wallwork, Ernest. 1972. *Emile Durkheim: Morality and Milieu.* Cambridge: Harvard University Press.

Zeitlin, Irving. 1968. *Ideology and Development of Sociological Theory.* Englewood Cliffs, N.J.: Prentice-Hall.

FIVE

Durkheimian Sociology and Cultural Studies Today

The human studies are in the midst of an explosion of cultural interest. In diverse disciplinary orientations throughout Europe and in literary studies in the United States, semiotics and structuralism—and the poststructuralist movements that have followed in their wake—have fundamentally affected contemporary understandings of social experience and ideas. In American social science there has emerged over the last twenty years a complementary movement within anthropology. This symbolic anthropology has begun to have powerful ramifications in related disciplines, especially in American and European social history.

In the discipline of sociology, however—particularly but not only in its American form—researchers and theorists are still fighting the last war. In the 1960s there was a general mobilization against the hegemony of structural-functional theory in the "idealist" form associated with Parsons. This challenge has triumphed, but theorizing of an equally one-sided sort has taken its place. The discipline is now dominated by micro and macro orientations which are either anti-systemic, anti-cultural, or both. The anti-cultural macro approach, which emphasizes conflict and social "structures," made positive, innovative contributions in the early phase of the fight against functionalism. It helped stimulate, for example, the reaction against the reigning consensus perspective in history. But the new social history, as it has been called for two decades, is by now old hat; it is in the process of being overtaken by a different kind of social history, one that has a pronounced cultural bent. Sociology, meanwhile, remains mired in presymbolic thought. It is as if in this small corner of the intellectual world the Reformation and Renaissance have been reversed. Sociologists are still trying to reform the Parsonian church. For them the cultural renaissance has yet to come. In sociology there is scarcely any cultural analysis at all.

The irony is that important intellectual roots of the current cultural revival can actually be traced to one of sociology's own founders, Emile Durkheim. Sociologists know Durkheim primarily through the works he published in the middle 1890s, *The Division of Labor in Society*, *The Rules of Sociological Method*, and *Suicide*. On the basis of these works sociologists have identified "Durkheimianism"—and to some extent sociology as such—with an emphasis on external constraint and "coercive social facts," on the one hand, and with positivistic, often quantitative methods, on the other.

But it was only after the completion of these works that Durkheim's distinctively cultural program for sociology emerged (see chapter 4, above).*It is true, of course, that even in his earlier works there is an unmistakable concern with subjectivity and solidarity. But only in the studies that began in the later 1890s did Durkheim have an explicit theory of symbolic process firmly in hand. It was at this time that he became deeply interested in religion. "A great number of problems change their aspects completely," Durkheim ([1899] 1960:351) wrote, "as soon as their connections with the sociology of religion are recognized." Durkheim came to believe, indeed, that theories of secular social process have to be modelled upon the workings of the sacred world. This turn to religion, he emphasized, was not because of an interest in churchly things. It was because he wanted to give cultural processes more theoretical autonomy. In religion he had discovered a model of how symbolic processes work in their own terms.

In scattered essays in the late 1890s, and in the monographs and lectures that followed until his death in 1914, Durkheim developed a theory of secular society that emphasized the independent causal importance of symbolic classification, the pivotal role of the symbolic division between sacred and profane, the social significance of ritual behavior, and the interrelation between symbolic classifications, ritual processes, and the formation of social solidarities. It was an unfortunate if largely fortuitous fact that the published work in which Durkheim announced and systematically developed this new theory—which he called his "religious

*For an overview and explication of Durkheim's intellectual development which emphasizes the shift toward subjectivity in his thought, see Alexander (1982, 1986).

sociology"—was devoted to archaic religion and to what would today be seen as anthropological concerns. Only in his unpublished lectures did Durkheim elaborate this new perspective in regard to the secular phenomena of modern life.

If Durkheim had lived beyond the First World War, the perspective of these lectures would be much more widely known today, for he would no doubt have converted them into published scholarly works. We would then have available to us systematic explorations of the "religious" structures and processes that continue to inform contemporary life. The posthumous publication of the lectures (Durkheim 1956, [1928] 1958, [1950] 1958, [1925] 1961, [1938] 1977) has certainly made his ambition and preliminary thinking in this regard perfectly clear (Alexander 1982:259–298). In a series of profound and probing discussions of education, politics, professional organization, morality, and the law, Durkheim demonstrated that these modern spheres must be studied in terms of symbolic classifications. They are structured by tensions between the fields of the sacred and profane; their central social processes are ritualistic; their most significant structural dynamics concern the construction and destruction of social solidarities. These lectures demonstrate the truth of Durkheim's remonstrance in the opening pages of *The Elementary Forms of Religious Life*, the late masterpiece in which he outlined his "religious sociology." He has not devoted himself to "a very archaic religion," Durkheim declares, "simply for the pleasures of telling its peculiarities." If he has taken Aboriginal religion as his subject, he (Durkheim [1911] 1965:1) argues, this is only "because it has seemed to us better adapted than any other to lead to an understanding of the religious nature of man, that is, to show us an essential and permanent aspect of humanity." His point, he insists, is that it is not only archaic man who has a religious nature, but also the "man of today."

The problem, however, is not only that Durkheim failed to enunciate this new and quite radical view of secular society in his published work. It is also that this late Durkheimian perspective eventually ceased to be articulated at all. For some years after his death, Durkheim's closest students, and those whom they influenced, continued to carry out studies that forcefully demonstrated the power of his later cultural approach. Halbwach's (e.g., 1913, 1950) research on working class consumption and collective memory, Simiand's (1934) on money, Mauss' ([1925] 1967) on exchange, Bouglé's (1908) on caste—these are merely the best known illustrations of how "late Durkheimianism" was carried into practice by the Durkheim school.

The possibilities that these studies opened up, however, were never extensively mined. In the aftermath of the First World War, the influence of the Durkheim school waned. The movements that sought to carry forward its legacy, moreover, distorted key elements of its thought. The *Annales* school of history began with a Durkheimian thrust, but its "sociological" emphasis soon tilted toward demographic and socio-political structures and away from consciousness. On the other hand, under Mauss' influence, what was left of the school proper veered increasingly toward ethnography (see Vogt 1976). Because of these and other developments, the theoretical ambitions manifest in Durkheim's later program gradually faded away. By the 1930s, the French intellectual community viewed Durkheimianism either as apolitical, archaicizing ethnography or as scientistic sociological determinism. It was rejected on both grounds.

As Durkheimian ideas made their way beyond French borders they were pushed in directions equally opposed to the symbolic interests of his later work. Radcliffe-Brown founded British social anthropology in Durkheim's name, but his mechanistic functionalism might be better identified with the theorizing against which Durkheim's later writing had been aimed. When Parsons (1937) initiated sociological functionalism, he declared Durkheim to be one of its founders. But while Parsons saw more of the cultural Durkheim than most interpreters, he explicitly criticized the later focus on autonomous symbolic processes. Rather than symbolic systems, Parsons insisted that sociology be concerned with social values and their institutionalization. He tied this value emphasis (e.g., Parsons 1967), moreover, to his search for the foundations of consensual social order.* In the post-Parsons period, sociologists who have conspicuously taken up Durkheim's mantle (e.g., Bloor 1976; Douglas and Wildavsky

---

* In the work of the other major American expositor of functionalism, Robert Merton, this distortion of Durkheim's actual theoretical intention took a much more radical form. Merton's ([1938] 1968) influential essay, "Social Structure and Anomie," came to be regarded as a prototypical application of the Durkheimian perspective. Merton drew here, however, entirely from Durkheim's earlier work. The extent to which he ignores the later sociology can be seen from the fact that when he labels one of his four categories of deviance "ritualistic," he does so in dismissive and pejorative terms.

1982; Traugott 1985) have tended to conceptualize culture in an even more reductive way.*

Yet, while the challenge of Durkheim's later writings has not been taken up by sociology, in other branches of the human studies it has been actively pursued (cf. Thompson 1982:138–145). The relationship has often been indirect, the influence subterranean. Those pursuing a "late Durkheimian" program are often unaware that such a link exists and when the possibility is recognized, it has often been denied. Nonetheless, a compelling case can be made that, more than to any other classical figure, it is to Durkheim that the contemporary cultural revival to which I earlier referred is most deeply in debt.

Consider, for example, Ferdinand Saussure, whose centrality is widely acknowledged because it was he who first conceived of modern structural linguistics and conceptualized "semiotics" as the science of signs. While Saussure never cites Durkheim directly—his major work, too, consisted of posthumously published lectures—parallels between his intellectual system and Durkheim's are striking indeed. In contrast with his linguistic contemporaries, Saussure ([1916] 1964: 107) insisted on the "institutional" character of language. He called language a social fact (*un fait social*) (p. 21), that emerged from the *"conscience collective"* (p. 104) of society, the linguistic elements of which were "consecrated through use" (Godel 1957:145). Saussure depended, in other words, on a number of key concepts that were identical with the controversial and widely discussed terms of the Durkheim school. Most historians of linguistics (e.g., Doroszewski 1933:89–90; Ardener 1971:xxxii–xiv) have interpreted these resemblances as evidence of Durkheim's very significant influence on Saussure. In doing so, moreover, they have conceived of Durkheim in his later, more symbolical guise.†

Whether a direct relationship can actually be demonstrated, however, is not the most important concern. The echoes in Saussurian linguistics

---

*My reference here is to Douglas' grid/group theory, which she identifies as the basis for a general theory of culture (cf., Douglas and Wildavsky 1982). In other parts of her work (e.g., Douglas 1966, Douglas and Isherwood 1979), as I will note below, she has, in fact, made important contributions to cultural theory in a late Durkheimian vein. Similar ambiguities mark Traugott's position (compare, e.g., Traugott 1984, 1985).

† E.g.: "One sees, in sum, that the *langue* of Saussure not only corresponds exactly to the *fait social* of Durkheim, but, in addition, that this *langue*, half physical and half social, exercising constraint on the individual and existing in the collective conscience of the social group, was in some way modelled on Durkheim's 'collective representations.' " (Doroszewski 1933: 90).

of Durkheim's symbolic theory are deep and substantial. Just as Durkheim insisted that religious symbols could not be reduced to their interactional base, Saussure emphasized the autonomy of linguistic signs vis-à-vis their social and physical referents. From his own insistence on cultural autonomy Durkheim was led to an interest in the internal dynamics of symbolic and ritual systems. From Saussure's emphasis on the arbitrariness of words there followed a similar concentration on the structures of symbolic organization in and of themselves.

Similar parallels exist between later Durkheimian theory and Lévi-Strauss' structural anthropology. Lévi-Strauss insists that societies must be studied in terms of symbolic classifications, that these symbolic systems are patterned as binary oppositions, and that social action (at least in premodern societies) is expressive and cultural rather than instrumental and contingent. Here is another influential cultural program, in other words, that bears a striking similarity to the late Durkheimian program I have outlined above. Once again, moreover, while direct linkage is impossible to establish, a compelling case of significant influence can be made. In linguistics, Lévi-Strauss acknowledges the influence not only of Jakobson but Saussure. In anthropology, he recognizes primarily his debt to Marcel Mauss, whose earlier work on symbols he (Lévi-Strauss 1968) praises for emphasizing the autonomy of classification and the antipathies and homologies of which it is composed. That Lévi-Strauss often takes sharp issue with Durkheim cannot, therefore, be taken at full face value. In the first place, such denials (e.g., Lévi-Strauss 1945) associate Durkheim with an antisymbolic "sociologism" that is at odds with the emphasis of Durkheim's own later work. In the second place, not only was Mauss himself Durkheim's closest student, but the work of Mauss that Lévi-Strauss (e.g., 1968:xxxi) most applauds, the essay translated as *Primitive Classification*, was co-authored with Durkheim and represents only one of many exemplifications of the later Durkheimian program.

From Saussure and Lévi-Strauss some of the most important contemporary cultural movements have been derived. It was structural thinking more than any other current that stimulated Roland Barthes to elaborate his enormously influential studies in social and literary semiotics. Over the last thirty years Barthes and other semioticians have explicated the codes—the systems of symbolic classification—that regulate a wide array of secular institutions and social processes, from fashions (Barthes 1983) and food production (Sahlins 1976) to civil conflict (Buckley 1984).

Poststructuralists like Foucault have carried this emphasis on the structuring power of symbolic patterns, or discourses, even further into the social domain.

On occasion these thinkers have made their relation to Durkheim explicit. These acknowledgments, however, often serve to emphasize rather than to reduce the distance between Durkheim's later program and sociology as it has come to be conventionally understood. Barthes (1983:10) insists in his methodological introduction to *The Fashion System*, for example, that while "the sociology of Fashion is entirely directed toward real clothing[,] the semiology of Fashion is directed toward a set of collective representations." He follows with the extraordinarily revealing statement that his own, semiotic emphasis leads "not to sociology but rather to the *sociologics* postulated by Durkheim and Mauss" (original italics), identifying the latter, nonsociological approach, by referring to the same essay on primitive classification cited by Lévi-Strauss.

In most cases, however, these Durkheimian roots are simply not recognized at all. In *A History of Sexuality*, Foucault devotes a major section of his argument to demonstrating the religious roots of the modern "rational" insistence on exposing the sexual basis of various activities. This contemporary discourse, he insists (1980:68), has "kept as its nucleus the singular ritual of obligatory and exhaustive confession, which in the Christian West was the first technique for producing the truth of sex." Secularization, then, consists in "this rite [having] gradually detached itself from the sacrament of penance." A more clear-cut exemplification of Durkheim's later program for sociology would be hard to find. It was Durkheim ([1899] 1960:350) who insisted that religious phenomena "are the germ from which all others . . . derived," and the treatment in his late lectures of such secular phenomena as contract and exchange find their echoes in Foucault. That Foucault himself never entertained the possibility of a Durkheimian link is in a certain sense beside the point. His work rests on an intellectual base to which late Durkheimian thought made an indelible contribution.

Both as theory and empirical investigation, poststructuralism and semiotic investigations more generally can be seen as elaborating one of the pathways that Durkheim's later sociology opens up. Indeed, they have demonstrated the importance of his later theory more forcefully than any discipline in the social sciences more narrowly conceived. As such, they constitute primarily theoretical resources from which the effort to create a cultural sociology will have to draw.

In emphasizing this extra-sociological Durkheimianism, however, I do not want to suggest that within the social science disciplines there has been no work related to late Durkheimian theory at all. There have, in fact, been some interesting developments, and, even if they have not been of comparable scope or influence, they are all endebted to late Durkheimian theory. Without, for the most part, explicitly acknowledging Durkheim's work, these efforts have joined his emphases to other theoretical frameworks in order to develop a more symbolic kind of discourse about secular life.

It is ironic, perhaps, that most of the important developments of this type emerged from the dissolution of the Parsonian camp. As disaffection with structural-functionalism increased, three of Parsons' most important students and co-workers tried to push his framework toward a distinctively Durkheimian emphasis on symbolism, sacredness, and ritual. Shils (1975) argued that secular, differentiated societies have symbolic "centers" which inspire awe and mystery and that it is the proximity to these sources of sacredness which allocates such "structural" qualities as social status. In a series of critical essays in the 1960s, Geertz (1973) argued that whether cultural systems are "religious" has nothing to do with their supernatural quality and everything to do with the degree to which they are sacralized, inspire ritual devotion, and mobilize group solidarity. Since that time, Geertz has interpreted secular phenomena from Balinese cockfighting (Geertz 1973a) to American political campaigns, (Geertz 1983) in more or less similar symbolic and culturalist terms.

Shils and Geertz never acknowledged their debt to Durkheim. It is true, of course, that they drew widely from cultural theory, and in this sense their failure to make the reference explicit merely reflects the permeation of later Durkheimian thinking into the general intellectual milieu. It also, however, reflects the resistance toward, and misunderstanding of, late Durkheimian ideas within social science itself. The result is that, while Geertz's work especially has been enormously influential outside the field of sociology, this turn toward cultural theorizing from within the social sciences has had only a limited impact on traditional sociological work (for exceptions, see Stivers 1982, Zelizer 1985, and Prager 1986).* It is only the third disaffected Parsonian, Robert Bellah, who openly acknowledged the link to Durkheim; indeed, he has made this connection the linchpin of his newly cultural work.

Bellah (1970, 1980b) has argued that secular nations have civic religions. These are symbolic systems that relate national political structures and events to a transcendent supra-political framework that defines some "ultimate" social meaning. Bellah calls this framework religious not because it must refer to God but, rather, in order to emphasize the sacredness of its symbols and the ritual power it commands. In these terms, even atheistic, communist nations possess civil religions. Not ontological properties but historically determined social conditions determine the effect of a civil religion on society.

More than any other social scientific formulation, the civic religion concept promised to open sociology to the power of Durkheim's later work. In the years since Bellah's original formulation, the concept has, indeed, been used to explain a wide variety of political and cultural situations (e.g., Coleman 1970; Moodie 1974; Wolf 1975; Bellah 1980a, 1980b, 1980c; Hammond 1980; Albanese 1976; Liebman and Don-Yehiya 1983; Rothenbuhler 1985). Yet civil religion has not, in fact, entered the language of social science in a central and powerful way. Rather, it has been taken up primarily in "religious studies," by historians and sociologists who specialize in religion (e.g., Hammond 1980a, 1980b) and by theologians (e.g., Lynn 1973; Marty 1974; Wilson 1979) with a special interest in society. The reasons, I think, have to do not only with the

---

*In addition to the quite profound effect Geertz has had on general intellectual life in the United States, his ideas have been closely associated with the cultural turn in American social history which I noted at the beginning of this essay. His influence can be seen directly, for example, in the work of Sewell (1980), Darnton (1984), and Wilentz (1985). That broader intellectual currents are also involved, however, is demonstrated by the more or less simultaneous development within France of more symbolic approaches to social history. In "The Sacred and the French Revolution," Hunt (1988) discusses the most important of these contributions—most of which concentrate on the French revolution— and she points out that they can be seen as elaborations of Mathiez (1904), who worked within a late Durkheimian program. Hunt's (1984) own major work on the French revolution represents an important combination of this French Durkheimian turn with Geertzean ideas and cultural theory. It is revealing of the lack of contact between sociology and this recent cultural turn in social history that Sewell's (1985) incisive culturalist critique of Skocpol's (1979) macro-structural theory of revolution appeared—along with Skocpol's response—not in a sociological review but in *The Journal of Modern History*.

resistance of social science to embracing cultural work but also with central ambiguities in the original concept.

Bellah first conceived the civil religion idea in a discussion that argued for the close relation between American politics and Protestant religiosity. He suggested that, while the connection was not necessary in principle, in practice the American civil religion did in fact center on traditional Christian symbols. Indeed, he argued that growing agnosticism could undermine the status of American civil religion vis-à-vis secular power. Moreover, the most significant expositor of Bellah's concept, the sociologist of religion Phillip Hammond (1980a, 1980b), has sought to limit civil religion explicitly to the kind of formation that exists in the American case. A nation has a civil religion, in his view, only if it has institutionalized a cultural system that ties politics to churchly symbols but is independent of an established church. But such an argument, while certainly illuminating particular empirical issues (cf., Thomas and Flippen 1972; Wimberly et al. 1976), narrows the more far-reaching and general implications of the concept, for it effectively cuts the concept off from its late Durkheimian base, although Hammond (1974) disagrees. Ironically, it was against precisely this kind of narrowing that Durkheim launched his later arguments, which in turn formed the basis for Bellah's original conception of the term.

While the innovative work of these American cultural theorists expands Parsonian functionalism, the other major development within the disciplinary matrix of sociology appropriates Durkheim from a Marxist and Weberian slant. Over the last two decades Bourdieu has elaborated a symbolically sophisticated theory of social conflict and class domination. From semiotics and structuralism he has accepted the notion that every facet of social life, from institution to individual act, is regulated by densely structured symbolic codes. Without learning these codes, individuals and groups cannot participate in the relevant social institution, whether work place, classroom (Bourdieu and Passeron 1977), or museum of art (Bourdieu 1968, 1984). Bourdieu believes that capitalist domination makes access to these institutions a privilege of birth and wealth, but he does not believe that the simple possession of wealth or birthright explains the reproduction of class power from one generation to the next. Position must be based on at least the appearance of personal prowess and only if an actor has internalized the appropriate system of representations can such achievement be made. To have learned these codes is to possess "cultural capital" (1968). To document the interrelation of cultural and economic capital has been the point of Bourdieu's work.

Yet, while Bourdieu's critical cultural sociology could not have been conceived outside of the intellectual milieu that Durkheim initiated, it is a theoretical connection that Bourdieu himself underplays. The reasons can be found primarily in the ruse of French intellectual history. It is to semiotics and structural anthropology, not to "Durkheim," that Bourdieu is conscious of owing a debt; if Lévi-Strauss cannot incorporate praxis, Durkheim is more determinist still (Bourdieu 1977:23). Bourdieu would prefer to present himself as the follower of Weber, although it is his Durkheimian revision of Weber's status theory that has allowed him to speak of class distinctions in fully symbolic ways.*

Bourdieu, Bellah, and Shils are sociologists, and while Geertz is not— he is an anthropologist—he was trained by Parsons, a theorist of sociology. The work of these four thinkers constitutes another significant resource from which cultural analysis must draw.

The other source of significant ideas that has emerged from within the social sciences comes from anthropology. The Durkheimian sociologists pushed theories about modern society to incorporate concepts previously applied only to premodern ones. Late-Durkheimian anthropologists have used Durkheim's theories of premodern society to move to a study of modern life. While beginning from opposite directions, in other words, they have ended up in much the same place.

Of these anthropological developments, Turner's work on the ritual process is undoubtedly the most important (see, e.g., Moore and Meyerhoff 1975). Turner (1969) argues that the basic components of ritual can be abstracted from the specific situations of archaic societies and treated as fundamental aspects of social behavior as such. Because all rituals involve transitions from one patterned position or structure to another, he suggests that ritual can be seen as possessing not simply an integrative but an "antistructural" dimension. During this antistructural, or liminal phase, he suggests, participants experience intense solidarity, or "communitas." Since this condition of liminal solidarity constitutes a deviant status, it often provides an an opening for social change. In his later work,

*The connection between Bourdieu and Durkheim is forcefully made by Collins (1988), who argues for the importance of a "conflict Durkheimian" strain more generally.

Turner (e.g., 1974) tried to separate these elements from an association with actual ritual events. He demonstrated that liminality and communitas could be seen as central features of such widely divergent secular phenomena as political confrontations, athletic contests, and countercultures.

Once again, the relationship between this new development in cultural theory and Durkheimian thought is never explicitly made. For his specific terminology, Turner drew on the work of Van Gennep, the contemporary of Durkheim's who criticized his explanation of Aboriginal religion. But the similarities between Turner's ideas and Durkheim's later project are plain, which is not to say that Turner did not go beyond his master in valuable ways. He demonstrated much more clearly than Durkheim, for example, how rituals can depend on contingent behavior and can be deeply involved in social change.

Much the same can be said for the work of Mary Douglas, the other anthropologist whose work has contributed significantly to broader currents in cultural studies. She has documented the classifying and symbolic functions of what are usually taken to be merely physical and adaptive activities (e.g., Douglas and Isherwood 1979). Most particularly, she (1966) has shown that pollution is a form of social control that societies use against symbolically deviant, profane things. Even in such clear efforts to generalize from religious to secular activity, however, Douglas dissociates her efforts from Durkheimian work. Still, it is the Durkheimianism of Radcliffe-Brown that she is fighting, not the symbolic theory of Durkheim's own later work. Her conception of pollution expands Durkheim's notion of profanation by relating it directly to issues of social control.*

My argument is that, even while references to Durkheim's later theory have virtually disappeared, his "religious sociology" has significantly influenced the developments in cultural studies that are invigorating the intellectual world today.† Two conclusions follow, both of which have to

---

*The connection becomes more easily seen if the "correction" of Caillois ([1939] 1959)—one of the last productive members of the Durkheimian school—is taken into account. Caillois argued that Durkheim's contrast between sacred and profane must be expanded to include a third term, because profane implied for Durkheim both routine (as compared with effervescent and charismatic) and evil (as compared with good).

†The only major contemporary current which is not at least indirectly indebted to Durkheim is the German hermeneutical tradition, which began its ambitious and distinctive program of cultural interpretation with Dilthey, whose writings (e.g., Dilthey 1976) ap-

do with the benefits of making this framework explicit. The first relates to cultural studies more generally. By making this Durkheimian framework explicit, the inner connections between these different developments can much more easily be seen. Only if these inner connections are established can the theoretical basis for contemporary cultural analysis be clearly articulated. The full array of theoretical resources is necessary if a general and comprehensive social scientific understanding of culture is finally to emerge (cf. Alexander, forthcoming).

The second conclusion is more limited. It has to do with cultural studies in a more disciplinary sense, specifically with the prospects for a cultural sociology. Disciplinary practice is defined by its classics (see chapter 1, above), and for sociology Durkheim's work is arguably the most classic of all. At the present time, "Durkheim" is perceived largely in terms of the structural concerns of his middle-period work. Insofar as the Durkheimian reference of contemporary cultural studies becomes explicit, however, this narrow understanding becomes increasingly difficult to sustain. If it cannot be sustained, if the understanding of Durkheim shifts toward the later work, then there will be increasing pressure to bring cultural analysis squarely into the practice of sociology. This, I have agreed, was precisely the ambition of Durkheim himself.

It is certainly not coincidental that it has been in the midst of this outpouring of Durkheim-inspired cultural work that a new and much more sophisticated phase of Durkheim scholarship has emerged. The scope of Durkheim's lectures in the later period was evident only after Lukes (1972) published the first fully annotated account of Durkheim's life and work. Lukes' research also brought to light biographical material that underscored not only the existence of Durkheim's turn to religion but also the personal significance religion may have had for him. Later in

---

peared over roughly the same period as Durkheim's own. In the present period, however, the significance of hermeneutics has been more directed to providing a philosophical justification for cultural analysis than toward carrying it out (e.g., Gadamer 1975; Bernstein 1976; Taylor [1971] 1979). In this context I would have to take issue with Lukes (1982), who draws a sharp line between Durkheimian sociology and contemporary cultural analysis on the grounds that Durkheim took a positivist rather than hermeneutic position. While there is no doubt about the limitations of the formal methodology to which Durkheim adhered, for example in a middle-period work like *Rules*, his later writing demonstrated a clear commitment to the hermeneutic method in practice. If this were not true, his ideas could not have provided the basis from the which so much of contemporary cultural analysis has drawn.

the 1970s there emerged a group of scholars around Philippe Bésnard and *La Revue francaise de sociologie* who initiated a new wave of historical explorations of Durkheim and his school. Once again, these historical investigations revealed the importance of the religious turn, not only for Durkheim himself but for the direction of his students' work (e.g., Birnbaum 1976; Bésnard 1979, 1983). Neither Lukes nor the French group argued that there emerged a later "religious sociology" more generally conceived. The interpretations that succeeded these pioneering studies, however (e.g., Filloux 1977; Jones 1977; Lacroix 1981; Alexander 1982), not only followed up on these leads but also, on the basis of this new understanding, read the extant Durkheim material in an altered way. Gradually, a more general perspective did begin to emerge. While some interpreters still do not accede (e.g., Giddens 1977; Traugott 1978), there is increasing agreement today that in the later period Durkheim's sociology underwent an important shift, even if there is little consensus about the precise nature of this shift or its ramifications in Durkheim's work. Only by recognizing the crucial distinctiveness of this later work, indeed, can the Durkheimian roots of contemporary cultural studies be traced.

It is time, now, for sociology finally and decisively to take up Durkheim's path. His mandate has been established. Contemporary work in cultural studies demonstrates where this mandate might lead. Significant exemplars of such work exist within the field of sociology itself.* It is not a question of adopting Durkheim's general theory of society, much less the ideological perspectives he brought to his work. The late Durkheimian perspective will be integrated with the traditions of Weber, Marx, and Parsons, or it will not be taken up at all. None of these other traditions, however, can supply the opening to cultural studies that sociology needs. For this, Durkheim's later program must be revived. In a fragmented way it has been at the heart of cultural analysis all along. In a more explicit form it can help to revitalize the practice of sociology today.

REFERENCES

Albanese, Catherine L. 1976. *Sons of the Fathers: The Civil Religion of the American Revolution.* Philadelphia: Temple University Press.

*The book for which this essay served as an introduction (Alexander 1988) is replete with the kinds of synthetic, "late Durkheimian" pieces I have in mind. See also chapter 6, below.

Alexander, Jeffrey C. 1982. *The Antinomies of Classical Thought: Marx and Durkheim.* Berkeley and Los Angeles: University of California Press.

—— forthcoming. "Analytic Debates: Understanding the 'Autonomy of Culture.'" In Alexander and Steven Seidman, eds. *Culture and Society: Contemporary Debates.* New York: Cambridge University Press.

Alexander, Jeffrey C., ed. 1988. *Durkheimian Sociology: Cultural Studies.* New York: Cambridge University Press.

Ardener, Edwin, ed. 1971. *Sociology and Language.*, pp. ix–cii (Introductory Essay). London: Tavistock.

Barthes, Roland. [1967] 1983. *The Fashion System.* New York: Hill and Wang.

Bellah, Robert N. 1970. "Civil Religion in America." In Bellah, *Beyond Belief*, pp. 168–189. New York: Harper and Row.

——1980a. "The Five Religions of Modern Italy." In Bellah and Hammond (1980):86–118.

—— 1980b. "Introduction." In Bellah and Hammond (1980):vii–xv.

—— 1980c. "The Japanese and American Cases." In Bellah and Hammond (1980):27–39.

Bellah, Robert N. and Phillip Hammond. 1980. *Varieties of Civil Religion.* New York: Harper and Row.

Bernstein, Richard J. 1976. *Restructuring Social and Political Theory.* Philadelphia: University of Pennsylvania Press.

Bésnard, Phillipe. 1979. "La Formation de l'équipe de *L'Année sociologique.*" *Revue française de sociologie* 20:7–31.

Bésnard, Phillipe, ed. 1983. *The Sociological Domain: The Durkheimians and the Founding of French Sociology:* London: Cambridge University Press.

Birnbaum, Pierre. 1976. "La Conception Durkheimienne de l'état: L'Apolitisme des fonctionnaires." *Revue française de sociologie* 17:247–258.

Bloor, David. 1976. *Knowledge and Social Imagery.* London: Routledge.

Bouglé, Célestin. 1908. *Essais sur le régime des castes.* Paris: Alkan.

Bourdieu, Pierre. 1968. "Outline of a Sociological Theory of Art Perception." *International Social Science Journal* 20(4):589–612.

—— 1977. *Outline of a Theory of Practice.* London: Cambridge University Press.

—— 1984. *Distinction.* Cambridge: Harvard University Press.

Bourdieu, Pierre and J-C Passeron, 1977. *Reproduction in Education, Society, and Culture.* Beverly Hills: Sage.

Buckley, Anthony York. 1984. "Walls within Walls: Religion and Rough Behavior in an Ulster Community." *Sociology* 18:19–32.

Callois, Roger. [1939] 1959. *Man and the Sacred.* New York: Free Press.

Coleman, John. 1970. "Civil Religion." *Sociological Analysis* 31:67–77.

Collins, Randall. 1988. "The Durkheimian Tradition in Conflict Sociology." In Alexander, ed. (1988):107–128.

Darnton, Robert. 1984. *The Great Cat Massacre and Other Episodes in French Cultural History.* New York: Basic.

Dilthey, Wilhelm. 1976. *Selected Writings.* London: Cambridge University Press.

Doroszewski, W. 1933. "Quelques remarques sur les rapports de la sociologie et de la linguistique: Durkheim et Saussure." *Journal de Psychologie* 30:83–91.

Douglas, Mary. 1966. *Purity and Danger*. London: Penguin.

—— 1982. *Risk and Culture*. Berkeley and Los Angeles: University of California Press.

Durkheim, Emile. [1899] 1960. "Preface to *L'année sociologique 2.*" In Kurt Wolff, ed. *Emile Durkheim et al. on Sociology and Philosophy*, pp. 347–352. New York: Free Press.

—— [1911] 1965. *The Elementary Forms of Religious Life*. New York: Free Press.

—— [1925] 1961. *Moral Education*. New York: Free Press.

—— [1928] 1958. *Socialism and Saint-Simon*. Yellow Springs, Ohio: Antioch University Press.

—— [1938] 1977. *The Evolution of Educational Thought*. London: Routledge and Kegan Paul.

—— [1950] 1958. *Professional Ethics and Civic Morals:* New York: Free Press.

—— 1956. *Education and Sociology*. New York: Free Press.

Filloux, Jean-Claude. 1977. *Durkheim et le socialisme*. Geneva: Librairie Droz.

Foucault, Michel. 1980. *A History of Sexuality*. New York: Vintage.

Gadamer, Hans-Georg. 1975. *Truth and Method*. New York: Crossroad.

Geertz, Clifford. 1973. *The Interpretation of Cultures*. New York: Basic.

—— 1983. *Local Knowledge*. New York: Basic.

Giddens, Anthony York: 1977. *Studies in Social and Political Theory*. New York: Basic.

Godel, Robert. 1957. *Les sources manuscrites du cours de linguistique generale*. Paris: Librarie Minard.

Halbwachs, Maurice. 1913. *La Classe ouvriére et les niveaux de vie*. Paris: Alcan.

—— 1950. *La Mémoire collective*. Paris: Press universitaires de France.

Hammond, Phillip. 1974. "Religious Pluralism and Durkheim's Integration Thesis." In A.W. Eister, ed. *Changing Perspectives in the Scientific Study of Religion*, pp. 115–142. New York: Wiley.

—— 1980a. "The Conditions for Civil Religion: A Comparison of the United States and Mexico." In Bellah and Hammond (1980):40–85.

—— 1980b. "The Rudimentary Forms of Civil Religion." In Bellah and Hammond (1980):121–137.

Hunt, Lynn. 1984. *Politics, Culture, and Class in the French Revolution*. Berkeley and Los Angeles: University of California Press.

—— 1988. "The Sacred and the French Revolution." In Alexander, ed. (1988):25–43.

Jones, Robert Alun. 1977. "On Understanding a Sociological Classic." *American Journal of Sociology* 83(2):279–319.

Lacroix, Bernard. 1981. *Durkheim et le politique*. Paris: Presses Universitaires de France.

Lévi-Strauss, Claude. 1945. "French Sociology." In Georges Gurvitch and Wilbert E. Moore, eds. *Twentieth Century Sociology.* New York: Philosophical Library.

—— 1968. Introduction to Marcel Mauss, *Sociologie et anthropologie.* Paris: Presses Universitaires de France.

Liebman, Charles C. and Eliezer Don-Yehiya. 1983. *Civil Religion in Israel.* Berkeley and Los Angeles: University of California Press.

Lukes, Steven. 1972. *Emile Durkheim: His Life and Work.* New York: Harper and Row.

—— 1982. Introduction to Lukes, ed. *Durkheim: Rules of Sociological Method.* London: Macmillan.

Lynn, Robert Wood. 1973. "Civil Catechetics in Mid-Victorian America: Some Notes About Civil Religion, Past and Present." *Religious Education* 68:5–27.

Marty, Martin. 1974. "Two Kinds of Civil Religion." In R. E. Richey and D. G. Jones, eds. *American Civil Religion.* New York: Harper and Row.

Mathiez, Albert. 1904. *Les Origines des cultures revolutionaires (1789–1792)* Paris: G. Bellais.

Mauss, Marcel. [1925] 1967. *The Gift.* New York: Free Press.

Merton, Robert. [1938] 1968. "Social Structure and Anomie." *Social Theory and Social Structure*, pp. 185–214. New York: Free Press.

Moodie, Dunbar. 1974. *The Rise of Afrikanerdom.* Berkeley and Los Angeles: University of California Press.

Moore, Sally F. and Barbara G. Myerhoff, eds. 1975. *Symbol and Politics in Communal Ideology.* Ithaca: Cornell University Press.

Parson, Talcott. 1937. *The Structure of Social Action.* New York: Free Press.

—— *Sociological Theory and Modern Society.* New York: Free Press.

Prager, Jeffrey. 1986. *Building Democracy in Ireland: Political Order and Cultural Integration in a Newly Independent Nation.* New York: Cambridge University Press.

Rothenbuhler, Eric. 1985. "Media Events, Civil Religion, and Sociological Solidarity: The Living Room Celebrations of the Olympic Games." PhD dissertation, University of Southern California.

Sahlins, Marshall. 1976. *Culture and Practical Reason.* Chicago: University of Chicago Press.

Saussure, Ferdinand. [1916] 1964. *A Course in General Linguistics.* New York: McGraw-Hill.

Sewell, William, Jr. 1980. *Work and Revolution in France.* New York: Cambridge University Press.

—— 1985. "Ideologies and Social Revolution: Reflections on the French Case." *Journal of Modern History* 57:57–85.

Shils, Edward. 1975. *Center and Periphery.* Chicago: University of Chicago Press.

Simiand, François. 1934. "La Monnaie, réalitié sociale." *Annalés sociologiques* ser. D., pp. 1–86.

Skocpol, Theda. 1979. *States and Social Revolutions*. New York: Cambridge University Press.

Stivers, Richards. 1982. *Evil in Modern Myth and Ritual*. Atlanta: University of Georgia Press.

Taylor, Charles. [1971] 1979. "Interpretation and the Sciences of Man." In Paul Rabinow and William M. Sullivan, eds. *Interpretive Social Science: A Reader*. Berkeley and Los Angeles: University of California Press.

Thomas, M.C. and C.C. Flippen. 1972. "American Civil Religion: An Empirical Study." *Social Forces* 51:218–225.

Thompson, Kenneth. 1982. *Emile Durkheim*. London: Tavistock.

Traugott, Mark. 1978. Introduction to Traugott, ed. *Emile Durkheim on Institutional Analysis*. Chicago: University of Chicago Press.

—— 1984. "Durkheim and Social Movements." *European Journal of Sociology* 25:319–325.

—— 1985. *Armies of the Poor*. Princeton: Princeton University Press.

Turner, Victor. 1969. *The Ritual Process*. Chicago: Aldine.

—— 1974. *Drama, Fields, and Metaphors*. Ithaca: Cornell University Press.

Vogt, W. Paul. 1976. "The Use of Studying Primitives." *History and Theory* 15(1):32–44.

Wilentz, Sean, ed. 1985. *Rites of Power*. Philadelphia: University of Pennsylvania Press.

Wilson, John F. 1979. *Public Religion in American Culture*. Philadelphia: Temple University Press.

Wimberly, R.C. et al. 1976. "The Civil Religious Dimension: Is It There?" *Social Forces* 54:890–900.

Wolfe, James. 1975. "The Kennedy Myth: American Civil Religion in the Sixties." PhD dissertation, Graduate Theological Union, Berkeley, California.

Wuthnow, Robert. 1987. *Meaning and Moral Order*. Berkeley and Los Angeles: University of California Press.

Zelizer, Viviana. 1985. *Pricing the Priceless Child*. New York: Basic.

Culture and Political Crisis:
'Watergate' and
Durkheimian Sociology

Durkheim's legacy has been appropriated by generations of social scientists in strikingly different ways. Each appropriation depends on a reading of Durkheim's work, of its critical phases, its internal crises and resolutions, and its culminating achievements. Such readings themselves depend upon prior theoretical understandings, for it is impossible to trace a textual development without seeing this part within some already glimpsed whole. The texts, however, have constituted an independent encounter in their own right, and new interpretations of Durkheim have given crucial impetus to the development of new theoretical developments in turn.

Almost every imaginable kind of sociology has been so inspired, for it is possible to see in Durkheim's development sharply contrasting theoretical models and presuppositions. Ecological determinism, functional differentiation, demographic expansion, administrative punishment and legal control, even the distribution of property—the study of each has been taken as sociology's decisive task in light of Durkheim's early work. From the middle and later work have emerged other themes. The centrality of moral and emotional integration is undoubtedly the most pervasive legacy, but anthropologists have also taken from this work a functional analysis of religion and ritual and a structural analysis of symbol and myth. None of these inherited exemplars, however, takes fully into consideration the actual trajectory of Durkheim's later and most sophisticated sociological understanding. Given Durkheim's classical stature, this failure is extraordinary, the importance of remedying it, very great.

I

It has become more widely accepted in recent years that Durkheim's work shifted sharply toward the subjective as early as 1894. Indeed, it was in the very first chapter of *Rules* that Durkheim ([1895] 1938) suggested that ecological forces, or social morphology, actually consisted in conceptual and emotional interaction. In *Socialism* ([1895-96] 1958) and *Suicide* ([1897] 1951) this insight was elaborated, yet, in fact, by 1896 and 1897 Durkheim was already engaged in extensive revision of this decisive break. Emotional interaction, he now perceived, never occurred separately from the symbolization of ideational values. Religion, and particularly religious ritual, now became the model for Durkheim's understanding of social life. Interaction produces an energy like the "effervescence" of religious ecstasy. This psychic energy attaches itself to powerful symbols—things or ideas—which in turn crystallize critical social facts. Symbols, in turn, have their own autonomous organization. They are organized into the sacred and profane, the latter being mere signs, the former being redolent with energy and mystery, and this symbolic division constitutes authority. These sacred symbols, Durkheim came to believe, could themselves control the structure of social organization. The liquid character of sacredness makes it contagious and precious. Societies must elaborate rules to contain it, for it must be rigorously separated not only from impure substances but from profane ones. Complicated ceremonies, furthermore, must be developed for its periodic renewal.

Although many interpreters have discussed this movement toward the sociology of religion, none have appreciated its full significance. From 1897 onward, Durkheim's intention was not just to develop a sociology of religion but, rather, a religious sociology. In everything he turned his hand to after that transitional time, his intention was always the same: to transform his earlier, secular analyses into religious ones. The division of labor and theory of history, the explanation of social pathology and crime, the theory of law, the analyses of education and family, the notions of politics and economics, and of course the very theory of culture itself—Durkheim sought in his later years to explain all these by analogy to the internal structuring of religious life (Alexander 1982: 259-298; cf. chapter 4, above). Each institution and process was made strictly analogous to the ritual model. Each structure of authority was conceived of as sacred in form, a sacralization that depended upon periodic propinquity and emotion. The developmental processes of each were alternating phases of sacred and profane, and the attenuation of effervescence constituted, for each, the turning points of its development.

Only by understanding the full scope of this theoretical shift can one appreciate the challenge that Durkheim's legacy poses to contemporary social science. Durkheim's challenge is to develop a cultural logic for society: to make the symbolic dimension of every social sphere a relatively autonomous domain of cultural discourse interpenetrated with the other dimensions of society. Few of Durkheim's own students picked up this gauntlet, some because they failed to understand it, others because they rejected it on some principled ground. It has taken the rest of us the better part of a century to come back to it. Durkheim's later religious sociology makes fundamental advances over the thought of his classical contemporaries. Marx developed scarcely any theory of contemporary culture, working instead at the other side of the epistemological continuum. Weber did make fundamental contributions to a theory of culture and society, but his historicist insistence on the modern destruction of meaning makes the incorporation of his insights extraordinarily difficult, though no less necessary (see chapter 2, above). Durkheim alone insisted on the centrality of meaning in secular society, and only in his work does a systematic theory of contemporary cultural life begin to emerge. This theory also goes beyond the most important postclassical theory—functionalism—in significant ways. Functionalism either has closely tied cultural values to social structual strain or, in Parsons' case, it has conceptualized culture's autonomy only by speaking of "values," an important but ultimately limiting framework for approaching the question of meaning and society.

For all of this, however, it must be frankly acknowledged that Durkheim's religious sociology is difficult to understand. This difficulty does not reside simply in the interpreter; it rests also on deep ambiguities in the theory itself. Durkheim's religious sociology works on three different levels: as a metaphor, as a general theory of society, and as a special theory of certain social processes. It is necessary to separate these theories from one another and to evaluate them independently if the permanent contributions of Durkheim's later work are to be properly understood and incorporated into contemporary thought.

It is clear that, in one sense, Durkheim's insistence after 1896 that society *is* religion plays a metaphorical role. He has invented here a vigorous and compelling way of arguing for the value-imbeddedness of action and order. Far from being a mundane utilitarian world, modern society still has a close relationship to strongly felt ends that compel the acquiescence of powerful means. These supra-individual ends are so strong, indeed, they may be likened to the other-wordly ends established by God. This metaphor of "religious society" produces accompanying similes: social symbols are *like* sacred ones, in that they are powerful and compelling; the conflict between social values is *like* the conflict between sacred and profane, or pure and impure sacredness; political interaction is *like* ritual participation in that it produces cohesion and value commitment.

Considered as metaphor and simile—as, in other words, a series of rhetorical devices—Durkheim's religious sociology is "true." It effectively communicates the importance of anti-utilitarian qualities in the modern world. As a conceptual or theoretical vocabulary, however, basic problems remain. For as a general theory of society—the second level at which it operates—Durkheim's religious sociology is certainly wrong. It is wrong in the first place for epistemological reasons, because it inscribes a dualistic social life that reflects Durkheim's overwhelming idealism. But Durkheim's religious sociology *qua* general theory is wrong also on empirical grounds. To make a strict analogy between society and religion leads to an overly condensed, undifferentiated, all-or-nothing understanding of social life. It implies that values can be communicated only through intensive high energy symbols that generate awe and mystery. These symbols are held to be constituted through "social experiences" with a capital "S," periods of renewal that are without conflict or material integument, whose integrative denouement is neat and complete. This world of symbol and ritual, moreover, is conceived as opposed to a profane world of individuals, economic institutions, and merely material structures. Because they are profane these objects are held to be nonsocial, and because they are nonsocial they are seen neither as socially structured nor as sociologically comprehensible.

But highly energized symbols are not, of course, the only way meaning is generated and maintained in modern societies. The profane world, defined as the routine world of relatively reduced excitation, remains firmly value-directed. It is also decidedly social and as ordered as it is conflictual. The social experiences that constitute intense and awesome symbols, moreover, are not necessarily harmonious and thoroughly integrating. They may be subject to intensely competitive processes, to individuation and reflexivity, and they may integrate some parts of society rather than the whole.

As a general theory, indeed, Parsonian functionalism seems in all these respects to be superior to Durkheim's later theory, and Parsons expressly sought to incorporate this later theory into his own. Parsonian theory clarifies levels of generality and establishes the independent social logics of various spheres. Rather than dichotomizing culture and material life, it argue for the simultaneous independence and interpenetration of personality, social system, and culture. Symbolism and values, then, are always part of social and individual life. While social system processes are not usually highly affective or intense, the specificity of role relationships is dependent, nonetheless, on normative prescriptions of more general cultural values. While functionalism acknowledges that value renewal occurs in time of crisis—though its analysis of such processes, I will argue, is seriously deficient—it also quite correctly sees that values are also acquired through more routine processes like socialization and learning, through leadership, and through exchange of the generalized media that facilitate communication between groups, individuals, and subsystems.

"Authority" presents a good example of the contrast between functionalism and Durkheimianism as general theory. For the religious theory, authority is always numinous; to the degree that it is profaned and routinized, it becomes meaningless, approximating mere power and force. By contrast, Parsonian functionalism draws upon Weber to argue that, in modern societies at least, routinized authority becomes "office." This designation implies a symbolic code that regulates power by condensing, indeed by secularizing, previously vivid, long-standing religious values, values like the impersonal transcendence of God and the duty for all men to carry out His will. Through the concept of office, Friedrichs (1964) has argued, mundane legal forms like constitutions can ensure the meaningful regulation of "profane" political life.

If this were the full extent of Durkheim's later sociology, if it were merely successful metaphor and failed general theory, we could leave Durkheim's legacy alone, satisfied with Parsons and Weber. But that is not so. Durkheim's later work also presents us with a special theory referring to specific kinds of empirical processes. This special theory is true and enlightening, and its implications have scarcely begun to be mined.

The ritualistic model of religious life that Durkheim developed in his later years is a hermeneutics of intense, direct value experience. It interprets the structure and effects of unmediated encounters with transcendent realities. The religious vocabulary of such experience, as Durkheim rightly insisted, derives not from the unique qualities of divine encounters but rather from the fact that such encounters typify transcendent experience as such. This religious experience, then, is one manifestation of a general form of social experience. These experiences are called religious simply because, in the course of human history, they have occurred most frequently in a religious form. In this sense, therefore, the "religious model" can indeed be taken not as metaphor, but as a strict analogy for certain universal processes of secular life.

Such a direct, unmediated encounter with transcendent experience is relevant to secular processes in at least two crucial ways. First, social system processes themselves are never thoroughly bound to normative prescriptions and differentiated roles. They are never, that is, completely routinized or profane. The terror and awe of simplified and general symbols—the purely cultural level that is experienced as religious or transcendent reality—always remains in the interstices of social life. We may continue here with our earlier example of political authority. While its use in modern societies is hedged in by elaborate norms of office, authority also carries with it the pregnant symbolism of sacred things. Roger Caillois ([1939] 1959) was the first Durkheimian to insist that sacredness often has the ecological corollary of centeredness, and that for this reason political power is often associated with the same kind of prohibitions and proscriptions as religious life. Edward Shils (1975) was the second Durkheimian to do so, and in his work the ambiguous interplay of the center's material and symbolic power is profoundly illuminated.* Bernard Lacroix (1981) is the third to pick up this theme. Though he is wrong, I believe, to insist that Durkheim's own analysis is concerned with power in a political sense, Lacroix is quite right to urge that the categories of this religious theory have an important political application.

Since this religious quality of secular power often, for better or worse, overpowers the specific role obligations of office, it is ironic that it recalls

---

*It is one of the ironies of the intellectual history of sociology that Shils has developed this Durkheimian insight under the ostensible rubric of Weberian thought (see chapter 5). Eisenstadt (1968) elaborates these Shilsian insights within a similarly "Weberian" framework.

the religious qualities from which specifically office obligations were derived. This concealed dialectic points to the profound relationship that exists between normative obligations and the much more generalized meaning-creating processes of cultural life. Values are created and renewed through episodes of directly experiencing and re-experiencing transcendent meaning. While these experiences are never completely shut out by the walls of routinized life, the periods of peak experience constitute an independent mode of "religious" experience.

In periods of social conflict and strain, the broad cultural framework for specific role definitions itself becomes an issue for examination. Parts of societies, or even societies as such, may be said to experience a "generalization" (Parsons and Smelser 1957, ch. 7; Parsons and Bales 1955: 353–396; Smelser 1959, 1963) away from the specificity of everyday social life. Though utilitarian factors like faction and interest are often crucial in determining the specific course of such generalized crisis, nonrational ritualization is the order of the day. This ritualization, which can occur massively or episodically, involves the direct reexperiencing of fundamental values (cf. Tiryakian 1967) and often their rethinking and reformulating as well as their reaffirmation. The classificatory system of collective symbols can sometimes be drastically changed through these experiences; the relation of social actors to these dominant classifications can also be shifted and transformed. Cultural myths are recalled and extended to contemporary circumstance. Social solidarities are reworked. Yet, while solidarity is always the concomitant of ritual, it may be expanded or contracted, depending on the specific case. Finally, role relationships are certainly changed, not only in terms of the structure of opportunities and rewards, but in terms of subjective role definitions.

II

A discussion of the Watergate crisis in the United States between 1972 and 1974 can continue, in a more detailed and specific way, this analysis of political authority. After analyzing Watergate, I will return to a more general consideration of the specific explanatory structure of Durkheim's religious theory.

In June 1972, employees of the Republican party made an illegal entry and burglary into the Democratic party headquarters in the Watergate Hotel in Washington, D.C. Republicans described the break-in as a "third-rate burglary," neither politically motivated nor morally relevant. Democrats said it was a major act of political espionage, a symbol, moreover, of a demagogic and amoral Republican president, Richard Nixon, and his staff. Americans were not persuaded by the more extreme reaction. The incident received relatively little attention, generating no real sense of outrage at the time. There were no cries of outrage. There was, in the main, deference to the president, respect for his authority, and belief that his explanation of this event was correct, despite what in retrospect seemed like strong evidence to the contrary. With important exceptions, the mass news media decided after a short time to play down the story, not because they were coercively prevented from doing otherwise, but because they genuinely felt it to be a relatively unimportant event. Watergate remained, in other words, part of the profane world in Durkheim's sense. Even after the national election in November of that year, after Democrats had been pushing the issue for four months, 80 percent of the American people found it hard to believe that there was a "Watergate crisis"; 75 percent felt that what had occurred was just plain politics; 84 percent felt that what they had heard about it did not influence their vote. Two years later, this same incident, still called "Watergate," had initiated the most serious peace-time political crisis in American history. It had become a riveting moral symbol, one which initiated a long passage through sacred time and space, and wrenching conflict between pure and impure sacred forms. It was responsible for the first voluntary resignation of a president.

How and why did this perception of Watergate change? To understand this we must see first what this extraordinary contrast in these two public perceptions indicates, namely that the actual event, "Watergate," was in itself relatively inconsequential. It was a mere collection of facts, and contrary to the positive persuasion, facts do not speak. Certainly, new "facts" seem to have emerged in the course of the two-year crisis, but it is quite extraordinary how many of these "revelations" actually were already leaked and published, in the pre-election period. Watergate could not, as the French might say, tell itself. It had to be told by society; it was, to use Durkheim's famous phrase, a social fact. It was the context of Watergate that had changed, not so much the raw empirical data themselves.

To understand how this telling of a crucial social fact changed, it is necessary to bring to the sacred/profane dichotomy the Parsonian concept of generalization. There are different levels at which every social fact can be told (Smelser 1959, 1963). These levels are linked to different kinds of social resources, and the focus on one level or another can tell us much about whether a system is in crisis—and subject, therefore, to the sacralizing process—or is operating routinely, or profanely, and in equalibrium.

First and most specific is the level of goals. Political life occurs most of the time in the relatively mundane level of goals, power and interest. Above this, as it were, at a higher level of generality, are norms—the conventions, customs, and laws that regulate this political process and struggle. At still a higher point there are values: those very general and elemental aspects of the culture that inform the codes which regulate political authority and the norms within which specific interests are resolved. If politics operates routinely the conscious attention of political participants is on goals and interests. It is a relatively specific attention. Routine, "profane" politics means, in fact, that these interests are not seen as violating more general values and norms. Nonroutine politics begins when tension between these levels is felt, either because of a shift in the nature of political activity or a shift in the general, more sacred commitments that are held to regulate them. In this situation, a tension between goals and higher levels develops. Public attention shifts from political goals to more general concerns, to the norms and values that are now perceived as in danger. In this instance we can say there has been the generalization of public consciousness I referred to earlier as the central point of the ritual process.

It is in light of this analysis that we can understand the shift in the telling of Watergate. It was first viewed merely as something on the level of goals, "just politics," by 75 percent of the American people. Two years subsequent to the break-in, by summer 1974, public opinion had sharply changed. Now Watergate was regarded as an issue that violated fundamental customs and morals, and eventually—by 50 percent of the population—as a challenge to the most sacred values that sustained political order itself. By the end of this two-year crisis period almost half of those who had voted for Nixon changed their minds, and two-thirds of all voters thought the issue had now gone far beyond politics.* What had happened was a radical generalization of opinion. The facts were not that

*These figures are drawn from the 1972-1974 panel survey taken by the American National Election study conducted by the University of Michigan's Institute for Social Science Research.

different, but the social context in which they were seen had been transformed.

If we look at the two-year transformation of the context of Watergate, we see the creation and resolution of a fundamental social crisis, a resolution that involved the deepest ritualization of political life. To achieve this "religious" status, there had to be an extraordinary generalization of opinion vis-à-vis a political threat that was initiated by the very center of established power and a successful struggle not just against that power in its social form but against the powerful cultural rationales it mobilized. To understand this process of crisis creation and resolution we must integrate Durkheim's ritual theory with a more muscular theory of social structure and process. Let me lay these factors out generally before I indicate how each relates to Watergate.

What must happen for an entire society to experience fundamental crisis and ritual renewal?

First, there has to be sufficient social consensus so that an event will be considered polluting, or deviant, by more than a mere fragment of the population. Only with sufficient consensus, in other words, can "society" itself be aroused and indignant.

Second, there has to be the perception by significant groups who participate in this consensus that the event is not only deviant but that it threatens to pollute the "center" of society.

Third, if this deep crisis is to be resolved, institutional social controls must be brought into play. However, even legitimate attacks on the polluting sources of crisis are often viewed as frightening. For this reason, such controls also mobilize instrumental force and the threat of force to bring polluting forces to heel.

Fourth, social control mechanisms must be accompanied by the mobilization and struggle of elites and publics that are differentiated and relatively autonomous from the structural center of society. Through this process there begins to be the formation of countercenters.

Finally, fifth, there has to be effective processes of symbolic interpretation, that is, ritual, and purification processes that continue the labeling process and enforce the strength of the symbolic, sacred center of society at the expense of a center which is increasingly seen as merely structural, profane, and impure. In so doing, such processes demonstrate conclusively that deviant or "transgressive" qualities are the sources of this threat.

In elaborating how each one of these five factors came into play in the course of Watergate, I will indicate how, in a complex society, reintegration and symbolic renewal are far from being automatic processes.* Much more than a simple reading of Durkheim's work might imply, reintegration and renewal rely on the contingent outcomes of specific historical circumstances.

First, the factor of consensus. Between the Watergate break-in in June of 1972 and the Nixon-McGovern election contest in November, the necessary social consensus did not emerge. This was a time during which Americans experienced intense political polarization, though most of the actual social conflicts of the '60s had significantly cooled. Nixon had built his presidency, in part, on a backlash against these '60s' conflicts, and the Democratic candidate, McGovern, was the very symbol of this "leftism" to many. Both candidates thought that they, and the nation, were continuing the battles of the '60s. McGovern's active presence during this period, therefore, allowed Nixon to continue to promote the authoritarian politics that could justify Watergate. One should not suppose, however, that because there was not significant social reintegration during this period that no significant symbolic activity occurred. It is terribly important to understand that agreement in complex societies occurs at various levels. There may be extremely significant cultural agreement (e.g., complex and systematic agreement about the structure and content of language) while more socially or structurally related areas of subjective agreement (e.g., rules about political conduct) do not exist. Symbolic agreement without social consensus can exist, moreover, within more substantive cultural arenas than language.

During the summer of 1972 one can trace a very complex symbolic development in the American collective conscience, a consensual development that laid the basis for everything that followed even while it did not produce consensus at more social levels.† It was during this four-month period that the meaning complex "Watergate," came to be defined. In the first weeks which followed the break-in to the Democratic headquarters, "Watergate" existed, in semiotic terms, merely as a sign, as a

*In developing this scheme, I have relied on—in addition to Shils and the other Durkheimians whose work I have already mentioned—Douglas (1966), Keller (1963), and Eisenstadt (1971), among others. For an application of this scheme to another empirical case, see Lewis and Veneman (1987).

† I am drawing here upon my reading of the televised news reports on Watergate-related issues available in the Vanderbilt Television Archives in Nashville.

denotation. This word simply referred, moreover, to a single event. In the weeks that followed, the sign "Watergate," became more complex, referring to a series of interrelated events touched off by the break-in, including charges of political corruption, presidential denials, legal suits, and arrests. By August of 1972, "Watergate" had become transformed from a mere sign to a redolent symbol, a word that rather than denoting actual events connotated multifold moral meanings.

Watergate had become a symbol of pollution, embodying a sense of evil and impurity. In structural terms, the facts directly associated with Watergate—those who were immediately associated with the crime, the office and apartment complex, the persons implicated later—were placed on the negative side of a system of symbolic classification. Those persons or institutions responsible for ferreting out and arresting these criminal elements were placed on the other, positive side. This bifurcated model of pollution and purity was then superimposed onto the traditional good/ evil structure of American civil religion, whose relevant elements appeared in the form indicated in figure 6.1. It is clear, then, that while significant symbolic structuring had occurred, the "center" of the American social structure was in no way implicated.

This symbolic development, it should be emphasized, occurred in the public mind. Few Americans would have disagreed about the moral meanings of "Watergate" as a collective representation. Yet while the social basis of this symbol was widely inclusive, the symbol just about exhausted the meaning complex of Watergate as such. The term identified a complex of events and people with moral evil, but the collective consciousness did not connect this symbol to significant social roles or institutional behaviors. Neither the Republican party, President Nixon's staff, and least of all, President Nixon himself had yet been polluted by the symbol of Watergate. In this sense, it is possible to say that some *symbolic* generalization had occurred but that value generalization within the social system had not.

It had not because the social and cultural polarization of American society had not yet sufficiently abated. Because there was continued polarization, there could be no movement upwards toward shared social values; because there was no generalization, there could be no societal sense of crisis. Because there was no sense of crisis, in turn, it became impossible for the other forces I have mentioned to come into play. There was no widespread perception of a threat to the center, and, because there

FIGURE 6.1

Symbolic Classification System as of August 1972

The Watergate "Structure"

Evil	Good
Watergate Hotel	Nixon and Staff/White House
The Burglars	FBI
Dirty Tricksters	Courts/Justice Department's Prosecution Team
Money Raisers	Federal "Watchdog" Bureaucracy

American Civil Religion

Evil	Good
Communism/Fascism	Democracy
Shadowy Enemies	White House-Americanism
Crime	Law
Corruption	Honesty
Personalism	Responsibility
Bad Presidents	Great Presidents
(e.g., Harding/Grant)	(e.g., Lincoln/Washington)
Great Scandals	Heroic Reformers
(e.g., Teapot Dome)	

was none, there could be no mobilization against the center. Against a powerful, secure, and legitimate center, social control forces like investigative bodies, courts, and congressional committees were afraid to act. Similarly, there was no struggle by differentiated elites against the threat to (and by) the center, for many of these elites were divided, afraid, and immobilized. Finally, no deep ritual processes emerged—that could have happened only in response to tensions generated by the first four factors.

Yet in the six months following the election the situation began to be reversed. First, consensus began to emerge. The end of an intensely divisive election period allowed a realignment that had been building at least for two years prior to Watergate. The social struggles of the 1960s had long been over and many issues had been taken over by centrist groups.*

---

*This observation is based on a systematic sampling of national news magazine and televised news reports from 1968 through 1976.

In the 1960s struggles, the left had invoked critical universalism and rationality, tying these values to social movements for equality and against institutional authority, including, of course, the authority of the patriotic state itself. The Right, for its part, evoked particularism, tradition, and the defense of authority and the state.

In the post-election period, critical universalism could now be articulated by centrist forces without being liked to the specific ideological themes or goals of the Left, indeed, in defense of American national patriotism itself. With this emerging consensus, the possibility for common feeling of moral violation emerged, and with it began the movement toward generalization vis-à-vis political goals and interests. Once this first resource of consensus had become available, the other developments I have mentioned could be activated.

The second and third factors were anxiety about the center and the invocation of institutional social control. Developments in the postelection months provided a much safer and less "political" atmosphere for the exercise of social control by the courts, the Justice Department, various bureaucratic agencies, and special congressional committees. The very operation of these social control institutions legitimated the media's efforts to extend the Watergate pollution closer to central institutions. It reinforced public doubt about whether Watergate was, in fact, only a limited crime. It also forced more facts to surface. Of course, at this point the ultimate level of generality and seriousness of Watergate remained undetermined. With this new public legitimation, and the beginnings of generalization it implied, fears that Watergate might pose a threat to the center of American society quickly spread to significant publics and elites. The question about proximity to the center preoccupied every major group during this early postelection Watergate period. Senator Baker, at a later time, articulated this anxiety with the question that became famous during the summertime Senate hearings: "How much did the President know, and when did he know it?" This anxiety about the threat to the center, in turn, intensified the growing sense of normative violation, increased consensus, and contributed to generalization. It further rationalized the invocation of coercive social control. Finally, in structural terms, it began to realign the "good" and "bad" sides of the Watergate symbolization. Which side of the classification system were Nixon and his staff really on?

The fourth factor was elite conflict. Throughout this period, the generalization process—pushed by consensus, by the fear for the center, and by the activities of new institutions of social control—was fueled by a desire for revenge against Nixon by alienated institutional elites. These elites had represented "leftism" or simply "sophisticated cosmopolitanism" to Nixon during his first four years in office, and they had been the object of his legal and illegal attempts at suppression or control. They included journalists and newspapers, intellectuals, universities, scientists, lawyers, religionists, foundations, and, last but not least, authorities in various public agencies and the U.S. Congress. Motivated by a desire to get even, to reaffirm their threatened status, and to defend their universalistic values, these elites moved to establish themselves as countercenters in the years of crisis.

By May of 1973, almost one year after the break-in and six months after the election, all of these forces for crisis creation and resolution were in motion. Significant changes in public opinion had been mobilized and powerful structural resources were being brought into play. It is only at this point that the fifth crisis factor could emerge. Only now could there emerge deep processes of ritualization—sacralization, pollution, and purification—though there had certainly already been important symbolic developments.

The first fundamental ritual process of the Watergate crisis involved the Senate Select Committee's televised hearings, which began in May and continued through August. This event had tremendous repercussions on the symbolic patterning of the entire affair. The decision to hold and to televise the Senate's hearings responded to the anxiety that had built up within important segments of the population. The symbolic process that ensued functioned to canalize this anxiety in certain distinctive, more generalized, and more consensual directions. The hearings constituted a kind of civic ritual which revivified very general yet nonetheless very crucial currents of critical universalism and rationality in the American political culture. It recreated the sacred, generalized morality upon which more mundane conceptions of office are based, and it did so by invoking the mythical level of national understanding in a way that few other events have in postwar history.

These hearings were initially authorized by the Senate on specific political and normative grounds, their mandate being to expose corrupt campaign practices and to suggest legal reforms. The pressure for ritual process, however, soon made this initial mandate all but forgotten. The hearings became a sacred process by which the nation could reach a judgment about the now critically judged Watergate crime. The consensus-building, generalizing aspect of the process was to some extent quite conscious. Congressional leaders assigned membership to the committee on the basis of the widest possible regional and political representation and excluded from the committee all potentially polarizing political personalities. Most of the generalizing process, however, developed much less consciously in the course of the event itself. The developing ritual quality forced committee members to mask their often sharp internal divisions behind commitments to civic universalism. Much of the committee staff, for example, had been radical or liberal activists during the '60s. They now had to assert patriotic universalism without any reference to specific left-wing issues. Other staffers, who had been strong Nixon supporters sympathetic to backlash politics, now had to forsake entirely that justification for political action.

The televised hearings, in the end, constituted a liminal experience (Turner 1969), one radically separated from the profane issues and mundane grounds of everyday life. A ritual *communitas* was created for Americans to share, and within this reconstructed community none of the polarizing issues that had generated the Watergate crisis, or the historical justifications that had motivated it, could be raised. Instead, the hearings revivified the civic religion upon which democratic conceptions of "office" have depended throughout American history. To understand how a liminal world could be created it is necessary to see it as a "phenomenological world" in the sense that Schutz described. The hearings succeeded in becoming a world "unto itself." It was *sui generis,* a world without history. Its characters did not have rememberable pasts. It was in a very real sense "out of time." The framing devices of the television medium contributed to the deracination that produced this phenomenological status. The in-camera editing, the repetition, juxtaposition, simplification, and other techniques that made the mythical story were invisible. Add to this "bracketed experience" the hushed voices of the announcers, the pomp and ceremony of the "event," and we have the recipe for constructing, within the medium of television, a sacred time and sacred space.*

At the level of mundane reality, two ferociously competitive political forces were at war during the Watergate hearings. These forces had to

*For an important general discussion about how the medium of television can transform social occasion into ritual "events," see Dayan and Katz (1988).

translate themselves into the symbolic idioms of the occasion; as a result, they were defined and limited by cultural structures even as they struggled to define and limit these structures in turn. For Nixon and his political supporters, "Watergate" had to be defined politically: what the Watergate burglars and cover-uppers had done was "just politics," and the anti-Nixon senators on the Watergate Committee (a majority of whom, after all, were Democratic) were characterized simply as engaged in a political witchhunt. For Nixon's critics on the committee, by contrast, this mundane political definition had to be opposed. Nixon could be criticized and Watergate legitimated as a real crisis only if the issues were defined as being above politics and involving fundamental moral concerns. These issues, moreover, had to be linked to forces near the center of political society.

The first issue was whether the hearings were to be televised at all. To allow something to assume the form of a ritualized event is to give participants in a drama the right to forcibly intervene in the culture of the society; it is to give to an event, and to those who are defining its meaning, a special, privileged access to the collective conscience. In primitive societies, ritual processes are ascribed: they occur at preordained periods and in preordained ways. In more modern societies, ritual processes are achieved, often against great odds. Indeed, in a modern society the assumption of ritual status often poses a danger and a threat to vested interests and groups. We know, in fact, that strenuous efforts were made by the White House to prevent the Senate hearings from being televised, to urge that less television time be devoted to them, and even to pressure the networks to cut short their coverage after it had begun. There were also efforts to force the committee to consider the witnesses in a sequence that was far less dramatic than the one eventually followed.

Because these efforts were unsuccessful, the ritual form was achieved.[1] Through television, tens of millions of Americans participated symbolically and emotionally in the deliberations of the committee. Viewing became morally obligatory for wide segments of the population. Old routines were broken, new ones formed. What these viewers saw was a highly simplified drama—heroes and villains formed in due course. But this drama created a deeply serious symbolic occasion.

If achieving the form of modern ritual is contingent, so is explicating the content, for modern rituals are not nearly so automatically coded as earlier ones. Within the context of the sacred time of the hearings, administration witnesses and senators struggled for moral legitimation, for definitional or ritual superiority and dominance. The end result was in no sense preordained. It depended on successful symbolic work. To describe this symbolic work is to embark on the ethnography, or hermeneutics, of televised ritual.

The Republican and administration witnesses who were "called to account for themselves" pursued two symbolic strategies during the hearings. First, they tried to prevent public attention from moving from the political/profane to the value/sacred level at all. In this way, they repeatedly tried to rob the event of its phenomenological status as a ritual. They tried to cool out the proceedings by acting relaxed and casual. For example, H. R. Haldeman, the presidential assistant who was compared to a Gestapo figure in the popular press, let his hair grow long so he would look less sinister and more like "one of the boys." These administrative witnesses also tried to rationalize and specify the public's orientation to their actions by arguing that they had acted with common sense according to pragmatic considerations. They suggested that they had decided to commit their crimes only according to standards of technical rationality. The secret meetings that had launched a wide range of illegal activities, and considered many more, were described not as evil, mysterious conspiracies but as technical discussions about the "costs" of engaging in various disruptive and illegal acts.

Yet the realm of values could not really be avoided. The symbol of Watergate was already quite generalized, and the ritual form of the hearings was already in place. It was within this value realm, indeed, that the most portentous symbolic struggles of the hearings occurred, for what transpired was nothing less than a struggle for the spiritual soul of the American republic. Watergate had been committed and initially justified in the climate of cultural and political "backlash," values which in basic ways contradicted the universalism, critical rationality, and tolerance upon which contemporary democracy must be based. Republican and administration witnesses evoked this subculture of backlash values. They urged the audience to return to the polarized climate of the 1960s. They sought to justify their actions by appealing to patriotism, to the need for stability, to the "un-American" and thereby deviant qualities of McGovern and the Left. They also justified it by arguing against cosmopolitanism, which in the minds of backlash traditionalists had undermined respect for tradition and neutralized the universalistic constitutional rules of the game. More specifically, administration witnesses appealed to loyalty as the ultimate standard that should govern the relationship between subordinates and authorities. An interesting visual theme which summed up both of these appeals was the passive reference by administration witnesses to family values. Each witness brought his wife and children if he had them. To see them lined up behind him, prim and proper, provided symbolic links to the tradition, authority, and personal loyalty that symbolically bound the groups of backlash culture.

The anti-Nixon senators, for their part, faced an enormous challenge. Outside of their own constituencies, they were not well-known; arrayed against them were representatives of an administration that six months before had been elected by the largest landslide vote in American history. This gigantic vote had been, moreover, partly justified by the particularistic sentiments of the backlash, the very sentiments that the senators were now out to demonstrate were deviant and isolated from the true American tradition.

What was the "symbolic work" in which the senators engaged? In the first instance, they denied the validity of particularist sentiments and motives. They bracketed the political realities of everyday life, and particularly the critical realities of life in the only recently completed 1960s. At no time in the hearings did the senators ever refer to the polarized struggles of that day. By making those struggles invisible, they denied any moral context for the witnesses' actions. This strategy of isolating backlash values was supported by the only positive explanation the senators allowed, namely, that the conspirators were just plain stupid. They poked fun at them as utterly devoid of common sense, implying that no normal person could ever conceive of doing such things.

This strategic denial, or bracketing in the phenomenological sense, was coupled with a ringing and unabashed affirmation of the universalistic myths that are the backbone of the American civic religion. Through their questions, statements, references, gestures, and metaphors, the senators maintained that every American, high or low, rich or poor, acts virtuously in terms of the pure universalism of the civic republican tradition. Nobody is selfish or inhumane. No American is concerned with money or power at the expense of fair play. No team loyalty is so strong that it violates common good or makes criticism toward authority unnecessary. Truth and justice are the basis of American political society. Every citizen is rational and will act in accordance with justice if he is allowed to know the truth. Law is the perfect embodiment of justice, and office consists of the application of just law to power and force. Because power corrupts, office must enforce impersonal obligations in the name of the people's justice and reason. Narrative myths which embodied these themes were often invoked. Sometimes these were timeless fables, sometimes they were stories about the origins of English common law, often they were the narratives about the exemplary behavior of America's most sacred presidents. John Dean, for example, the most compelling anti-Nixon witness, strikingly embodied the American detective myth (Smith 1970). This figure of authority is derived from the Puritan tradition, and in countless different stories is portrayed as ruthlessly pursuing truth and injustice without emotion or vanity. Other narratives developed in a more contingent way. For administration witnesses who confessed, the committee's "priests" granted forgiveness in accord with well-established ritual forms, and their conversions to the cause of righteousness constituted fables for the remainder of the proceedings.

These democratic myths were confirmed by the senator's confrontation with family values. Their families were utterly invisible throughout the hearings. We don't know if they had families, but they certainly were not presented. Like the committee's chairman, Sam Ervin, who was always armed with the Bible and the Constitution, the senators embodied transcendent justice divorced from personal or emotional concerns.

Another confrontation that assumed ritual status was the swearing in of the witnesses. Raising their right hands, each swore to tell the truth before God and man. While this oath did have formal legal status, it served the much more important function of ensuring moral degradation. It reduced the famous, powerful people who were involved to the status of "Everyman." It placed them in subordinate positions vis-à-vis the overpowering and universalistic law of the land.

In terms of more direct and explicit conflict, the senators' questions centered on three principle themes, each fundamental to the moral anchoring of a civic democratic society. First, they emphasized the absolute priority of office obligations over personal ones: "This is a nation of laws not men" became a constant refrain. Second, they emphasized the embeddedness of such office obligations in a higher transcendent authority: "The laws of men" must give way to the "laws of God." Or as Sam Ervin, the committee chairman, put it to Maurice Stans, the ill-fated treasurer of Nixon's campaign committee, "Which is more important, not violating laws or not violating ethics?" Finally, the senators insisted that this transcendental anchoring of interest conflict allowed America to be a true *Gemeinschaft,* in Hegel's terms, a true "concrete universal." As Senator Wiecker put it in a famous statement: "Republicans do not cover up, Republicans do not go ahead and threaten . . . and God knows Republicans don't view their fellow Americans as enemies to be harassed [but as] human being[s] to be loved and won."

In normal times many of these statements would have been greeted with derision, with hoots and cynicism. In fact, many of them were lies in terms of the specific empirical reality of everyday political life, and especially in terms of the political reality of the 1960s. Yet they were not laughed at or hooted down. The reason was because this was not everyday life. This was a ritualized and liminal event, a period of intense generalization that had powerful claims to truth. It was a sacred time and the hearing chambers had become a sacred place. The committee was evoking luminescent values, not trying to describe empirical fact. On this mythical level the statements could be seen and understood as true, as, indeed, embodying the normative aspirations of the American people. They were so seen and understood by significant portions of the population.

The hearings ended without laws or specific judgments of evidence, but they nevertheless had profound effects. They helped to establish and fully to legitimate a framework that henceforth gave the Watergate crisis its meaning. They accomplished this by continuing and deepening the cultural process which had begun before the election itself. Actual events and characters in the Watergate episode were organized in terms of the higher antitheses between the pure and the impure elements of America's civil religion. Before the hearings "Watergate" was already a symbol redolent with the structured antitheses of American mythical life, antitheses which were implicitly linked by the American people to the structure of their civil religion. What the hearings accomplished, first, was to make this linkage to civil religion explicit and pronounced. The "good guys" of the Watergate process—their actions and motives—were purified in the resacralization process through their identification with the Constitution, norms of fairness, and citizen solidarity. The perpetrators of Watergate, and the themes which they evoked as justification, were polluted by association with symbols of civil evil: sectarianism, self-interest, particularistic loyalty. As this description implies, moreover, the hearings also restructured the linkages between Watergate elements and

FIGURE 6.2
Symbolic Classification System as of August 1973

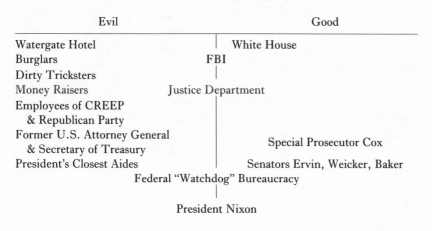

The Watergate "Structure"

Evil	Good
Watergate Hotel	White House
Burglars	FBI
Dirty Tricksters	
Money Raisers	Justice Department
Employees of CREEP & Republican Party	
Former U.S. Attorney General & Secretary of Treasury	Special Prosecutor Cox
President's Closest Aides	Senators Ervin, Weicker, Baker

Federal "Watchdog" Bureaucracy

President Nixon

American Civil Religion

Evil		Good
Communism/Fascism		Democracy
Shadowy Enemies		White House-Americanism
Crime		Law
Corruption		Honesty
Personalism		Responsibility
Bad Presidents		Great Presidents
(e.g., Harding/Grant)	President Nixon	(e.g., Lincoln/Washington)
Great Scandals		Heroic Reformers
(e.g., Watergate)		(e.g., Sam Ervin)

the nation's political center. Many of the most powerful men surrounding President Nixon were now implacably associated with Watergate evil, and some of Nixon's most outspoken enemies were linked to Watergate good. As the structural and symbolic centers of the civil religion were becoming so increasingly differentiated, the American public found the presidential party and the elements of civic sacredness more and more difficult to bring together (see figure 6.2).

While this reading of the events is based on ethnography and interpretation, the process of deepening pollution is also revealed by poll data. Between the 1972 election and the very end of the crisis in 1974, there was only one large increase in the percentage of Americans who considered Watergate "serious." This occurred during the first two months of the Watergate hearings, April through early July 1973. Before the hearings, only 31 percent of Americans considered Watergate a "serious" issue. By early July 50 percent did, and this figure remained constant until the end of the crisis.

Although an enormous ritual experience had clearly occurred, any contemporary application of Durkheimianism must acknowledge that such modern rituals are never complete. In the first place, ritual symbols must be carefully differentiated. Despite the frequent references to presidential involvement, and despite the president's shadow throughout the hearings, poll data reveal that most Americans did not emerge from the ritual experience convinced of President Nixon's involvement. In the second place, the ritual effects of the hearings were unevenly felt. The Senate hearings were most powerful in their effect on certain centrist groups and left-wing groups: (1) among McGovern voters whose outrage at Nixon was splendidly confirmed; (2) among moderate Democrats who even if they had voted for Nixon were now outraged at him, particularly after many had crossed party lines to vote for him; (3) among moderate or liberal Republicans and independents who while disagreeing with many of Nixon's positions had voted for him anyway. The latter groups were particularly important to the entire process of Watergate. They were prototypically cross-pressured, and it was the cross-pressured groups who along with radical McGovern supporters became most deeply involved in the hearings. Why? Perhaps they needed the hearings to sort out confused feelings, to clarify crucial issues, to resolve their uncomfortable ambivalence. Certainly such a relative stake can be found in the poll data. In the period mid-April 1973 to late June 1973—the period of the hearings' beginnings and its most dramatic revelations—the growth among Republicans who thought Watergate "serious" was 20 percent, and among independents, 18 percent; for Democrats, however, the percentage growth was only 15 percent.*

*The figures in these last two paragraphs are drawn from the poll data presented in Lang and Lang (1983:88–93, 114–117). Appropriating the term "serious" from the polls, however, the Langs do not sufficiently differentiate the precise symbolic elements to which the designation referred.

The year-long crisis which followed the hearings, from August 1973 to August 1974, was punctuated by episodes of moral convulsion and public anger, by renewed ritualization, by the further shifting of symbolic classification to include the structural center—the Nixon presidency—and by the further expansion of the solidary base of this symbolism to include most of the significant segments of American society. In the wake of the Senate hearings, a Special Prosecutor's Office was created. It was staffed, though not chaired, almost entirely by formerly alienated members of the left-wing opposition to Nixon, who with their assumption of office made publicly accepted professions of their commitments to impartial justice, a process that further demonstrated the powerful generalizing and solidarizing phenomenon underway. The first special prosecutor was Archibald Cox, whose Puritan and Harvard background made him the ideal embodiment of the civil religion. Nixon fired Cox in October 1973 because he had asked the courts to challenge the president's decision to withhold information from the Special Prosecutor's Office. In response, there was a massive outpouring of spontaneous public anger, which newspaper reporters immediately dubbed the "Saturday Night Massacre."

Americans seemed to view Cox's firing as a profanation of the attachments they had built up during the Senate hearings, commitments to newly revivified sacred tenets and against certain diabolical values and tabooed actors. Because Americans had identified their positive values and hopes with Cox, his firing made them fear pollution of their ideals and themselves. This anxiety caused public outrage, an explosion of public opinion during which three million protest letters were sent to the White House over a single weekend. These letters were labelled a "flashflood," a metaphor that played on the pre-crisis signification of the word Watergate. The metaphor suggested that the scandal's polluted water had finally broken the river gates and flooded surrounding communities. The term "Saturday Night Massacre" similarly intertwined deeper rhetorical themes. In the 1920s a famous mob killing in gangland Chicago had been called the "St. Valentine's Day Massacre". "Black Friday" was the day in 1929 when the American stockmarket fell, shattering the hopes and trust of millions of Americans. Cox's firing, then, produced the same kind of symbolic condensation as dream symbolism, but on a mass scale. The anxiety of the citizenry was deepened, moreover, by the fact that pollution had now spread directly to the very figure who was supposed to hold American civil religion together, the president himself. By firing Cox,

President Nixon came into direct contact with the molten lava of sacred impurity. The pollution that "Watergate" carried had now spread to the very center of American social structure. While support for Nixon's impeachment had gone up only a few points during the Senate hearings, after the "Saturday Night Massacre" it increased by fully 10 points. From this flashflood came the first congressional motions for impeachment and the instauration of the impeachment process in the House of Representatives.

Another major expansion of pollution occurred when the transcripts of White House conversations secretly taped during the Watergate period were released in April and May 1974. The tapes contained numerous examples of presidential deceit, and they were also laced with presidential expletives and ethnic slurs. Once again, there was tremendous public indignation at Nixon's behavior. By his words and recorded actions he had polluted the very tenets which the entire Watergate process had revivified: the sacredness of truth and the image of America as an inclusive, tolerant community. The symbolic and structural centers of American society were further separated, with Nixon (the representative of the structural center) increasingly pushed into the polluted, evil side of the Watergate dichotomies. This transcript convulsion helped define the symbolic center as a distinct area, and it demonstrated that this center was neither liberal nor conservative. Indeed, most of the indignation over Nixon's foul language was informed by conservative beliefs about proper behavior and civil decorum, beliefs which had been flagrantly violated by Nixon's enemies, the Left, during the polarized period that preceded the Watergate crisis.

In June and July of the year following, legal proceedings began against Nixon in the U.S. House of Representatives. These impeachment hearings were conducted by the House Judiciary Committee, and they marked the most solemn and formalized ritual of the entire Watergate episode. This proved to be the closing ceremony, a rite of expulsion in which the body politic rid itself of the last and most menacing source of sacred impurity. By the time of these hearings the symbolization of Watergate was already highly developed; in fact, Watergate had become not only a symbol with significant referents but also a powerful metaphor whose self-evident meaning itself served to define unfolding events. The meaning structure associated with "Watergate," moreover, now unequivocally placed a vast part of White House and "center" personnel on the side of civil pollution and evil. The only question that remained was whether President Nixon himself would finally be placed alongside them as well.

The House hearings recapitulated the themes which had appeared in the Senate hearings one year before. The most pervasive background debate was over the meaning of "high crimes and misdemeanors," the constitutional phrase which set forth the standard for impeachment. Nixon's supporters argued for a narrow interpretation which held that an officer had to have committed an actual civil crime. Nixon's opponents argued for a broad interpretation which would include issues of political morality, irresponsibility, and deceit. Clearly, this was a debate over the level of system crisis: were merely normative, legal issues involved, or did this crisis reach all the way to the most general value underpinnings of the entire system? Given the highly ritualized format of the hearings, and the tremendous symbolization which had preceded the committee's deliberations, it hardly seems possible that the committee could have adopted anything other than the broad interpretation of "high crimes and misdemeanors."

This generalized definition set the tone for the hearings' single most distinctive quality: the ever-recurring emphasis on the members' fairness and the objectivity of its procedures. Journalists frequently remarked on how congressmen rose to the sense of occasion, presenting themselves not as political representatives of particular interests but as embodiments of sacred civil documents and democratic mores. This transcendence of wide partisan division was echoed by the cooperation among the Judiciary Committee's staff, which, in fact, had actually set the tone for the committee's formal, televised deliberations. Key members of the staff had, in the '60s, been critics of establishment activities like the Vietnam War and supporters of antiestablishment movements like civil rights. Yet this partisan background never publicly surfaced during the vast journalistic coverage of the committee's work; even right-wing conservatives never made an issue of it. Why not? Because this committee, like its Senate counterpart one year before, existed in a liminal, detached place. They, too, operated within sacred time, their deliberations continuous not with the immediate partisan past but with the great constitutive moments of the American republic: the signing of the Bill of Rights, the framing of the Constitution, the crisis of the Union which marked the Civil War.

This aura of liminal transcendence moved many of the most conservative members of the committee, Southerners whose constituents had voted for Nixon by landslide proportions, to act out of conscience rather than political expediency. The Southern bloc, indeed, formed the key to the coalition that voted for three articles of impeachment. These final articles, revealingly, purposefully eschewed a fourth article, earlier proposed by liberal Democrats, which condemned Nixon's secret bombing of Cambodia. Though this earlier article referred to a real violation of law, it was an issue that was interpreted by Americans in specifically political terms, terms about which they widely disagreed. The final three impeachment articles, by contrast, referred only to fully generalized issues. At stake was the code that regulated political authority, the question of whether impersonal obligations of office can and should control personal interest and behavior. It was Nixon's violation of the obligations of his office which made the House vote his impeachment.

After Nixon resigned from office, the relief of American society was palpable. For an extended period the political community had been in a liminal state, a condition of heightened anxiety and moral immersion which scarcely allowed time for the mundane issues of political life. When Vice-President Ford ascended to the presidency, there were a series of symbolic transformations which indicated ritualistic reaggregation. President Ford, in his first words after taking office, announced that "our long national nightmare is over." Newspaper headlines proclaimed that the sun had finally broken through the clouds, that a new day was being born. Americans effused about the strength and unity of the country. Ford himself was transformed, through these reaggregating rites, from a rather bumbling partisan leader into a national healer, the incarnation of a "good guy" who embodied the highest standards of ethical and political behavior.

Before continuing with the symbolic process after this reaggregation, I would like to return, once again, to the fact that modern rituals are never complete. This incompleteness represents the impact of relatively "autonomous" social system forces which Durkheim's sociological idealism made it impossible to consider. Even after the ritual ceremony which consensually voted articles of impeachment and the ritual renewal with President Ford, poll data reveal that a surprising segment of American society remained unconvinced. Between 18 and 20 percent of Americans did not find President Nixon guilty, either of a legal crime or of moral turpitude. These Americans, in other words, did not participate in the generalization of opinion which drove Nixon from office. They interpreted the Watergate process, rather, as stimulated by political vengeance by Nixon's enemies. The demographics of this loyalist group are not particularly revealing. They were of mixed education and from every class and occupation. One of the few significant structural correlations was their tendency to be from the South. What did, apparently, really distinguish this group was their political values. They held a rigid and narrow idea of political loyalty, identifying the belief in God, for example, with commitment to Americanism. They also held a deeply personalized vision of political authority, tending much more than other Americans to express their allegiance to Nixon as a man and to his family as well. Finally, and not surprisingly, this group had reacted much more negatively than other Americans to the left-wing social movements of the 1960s. The fact that they were committed to a polarized and exclusivist vision of political solidarity reinforced their reluctance to generalize from specifically political issues to general moral concerns. Such generalization would have involved not only criticism of Nixon but the restoration of a wider, more inclusive political community. In voting for Nixon they had supported a candidate who promised to embody their backlash sentiments and who had appeared, during his first years in office, inclined to carry out their wishes for a narrow and primordial political community.

The period of social reaggregation after Watergate's liminal period—the closure of the immediate ritual episode—raises, once again, the problem of the dichotomizing nature of Western social theory, for it involves the relationship between such categories as charisma/routine, sacred/profane, generalization/institutionalization. On the one hand, it is clear that with Ford's ascension a much more routine atmosphere prevailed. Institutional actors and the public in general seemed to return to the profane level of goal and interest conflict. Political dissensus once again prevailed. Conflicts over the inflationary economy captured the news for the first time in months, and this issue, along with America's dependence on foreign oil, loomed large in the autumn congressional elections of 1974.

According to the theories of routinization and specification, or institutionalization, the end of ritualization ushers in a new, completely post-spiritual phase, in which there is the institutionalization or crystallization of ritual spirit in a concrete form. The most elaborated theory of this transition is found in the works of Smelser (1959, 1963) and Parsons (Parsons and Bales 1955:35–132). In these works, post-crisis structures are described as evolving because they are better adapted to deal with the source of initial disequilibrium. Generalization is ended, then, because of the "efficiency" with which newly created structures deal with concrete role behavior. Now, to a certain extent, such new and more adaptive institution building did occur in the course of the Watergate process. New structures emerged that allowed the political system to be more differentiated, or insulated, from interest conflict, and which allowed universalism to be more strongly served. Conflict-of-interest rules were developed and applied to presidential appointments; congressional approval of some of the president's key staff appointments, like Director of the Office of Management and Budget, was instituted; a standing Special Prosecutor's Office was created, the attorney general being required to decide within thirty days of any congressional report on impropriety whether a prosecutor should actually be called; finally, federal financing of presidential election campaigns was passed into law. There were, in addition, a range of more informally sanctioned institutional innovations: the post of "chief of staff" became less powerful; the doctrine of "executive privilege" was used much more sparingly; Congress was consulted on important matters.

Durkheim and Weber would tend to support this dichotomous picture of crisis resolution. Weber, of course, saw most political interaction as instrumentally routine. The transition from charisma (Weber 1978:246–255) was preceded by structural innovation on the part of the leader's self-interested staff and triggered automatically and conclusively by the leader's death.* Durkheim's understanding is more complex. On the one hand—and this, of course, is the problem with which we began our inquiry—Durkheim saw the non-ritual world as thoroughly profane, as non-valuational, as political or economic, as conflictual, and even in a certain sense as nonsocial (Alexander 1982: 292–306). At the same time, however, Durkheim clearly overlaid this sharp distinction with a more continuous theory, for he insisted that the effervescence from rituals

---

*Shils' (1975; cf. Eisenstadt 1968) reading of Weber's charisma theory has been an important exception that has significantly influenced my own treatment. Shils makes routinization the corollary of institutionalization and does so with a reference to continuing sacrality. Shils' overt reliance on Weber and charisma, however, tells us more about what Bloom calls the anxiety of influence than it does about the real theoretical origins of his work, for he clearly draws more on Parsons' and Durkheim's later thought than on Weber himself (see chapter 5). For an extremely interesting extension of the Shils-Eisenstadt charisma theory, see Seligman's (1987) discussion of the relationship between routinization, institutionalization, and primordiality in early New England.

continued to infuse post-ritual life for some time after the immediate period of ritual interaction. Once again, I believe that this profound empirical insight can be understood only by reconceptualizing it, specifically by using it to critique and reorient the generalization-specification theory of the Parsonian tradition.

Though the crisis model of generalization-specification has been taken from functionalist analysis, the notion of generalization as ritual has been drawn from Durkheim. The analysis of social crisis presented here, therefore, has given much more autonomy to symbolic process than would a purely functionalist one. Generalization and ritualization are not engaged, in my view, purely for psychological or social-structural reasons—either because of anxiety or the inefficiency of social structures—but also because of the violation of ardently adhered to moral beliefs. Symbolic processes, therefore, occur as much to work out issues on this level as to provide more efficient structures for addressing specific, "real" disequilibriating problems. It is for this reason that ritualization is succeeded not by merely structural change but also by continued cultural effervescence. The recharged antinomies of the cultural order, and the emotional intensity which underlies them, continue to create moral conflict and, often, to support significantly different cultural orientations.

As compared, for example, to the aftershocks of the Dreyfus Affair, the effervescence of Watergate must be understood in terms of relative cultural unity. "Watergate" had come to be viewed—and this is extraordinarily significant in comparative terms—not as an issue of the Left or the Right but rather as a national issue about which most parties agreed. There were, it was universally agreed, certain "lessons of Watergate" from which the nation had to learn. American talked incessantly in the period between 1974 and 1976 about the imperatives of what was referred to as "post-Watergate morality." They experienced this as an imperious social force which laid waste to institutions and reputations. "Post-Watergate morality" was the name given to the effervescence from the ritual event. It named the revivified values of critical rationality, anti-authoritarianism, and civil solidarity, and it named the polluted values of conformity, personalistic deference, and factional strife. For several years after the end of liminality, Americans applied these highly charged moral imperatives to group and interest conflict and to bureaucratic life, demanding radical universalism and heightened solidarity at every turn.

For the adult population, therefore—the case seems to have been somewhat different for children—the effect of Watergate was not increased cynicism or political withdrawal. Quite the opposite. Ritual effervescence increased faith in the political "system" even while the distrust it produced continued to undermine public confidence in particular institutional actors and authorities. Institutional distrust is different from the delegitimation of general systems per se (Lipset and Schneider 1983). If there is trust in the norms and values which are conceived as regulating political life, there may actually be more contention over the wielding of power and force (cf. Barber 1983). In this sense, political democracy and political efficiency may be opposed, for the first lends itself to conflict while the second depends on order and control.

In the immediate post-Watergate period, a heightened sensitivity to the general meaning of office and democratic responsibility did indeed lead to heightened conflict and to a series of challenges to authoritative control. Watergate became more than ever before a highly charged metaphor. No longer was it simply a referent for naming events which objectively occurred, but a moral standard which helped subjectively to create them. Members of the polity, inspired by its symbolic power, sought out sinful behavior and tried to punish it. The result was a series of scandals: "Koreagate" and "Billygate" on the American scene, for example, and "Winegate" abroad.

The giant explosion of Watergate into the American collective conscience vented a series of aftershocks of populist anti-authoritarianism and critical rationality.

1. Almost immediately after the reaggregation ceremonies, there unfolded in close succession a series of unprecedented congressional investigations. Nelson Rockefeller, Ford's vice-presidential nominee, was subjected to a long and heated televised inquiry into the possible misuses of his personal wealth. Enormous televised investigations were also launched by the Congress into the secret, often anti-democratic working of the Central Intelligence Agency (CIA) and the Federal Bureau of Investigation (FBI), institutions whose patriotic authority had previously been unquestioned. This outpouring of these "little Watergates," as they were called, extended well into the Carter administration of 1976–1980. Carter's chief assistant, Bert Lance, was forced out of office after highly publicized hearings that badly impugned his financial and political integrity. Each of these investigations created a scandal in its own right; each

followed, often down to the smallest detail and word, the symbolic model established by Watergate.

2. Whole new reform movements were generated from the Watergate spirit. There emerged a Society for Investigative Reporting, a new organization that responded to the spurt of morally inspired, critical journalism by those journalists who had internalized the Watergate experience and sought to externalize its model. Federal crime investigators—lawyers and policemen—formed white-collar crime units throughout the United States. For the first time in American history significant prosecutorial resources were shifted away from the conventionally defined, often lower-class, criminals to high-status office holders in the public and private domains. Inspired by the Watergate model, it became the established, *a priori* conviction of many city, state, and federal prosecutors that office holders might well commit crimes against the public. By ferreting them out and prosecuting them, they tried to maintain the moral alertness of all authorities to the responsibility of office as such.

3. In the months subsequent to reaggregation, authority was critically examined at every institutional level of American society, even the most mundane. The Boy Scouts, for example, rewrote their constitution to emphasize not just loyalty and obedience but critical questioning. The judges of the Black Miss America beauty pageant were accused of personalism and bias. Professional groups examined and rewrote their codes of ethics. Student-body officers of high schools and universities were called to task after little scandals were created. City councillors and mayors were "exposed" in every city, great and small. Through most of these controversies, specific issues of policy and interest were not significantly considered. It was the codes of office themselves which were at stake.

These concrete, institutional events, in other words, were actually motivated by the continuing "religious" struggles within post-Watergate culture. This connection is further demonstrated by the continuation in that period of even more specific Watergate-related themes. There were continuous assertions, for example, that America was morally unified. Groups which had been previously excluded or persecuted, most particularly those associated with the Communist party, were publicly cleansed. I have already mentioned that those institutions most responsible for political witch hunts, particularly the FBI, were reprimanded for their un-Americanism. Alongside this there occurred a more subtle outpouring from the collective conscience: books, articles, movies, and television shows appeared about the immorality and tragedies associated with "McCarthyism," all painting persecuted fellow-travellers and Communists in a sympathetic and familiar light. The anti-war movement assumed, through this same retrospective figuratorial process, a respectable, even heroic light. No doubt inspired by this rebirth of community, leaders of New Left underground organizations began to give themselves up, trusting the state but particularly the American opinion-making process to give them a fair hearing.

Through it all the vividness of Watergate's impure symbols remained strikingly intact. Trials of the Watergate conspirators, former cabinet officers and high-ranking aids generated large headlines and great preoccupation. Their published confessions and *mea culpas* were objects of intensely moral, even spiritual dispute. Richard Nixon, the very personification of evil, was viewed by alarmed Americans as a continuing source of dangerous pollution. Still a source of symbolic power, his name and his person were forms of what Durkheim called the "liquid impure." Americans tried to protect themselves from this polluting Nixonian lava by building walls. They sought to keep Nixon out of "good society" and isolated in San Clemente, his former presidential estate. When Nixon tried to buy an expensive apartment in New York, the building's tenants voted to bar the sale. When he travelled around the country, crowds followed to boo him, and politicians shunned him. When he reappeared on television, viewers sent indignant, angry letters. Indeed, Nixon could escape this calumny only by travelling to foreign countries, though even some foreign leaders refused to associate with him in public. For Americans, there was an extraordinary fear of being touched by Nixon or his image. Such contact was believed to lead to immediate ruin. When President Ford pardoned Nixon several months after assuming office, Ford's honeymoon with the public abruptly ended. Tarnished by this (however brief) association with Nixon, he alienated such a large body of the electorate that it cost him the subsequent presidential election.

The spirit of Watergate did eventually subside. Much of the structure and process which had stimulated the crisis reappeared, although it did so in a significantly altered form. Nixon had ridden a backlash against modernity into office, and after his departure this movement against liberal and inclusive secularism continued. But this conservatism now emerged in a much more anti-authoritarian form. Social movements like the tax revolt and the anti-abortion movement combined the post-Watergate spirit of critique and challenge with particularistic and often reactionary political issues. Ronald Reagan was swept into office on many of the old backlash issues, yet upon the Reagan presidency, too, there continued to be a noticeable post-Watergate effect. For if Reagan was even more conservative than Nixon, he was committed to carrying out his reaction against the Left in a democratic and consensual way. This commitment may not have been a personal one, but it was enforced unequivocally by the public mood and by the continuing vitality of the potential counter centers to presidential power.

Not only did the rightward movement of American politics reappear, but the authoritarianism of the "imperial presidency" regained much of its earlier force. As the distance from Watergate increased, concrete economic and political problems assumed greater importance. Solving foreign crises, inflation, energy problems—the American people focused more and more on attaining these elusive "goals." These generated demands for specificity and efficacy, not for generalized morality. Given the structure of the American political system, these demands for efficacy necessitated a strong executive. The concern about the morality of authority became increasingly blunted by demands for strong and effective authority. Jimmy Carter began his presidency by promising the American people, "I will never lie to you." He ended it by making a strong presidency his principal campaign slogan. By the time Reagan became president, he could openly disdain some conflict-of-interest laws, re-employ some of the lesser-polluted Watergate figures, and move to wrap executive authority once again in a cloak of secrecy and charisma. These later developments do not mean that Watergate had no effect. The codes that regulate political authority in America had been forcibly renewed, codes which, even when they are latent, continue to affect concrete political activity. Politics in America had simply, and finally, returned to the "normal" level of interests and roles.

The Iran-Contra affair of 1986–1987 demonstrated both sides of the Watergate denouement—social normalization and political conservatism, on the one hand, continuing normative vitality and broad democratic conventions, on the other. Like Nixon and other presidents who were confronted with institutional blockages, Reagan subverted office obligations to attain his goals by illegal means. With the Democratic takeover of the Senate in November 1986, and the gradual shift of American public opinion away from a conservative, anti-government stance, the social environment that had legitimated these actions begin to change. As a result of these and other contextual shifts, strong barriers were thrown up against what became "Contragate." In the midst of the furor in the public media and contentious Congressional hearings, Reagan's actions were transformed for many Americans from a questionable political strategy into an abuse, or even usurpation, of power. Because this attack on earthly power was intertwined, once again, with a renewal of ideal codes, this usurpation was described as a polluting aberration. These events never reached the crisis proportions of Watergate; few events in a nation's history ever do.* Still, without the "memory of justice" provided by that earlier crisis, it is doubtful that the administration's actions would so easily and quickly have been transformed into an affair.

III

In the first part of this essay I maintained the importance of Durkheim's later, "religious" sociology. At the same time, I argued that it should be accepted more as an empirical theory of specific social processes than as a general theory of societies. In the second section I explored what these specific social processes are with reference to the Watergate crisis in the United States, placing the religious sociology within a more general theoretical and empirical framework. In this concluding section, I would like to focus briefly on the status of this later religious theory in a more general and abstract way.

There are three dimensions of Durkheim's later religious theory: morphology, solidarity, and classification. Each of these dimensions refers to a different empirical element in Durkheim's later work, yet, at the same time, Durkheim often conflates and reduces each element to the other. Each of these three elements, moreover, becomes the focus for independent strands of the Durkheimian tradition after Durkheim's death. Before a satisfactory cultural sociology can be developed, these traditions must be brought back together, the elements of each reconceptualized and analytically intertwined (see Alexander 1988a, and chapter 5, above).

Durkheim's theory of classification relates purely to the organization of symbols, and his major contribution in this regard is to suggest that the

---

*For an examination of the Iran-Contra scandal in terms of the framework I have set out here, see Alexander (1987).

antipathy between sacred and profane presents a fundamental structure of symbolic organization. Certainly the structuralism of Lévi-Strauss (1966) represents the foremost contribution to expanding, systematizing, and applying this classificatory scheme.* But because of its purely cognitive focus, structuralism ignores the manner in which such bifurcating classification is oriented not simply to mind but to affect and society. These emphases can be brought into the abstract schema of structuralism by reinvoking the charged terms "sacred" and "profane." Sacred symbols are not simply one side of an abstract dichotomy. They are the focus of heightened affect, reflecting the emotional desirability of achieving the good. The opposite, antagonistic side of Durkheim's classification system must, however, undergo further reconstruction. As Caillois ([1939] 1959) first demonstrated, Durkheim often confused the profane-as-routine with the sacred-as-impure. It is necessary, therefore, to develop the three-fold classification of pure-sacred/impure-sacred/profane. Mary Douglas (1966), building upon notions of taboo, has expanded Durkheim's original understanding in a similar way, demonstrating that every symbolization of sacred purity is classified with an impure element that is given enormous polluting power. Because the fear of pollution is motivated by psychological anxiety and is directed, as well, to deviant social forces and groups, this revised understanding allows Durkheim's classificatory theory to be set forth in a manner that avoids the idealist and abstract implications of structural theory.

Yet the theory of symbolic antagonism must be complemented by other theories of symbolic classification. Symbols are also powerfully organized by myths, by narratives that assemble and reassemble symbols into dramatic forms. Eliade (1959) has elaborated mythical organization in historical and archeological ways. Ricoeur has developed perhaps the most elaborate contemporary phenomenology of mythical organization, particularly in his work (Ricoeur 1967) on the symbolism of evil. But more present-oriented myth analyses must also be explored, for example, the work of Henry Nash Smith, *Virgin Land* (1970), which builds upon Levy-Bruhl to explore how myths about the Yoeman Farmer guided the Western movement of the American nation.

Neither myth nor structural analysis address the issue of temporality, the actual historical development that often occurs within the realm of

---

*For an example of the best recent work in this tradition see Sahlins (1976).

symbolic classification itself. Here, one turns to the contribution of Weber and others in the German Idealist school (chapter 2, above). In his account of the movement from this-worldly mysticism to this-worldly asceticism (1978:541–635) Weber systematically demonstrated the evolution of religious ideas about salvation. Troeltsch ([1911] 1960) followed up Weber's contribution by demonstrating historical evolution in ideas about individual autonomy. Jellinek's writings ([1885] 1901) on the origins of the Declaration of the Rights of Man represents a less-known work in this genre, that later inspired Weber himself. Among contemporaries, Bellah's (1970 and Bellah and Hammond 1980) theory about the comparative evolution of "civil religions" is the most significant secular transformation of Weberian ideas, although Walzer's (1965) work on Puritanism and the English Revolution and Little's (1969) on Puritanism and law are also exemplary.

This historical dimension of the Weberian approach to symbolic organization feeds into the Parsonian-functionalist concentration on values. "Values" refers to explicit cognitive ideas about the meaning of social structure. Value analysis has often functioned as a cover for the reduction of culture to social structure, and it has also tended to produce a fragmentary description of culture as composed of discrete and unconnected units of meaning. It need not do so, however, particularly if it is combined with the thematic approach of intellectual history. Martin Wiener's (1981) analysis of the rise of anti-industrial values in English history is just such a case. Sewell's (1980) work on the value of corporatism in French working-class history is another. Viviana Zelizer's (1979) analysis of how shifting ideas related to the development of the American life insurance industry is a fine example of value analysis in the functionalist tradition (see also Zelizer 1985).

Finally, as Lukes (1982) has reminded us in his recent introduction to Durkheim's writing on sociological method, any contemporary extension of Durkheimian "classification" theory must come firmly to grips with the hermeneutical and interpretive tradition. Rhetorical theories of textual analysis—so brilliantly elaborated by Geertz (1973)—must be incorporated into the tools of cultural sociology. So must the general stricture, first insisted upon by Dilthey (1976:155–263) and most recently articulated by Ricoeur (1971), that for purposes of symbolic analysis social action must be read as a text. Semiotics, both as literary method and as social theory, can be incorporated into cultural sociology only in this way (cf. Sahlins 1976; Barthes 1983).

Yet Durkheim's analysis of solidarity is just as significant, I believe, as his theory of symbolic organization. He leads classification to solidarity through his ritual theory; hence it is not only solidarity but ritual that symbolic structuralism ignores. Ritual theory provides the social process and action for symbolic classification; solidarity provides the link between ritual, symbolization, and the concrete social community. Together, ritual and solidarity allow the cultural analyst to discuss social crisis and renewal, and their relation not only to symbolic organization but to institutions and social groups.

Durkheim tied solidarity too closely to classification. Although he implied an independent power for the sacred and profane (here Lévi-Strauss's critique [e.g., 1966:214] is wrong), he just as often explained classification merely as the reflection of solidary forms (here Lévi-Strauss was right). Not only must symbolic organization be treated as an independent dimension, but solidarity itself must be internally differentiated. The renewal of solidarity that ritual provides must be considered separately from the degree of its empirical reach, apart, that is, from the question of just how far such solidarity extends.* Both these issues, moreover— renewal and integration—must be dissociated from the unreflexive, automatic quality that accrues to them in Durkheim's original work. Not only must the initiation of ritual be treated in an historically specific way, but the course that ritualization and solidarizing processes take once they are initiated must be theorized in a manner that allows an open-ended understanding. Evans-Pritchard's (1953) demonstration of how ritual activity can re-establish the relationship between socially refracted cultural themes is a crucial early contribution to this problem (cf. Alexander 1988c). Victor Turner (e.g., 1969) has made the most explicit effort to expand Durkheim's solidary/ritual theory. Turner's generalization and abstraction of Van Gennep's stages of ritual process—separation, liminality, reaggregation—is important because it allows ritual analysis to be applied outside of tightly structured domains. Liminality, and the communitas that accompanies it, can now be seen more clearly as typical responses to status reversal and instability at any level of social life. Yet Turner's work

---

*I believe that Lukes (1975) was getting at this separation in another way in his important piece on neo-Durkheimian treatments of ritual life.

still suffers from the rigid dichotomies of Durkheim's original, particularly from the idealistic reification of solidarity and from his insistence that liminality is astructural rather than simply less specified and routinized. Sewell's detailed and historically specific description of the episodic eruption of working-class solidarity and the gradual expansion of worker cooperation avoids these problems while maintaining a close, if implicit, faithfulness to the central core of Durkheim's work. Moore's (1975) insistence on the processual and contingent within ritual process, by contrast, tries to push contemporary ritual analysis toward the flux and flow of social life.

Finally, there is the problem of morphology. For Durkheim, morphology is social structure. Yet, though he insisted that classification and solidarity must be linked to morphology, once he abjures the morphological determinism of his early work he seems unable to tell us how such a link might take place. One problem is that his theoretical dichotomies force him to work with a correspondence theory of interrelationship. A more multidimensional stance, by contrast, would make morphology the continuous referent for a symbolizing process that simultaneously refers to the personality and cultural orders. Most contemporary work on culture and social structure, however, repeats Durkheim's mistake, what Sahlins (1976) describes—in reference to Marx—as giving morphology temporal if not ontological priority over symbolization. This is especially true, for example, in the later work of Mary Douglas (Douglas and Wildavsky 1982), which describes pollution symbols as if they were mere reflections of core group/out group relations. In his discussion of solidarity, Turner makes much the same mistake. He describes it as propelled by concrete social arrangements without any prior relationship to cultural codes. Sewell, too, derives his French workers' initial ideas about solidarity from the "real" structures of their economic life.

The only way to avoid this false prioritizing is to appreciate Parsons's insistence that there is only an *analytical* (never empirical or historical) differentiation between culture and social system. Social structural components are never without symbolic internalization or institutionalization, nor are symbolic classifications ever without some element of socialized form.* The only way to capture this analytic point empirically is to acknowledge that every structural event, and even every specific social

---

*While the latter point is often denied by Sahlins (1976), his analysis of food symbolism as structured by the value placed on human life actually demonstrates its truth.

value, exists within a very broad matrix of cultural tradition. Until recently, this matrix has been religion, and morphological analysis that separates material from religious structure does so at its peril. Walzer's (1965) analysis of the interrelation of class, Christianity, education, political exile, and social change remains the most successful analysis of interrelation of which I am aware.

But the problem of morphology extends beyond the problem of interrelationship alone. It is based as well on the very difficulty of conceptualizing morphology itself. Durkheimian theory has had a very underdeveloped sense of the nature of social structure. One needs to turn to the functionalist and Weberian traditions to find a more complex and dynamic referent for symbolization and solidarity. Only after this referent is discovered can the most interesting substantive processes of contemporary symbolization be studied—for example, the Weberian problem of authority—and can questions like the degree of ritual integration finally be addressed. It has been a working hypothesis of this essay that the ability to reconstitute solidarity in social crises is related to the degree of social structural differentiation, on the one hand, and to the degree to which a given culture defines symbolic authority in universalistic terms, on the other.

If social science today is to develop a cultural theory, it must build on Durkheim's "religious" sociology. If it is to do this, however, it must reconstruct this later writing in a serious and ambitious way. I have tried, in the present essay, to lay out some of what this reconstruction entails and to offer an extended example of what such a reconstructed theory might look like in action.

NOTE

1. That Nixon struggled against television in order to prevent ritualization underscores the peculiar qualities of this medium's esthetic form. In his pioneering essay, *What Is Cinema?* André Bazin (1958) suggested that the unique ontology of cinema, as compared to written art forms such as novels, is realism. Bazin meant not that artifice is absent from cinema but that the end results of cinema artifice gives the unmistakable impression of being real, lifelike and true. The audience cannot distance itself from talking and speaking images as easily as it can

from static, impersonal, literary forms. This forceful realism is as true for television, particularly documentary and news television, as for the classic cinema, though in this case the medium of contrast is the newspaper rather than the novel. Thus, ever since its appearance after World War II, political leaders have sensed that to command the medium of television, with the hidden artifice of it *mis-en-scène,* means that one's words will possess—in the public's mind—the ontological status of truth.

In this sense, Nixon's struggle against televising the hearings was a struggle to contain information about the Senate hearings within the less-convincing aesthetic package of newsprint. He and his supporters sensed that if the televised form were to be achieved, the battle already would be partly lost.

This insight from the philosophy of aesthetics should, however, be modified in two ways. First, because live television coverage of news events is contingent, the realism of the Senate hearings was necessarily uncertain. The "possession" of the Watergate *mis-en-scène*—the play-by-play of the hearings—was far from determined. But Bazin's aesthetic dictum must be modified in another sociological way as well. Television, even "factual" television, is a medium that depends on influence, and the willingness to be influenced—to accept statements of fact at face value—depends on trust in the persuader. The degree to which factual television is believed—how and to what degree it achieves the ontological status to which it is, as it were, aesthetically entitled—depends on the degree to which it is viewed as a differentiated, unbiased medium of information (see Alexander 1988b).

Indeed, the analysis of poll data from this period suggests that one of the strongest predictors of support for impeachment was the belief that television news was fair. It follows that one of the primary reasons for the failure to accept Watergate as a serious problem—let alone Nixon's culpability—before the 1972 election was the widespread perception that the media was not independent but part of the vanguard modernist movement, a linkage which was, of course, strongly promoted by Vice-President Spiro Agnew. Because of the processes I have described, however, between January and April, 1973, the media was gradually rehabilitated. Feelings of political polarization had ebbed, and other key institutions now seemed to support the media's earlier reported "facts." Only because the medium of television now could draw upon a fairly wide social consensus, I believe, could its message begin to attain the status of realism and truth. This shifting social context for the aesthetic form is therefore critical for understanding the impact of the Senate hearings.

REFERENCES

Alexander, Jeffrey C. 1982. *The Antinomies of Classical Thought: Marx and Durkheim.* Berkeley and Los Angeles: University of California Press.

—— 1987. "Constructing Scandal." *The New Republic,* June 8, pp. 18–20.

—— 1988a. *Action and Its Environments.* New York: Columbia University Press.

—— 1988b. "The Mass News Media in Systemic, Historical, and Comparative Perspective." In Alexander (1988a):107–152.

—— 1988c. "Three Models of Culture and Society Relations: Toward an Analysis of Watergate." In Alexander (1988a):153–174.

Barber, Bernard. 1983. *The Logic and Limits of Trust.* New Brunswick, N.J.: Rutgers University Press.

Barthes, Roland. 1983. *The Fashion System.* New York: Hill and Wang.

Bazin, André. 1958. *Qu' est-ce que le cinéma?* Vol. 1. Paris: Editions du Cerf.

Bellah, Robert N. 1969. "Civil Religion in America." In Bellah, *Beyond Belief,* pp. 168–189. New York: Harper and Row.

Bellah, Robert N., and Phillip E. Hammond. 1980. *Varieties of Civil Religion.* New York: Harper and Row.

Callois, Roger. [1939] 1959. *Man and the Sacred.* New York: Free Press.

Dayan, Daniel, and Elihu Katz. 1988. "Articulating Consensus: The Ritual and Rhetoric of Media Events." In Alexander, ed., *Durkheimian Sociology: Cultural Studies,* pp. 161–186. New York: Cambridge University Press.

Dilthey, Wilhelm. 1976. *Selected Writings.* London: Cambridge University Press.

Douglas, Mary. 1966. *Purity and Danger.* London: Penguin.

Douglas, Mary, and Aaron Wildavsky. 1982. *Risk and Culture.* Berkeley and Los Angeles: University of California Press.

Durkheim, Emile. [1895] 1938. *The Rules of Sociological Method.* New York: Free Press.

—— [1895–96] 1958. *Socialism and Saint-Simon.* Yellow Springs, Ohio: Antioch University Press.

—— [1897] 1951. *Suicide.* New York: Free Press.

Eliade, Mircea. 1959. *The Sacred and the Profane.* New York: Harcourt, Brace.

Eisenstadt, S. N. 1968. "Charisma and Institution Building: Max Weber and Modern Sociology." In Eisenstadt, ed., *Max Weber on Charisma and Institution Building,* pp. ix–lvi. Chicago: University of Chicago Press.

Evans-Pritchard, E. E. 1953. "The Nuer Concept of the Spirit in Its Relation to Social Order." *American Anthropologist* 55:201–241.

Friedrichs, Carl J. 1964. *Transcendent Justice.* Durham, N.C.: Duke University Press.

Geertz, Clifford.1973. *The Interpretation of Cultures.* New York: Basic Books.

Jellinek, Georg. [1885] 1901. *The Declaration of The Rights of Man and of Citizens: A Contribution to Modern Constitutional History.* New York: Holt.

Keller, Suzanne. 1963. *Beyond the Ruling Class.* New York: Random House.

Lacroix, Bernard. 1981. *Durkheim et la politique.* Paris: Presses Universitaires de France.

Lang, Gladys, and Kurt Lang. 1983. *The Battle for Public Opinion.* New York: Columbia University Press.

Lévi-Strauss, Claude. 1966. *The Savage Mind.* Chicago: University of Chicago Press.

Lewis, Jerry M. and J. Michael Veneman. 1987. "Crisis Resolution: The Bradford Fire and English Society." *Sociological Focus* 20(2):155–168.

Lipset, Seymour Martin, and William Schneider. 1983. *The Confidence Gap*. New York: Free Press.

Little, David. 1969. *Religion, Order, and Law*. New York: Harper and Row.

Lukes, Stephen. 1975. "Political Ritual and Social Integration." *Sociology* 2: 289–308.

—— 1982 Introduction to *Emile Durkheim: Rules of Sociological Method*, ed. by Lukes. London: Macmillan.

Moore, Sally F. 1975. "Uncertainties in Situations: Indeterminates in Culture." In Moore and Barbara Meyerhoff, eds., *Symbol and Politics in Communal Ideology*, pp. 210–239. Ithaca, N.Y.: Cornell University Press.

Parson, Talcott, and Robert F. Bales, eds. 1955. *Family, Socialization, and Interaction Process*. New York: Free Press.

Parsons, Talcott, and Neil J. Smelser. 1957. *Economy and Society*. New York: Free Press.

Ricoeur, Paul. 1967. *The Symbolism of Evil*. Boston: Beacon.

—— 1971. "The Model of the Text: Meaningful Action Considered as Text." *Social Research* 38:529–562.

Sahlins, Marshall. 1976. *Culture and Practical Reason*. Chicago: University of Chicago Press.

Seligman, Adam. 1987. *Human Agency, The Millenium, and Social Change*. Ph.D. dissertation, Hebrew University, Jerusalem.

Sewell, William H., Jr. 1980. *Work and Revolution in France*. New York: Cambridge University Press.

Shils, Edward. 1975. *Center and Periphery: Essays in Macrosociology*. Chicago: University of Chicago Press.

Smelser, Neil J. 1959. *Social Change in the Industrial Revolution*. Chicago: University of Chicago Press.

—— 1963. *Theory of Collective Behavior*. New York: Free Press.

Smith, Henry Nash. 1970. *Virgin Land*. New York: Vintage.

Tiryakian, Edward A. 1967. "A Model of Societal Change and Its Lead Indicators." In Samuel Z. Klausner, ed., *The Study of Total Societies*, pp. 69–97. New York: Praeger.

Troeltsch, Ernst. [1911] 1960. *The Social Teachings of the Christian Church*. Chicago: University of Chicago Press.

Turner, Victor. 1969. *The Ritual Process*. Chicago: Aldine.

Walzer, Michael. 1965. *The Revolution of the Saints*. Cambridge: Harvard University Press.

Weber, Max. 1978. *Economy and Society*. Berkeley and Los Angeles: University of California Press.

Weiner, Martin J. 1981. *English Culture and the Decline of the Industrial Spirit, 1850–1980*. New York: Cambridge University Press.

Zelizer, Viviana. 1979. *Morals and Markets*. New York: Columbia University Press.

—— 1985. *Pricing the Priceless Child*. New York: Basic Books.

SEVEN

Habermas and Critical Theory: Beyond the Marxian Dilemma?

Every critical social theory is faced with the problem of constituting its grounds for critique. Of course, even empirical, "positive" theory contains an ideological dimension, but because its main ambition is explanatory rather than evaluative it can—indeed, must—leave this normative source implicit and diffuse. For critical theory, the situation is quite different. It is explicitly political, seeking to draw readers toward a normative position and often to a political stance. Because this is so, its grounds for moral judgment are explicitly called into question.

There seem to be three ways that the grounds for a critical theory can be constituted. The first is through relativism: "I criticize society because it violates my principles." The sources of critique are presented as subjective, as emerging from personal convictions. Here is the "humanistic" position that became so popular in the non-Marxist critical sociology of the late '60s and early '70s, the "self-reflexive" sociology that eschews the bindingness of objectivity and calls upon the theorist to be forthright about his or her own personal values.

In intellectual and political terms, however, this relativist position has seemed unsatisfactory. Critical theorists have usually sought a position that at least appears to be more objective and, hence, less challengeable. The alternative strategy has been to seek an immanent critique, to try to demonstrate that the critical standard grows naturally and inevitably out of the conditions of the society against which the critique is aimed. Two kinds of immanent justification have been offered, the objective and the subjective. Marx is the great exemplar of the former. The communist demands of the proletariat, he insisted, grow not from the head of this or that philosopher or from some free-floating idealistic hope but from the

concrete conditions of real social life. While the dominant thrust of capitalist society is irrational, a more rational form of social organization can,
in fact, be gleaned from the actual social conditions of capitalism, from
its objectivity, its cosmopolitanism, its universalism, and the egalitarian
cooperation it forces upon its working class. Hegel represents the exemplar of the alternative approach, seeking an immanent justification in a
subjective, idealist form. In his *Phenomenology of Spirit* he laid out a
developmental sequence that was simultaneously logical, psychological,
and historical, and he argued that the sources for moving beyond each
stage would inevitably be discovered in the experienced inadequacies
(illogic, frustrations, social tensions) of each state itself. For both Marx
and Hegel, then, an appropriate standard of critical reason was immanent
at every historical stage.

The tradition of twentieth-century theory associated with the Frankfurt
school of Marxism, initiated by Horkheimer and Adorno and associated
most famously with the political theories of Herbert Marcuse, must be
credited with making this issue of critical justification completely explicit.
Rather than Marxist or Hegelian, it called itself quite simply "critical
theory," and it explicitly adopted the transcendent criterion of "rationality" as the basis for its anti-capitalist critique. This position clearly followed the normative path; the Frankfurt school found only moral bank-
ruptcy in objectivist theories like those of the orthodox Marx. But since
the Frankfurt Marxists had abandoned Hegel's faith in God, they had no
firm basis for their own moral criticism. Though they postulated an
immanent rationality, their work became mystical and arbitrary when
they tried to define rationality's source. Perhaps inevitably, this source
came to be associated with the prerogative of intellectuals. With this
development the universalistic ambition of this Frankfurt Marxist criticism came to seem more and more particularistic. It became an increasingly serious problem in the 1960s, when Marcuse defended critical reason by opposing "pure tolerance" and at least appeared to apologize for
revolutionary coercion in Western societies in a manner that paralleled
Fanon's defense of it in the Third World.

It is in the context of this historical and theoretical juncture that Jürgen
Habermas' work must be understood. Habermas is a radical, but he is not
a revolutionary. Whereas Marcuse celebrated the excesses of the 1960s,
Habermas was appalled by them, and he earned the permanent contempt
of some German student radicals for his public opposition. As a left-wing

humanist and democrat, Habermas has always been acutely aware of the theoretical and political degeneration of critical theory. In a recent "Reply to My Critics," many of whom were orthodox representatives of the critical school, Habermas insists (1982:222) that "revolutionary self-confidence and theoretical self-certainty are gone." To regain them critical theory must find a way to justify its standard of immanent rationality. This is what Habermas set out to do.

To restore universality to critical rationality and to cleanse the critical tradition of its elitism, Habermas seeks to return to key aspects of Marx's original strategy. He does not do this by embracing an objectivist criterion, for he maintains the moral tone of the "Western Marxist" tradition. Rather, he returns to Marx in the sense of embracing empirical social science and empirically based philosophy. Earlier generations of the Frankfurt school attacked social science as inevitably "positive," bourgeois and conservative. In contrast, Habermas embraces the most advanced empirical theorizing of his day. As Marx sought to turn political economy against itself in the name of socialism, so Habermas seeks to demonstrate that the empirical processes illuminated by contemporary theories—processes there for all to see—carry inside themselves the potential for critique and transcendence of the status quo.

I

Over the last fifteen years there have been three traditions of empirical social theory upon which Habermas has drawn. Perhaps the least remarked upon by either Habermas or his interpreters is the Parsonian.* Habermas began teaching Parsons in the early 1960s and, though rarely footnoted, Parsonian themes like systems, pattern-variables, and the centrality of socialization permeate his thought. Only in the 1980s has Habermas made this debt explicit, as his work has taken a formidable Parsonian turn. As he remarks in the second volume of *The Theory of Communicative Action* (1981:297), "though Parsons' later work has at times been pushed into the background by hermeneutically and critically-oriented

---

*It is remarkable, for example, that in the comprehensive collection of critical essays on Habermas collected by Thompson and Held (1982), there is only a single reference to the Habermas-Parsons link. It is Giddens (1982:160) who notices and regrets the connection; he refers to the link, however, only in connection with Habermas' internalization theory, neglecting the much more important theme of normative evolution.

investigations, no social theory can be taken seriously today which does not—at the very least—clarify the relationship to Parsons."

But Habermas does more than simply clarify the relationship; he takes Parsons' work as embodying the highest level of contemporary theoretical work. "As it stands today," he writes, "the work is unparalleled in regard to its level of abstraction, internal differentiation, theoretical breadth and systematicity—all of which is, simultaneously, connected to the literature of each particular empirical field." In fact, he issues a warning to any "neo-Marxism which wishes simply to bypass Parsons," averring that "in the history of social science errors of this type are normally quickly corrected" (1981:297).

Habermas sees that Parsons was centrally concerned with the sociological preconditions of universalism, which is, as Hegel clearly saw, perhaps the most crucial dimension of rationality. More recently, Habermas has relied heavily on the historical twist that Parsons gave to the sociology of universalism in his evolutionary theory. Terms like "learning processes" and "normative integration" have become central to Habermas' critical vocabulary. In the book of essays that adumbrated the present work, Habermas (1979:120) wrote: "I would even defend the thesis that the development of . . . normative structures is the pacemaker of social evolution." He is aware that this Parsonian theme turns the tables on Marx: "Whereas Marx localized the learning processes important for evolution in the dimension of objectivizing thought—of technical and organizational knowledge, of instrumental and strategic action, in short, of productive forces—there are good reasons meanwhile for assuming that learning processes also . . . are deposited in more mature forms of social integration, in new productive relations, and that these in turn first make possible the introduction of new productive forces" (p. 98).

The second line of empirical theorizing upon which Habermas has drawn is Piaget's work on cognitive and moral development. Whereas Parsons allows Habermas to claim that universalistic and solidary relationships are grounded in the historical development of real societies, Piaget allows him to argue that universalistic, critical thought is grounded in the normal development of the human mind. The internal emphasis of Piaget—the vocabulary of "interiorization," "representation," "generalization"—complements the normative reference of Habermas' critique; it also clearly articulates with the Freudian vocabulary of Parsons' socialization theory, upon which Habermas also relies (for his interweaving of these traditions, see 1979:81–88). Indeed, Habermas uses Piagetian theory to conceptualize a point that Parsons' critics have somehow seemed unable to grasp: developmental theory conceives socialization as learning to be rational and autonomous, not dependent and submissive. Piaget insists that human intelligence moves from the concrete to the formal and in the process gains a critical distance from and mastery over the objects in its environment. These are precisely the qualities that allow Habermas to extend his empirical theorizing about the immanent source of critical rationality. By the mid-1970s the key terms of Piagetian theory have been thoroughly incorporated into Habermas' discussion of contemporary reality. Consciousness is "decentered" and "objective"; it "goes beyond reality" to think the "possible"; it seeks universal, generalizable principles, "the rules behind rules" (compare, e.g., Piaget 1972 with Habermas 1979:69–94). Finally, Piaget's emphasis on the pragmatic, concrete character of the developmental crises that promote learning allows Habermas to conceptualize the immanent growth of mental rationality without falling into the trap of Hegel's idealism.

What Habermas has taken from Parsons and Piaget is not simply a theory of the empirical development of rationality, but also the notion that a great deal of rationality is already realized in the world as structured today. This is the price of buying into empirical theorizing, and it is the very price that earlier generations of critical theorists were unwilling to pay. Horkheimer and Adorno learned a great deal from Hegel's *Phenomenology,* but they seem to have stopped learning after his discussion of the Enlightenment, which Hegel ([1807] 1977:6. B. 1–2.a) criticized for its mechanistic version of rationality. For Horkheimer and Adorno, Western cultural development evidently stopped at that point, hence their equation Enlightenment = Capitalism = Instrumental Reason. Hegel, in contrast, believed that the reigning conception of reason continued to grow (e.g., [1807] 1977:6.c, passim) in the course of subsequent Western development. By passing through later phases of expressive, ethical, and eventually religious experience, the conception of rationality became enriched and multivalent. Habermas follows Hegel himself rather than the Horkheimer/Adorno caricature, though he does not follow him to the point of believing that a completely satisfactory "rationality" is enshrined in the status quo. Having learned from Parsons and Piaget, Habermas can describe how cognitive, expressive, and moral rationality have developed in the present day. He can also argue, in light of his own more critical ambitions, that their theories provide an explanation not only of contemporary society but of a rational standpoint from which to go beyond it.

But neither Parsons nor Piaget plays a central role in the first volume of Habermas' most recent and most systematic work, *The Theory of Communicative Action*. Parsons receives major consideration in the second volume; Piaget is discussed only passingly in both volumes, though his ideas continue to permeate Habermas' theoretical vocabulary. In this volume pride of place is given to the third empirical tradition that Habermas uses to remake his critical theory, the speech-act theory which derives from ordinary language philosophy. To "scientific" sociologists, it may seem strange to claim a modern philosophical tradition as an empirical, or at least empirically related theory. But speech-act theory and the "analytic" movement out of which it grew are directed toward the study of empirical processes in a way that is antithetical to the metaphysical traditions of continental philosophy. This contrast, of course, is exactly what attracts Habermas. By developing a theory of "communicative action," he wants to use speech-act theory to extend his empirical analysis of immanent rationality.

Habermas seems to have been drawn to ordinary-language analysis under the influence of Karl-Otto Apel. In a major essay first published in 1965, *Analytic Philosophy of Language and the Geisteswissenschaften,* Apel demonstrated a convergence between later trends in English, analytic philosophy and the interpretive tradition of German hermeneutics. He demonstrated (1967:37) that the rationalistic intentionalist bias that had given early analytic philosophy an atomistic and empiricist approach to meaning had been superceded by Wittgenstein's later "revolution." Wittgenstein had shown that rather than denoting intended objects, words really denote simply other words. Wittgenstein believed that words are arbitarily arranged in language games, and that such games must be interpreted from within. In Apel's view (1967:33) this opened the way for reconciling ordinary-language theorizing with the *Geisteswissenschaften* (i.e., cultural studies) tradition.

Habermas, then, uses post-Wittgensteinian analytic philosophy to root his standard of rationality more firmly in immanent, empirical processes, this time in the nature of ordinary language itself. Though he did not pursue the issue at this early point, Habermas (1971:314) articulated precisely this connection in his inaugural lecture at Frankfurt in 1965:

"The human interest in autonomy and responsibility is not mere fancy, for it can be apprehended *a priori*. What raises us out of nature is the only thing whose nature we can know: language."* Habermas argues that in ordinary speech actors make implicit claims about the validity of their statements, claims which, in a crunch, they are prepared to justify through argument. On these grounds, he suggests that rationality "is ingrained in the very structure of action oriented toward reaching understanding" (1984:130). Perhaps the most eloquent expression of the peculiar marriage of Hegelianism and empiricism that inspires Habermas' turn to language can be found in an earlier work. "In action oriented toward reaching understanding," Habermas writes (1979:97), and here he means to include most ordinary language, "validity claims are 'always already' implicitly raised." It is "in these validity claims," he goes on to argue, that "communication theory can locate a gentle but obstinate, a never silent although seldom redeemed claim to reason."

In his communication theory, Habermas defines rationality as the quality that makes action "defendable against criticism" (1984:16). To be rational, acts must rest upon "criticizable validity claims" (p. 15) rather than on unchallengeable authority or physical force. If challenged, then, rational actors will cite potentially consensual grounds that justify their statements or actions. In doing so they will be engaging in "argumentation." Argumentation is speech that "thematizes" contested validity claims, explicitly supporting or criticizing them. Ordinary language, Habermas believes, can rest on four kinds of implicit validity claims, each of which in the ideal speech situation can be justified through argument. These claims refer to cognitive, moral, and expressive dimensions. In instrumental and strategic action (which Habermas also calls teleological), the claim is made for efficiency; the discourse that thematizes this action— though it is rarely, in fact, subject to such argumentation—is empirical. Related to this, but more generalized, is the kind of speech act that Habermas calls assertive or constative. These are statements of fact. They refer to actions that rest on purely factual claims, and they are ultimately validated by claims to truth in the cognitive sense. The discourse that thematizes this claim Habermas calls theoretical. While both strategic and constative speech acts are located within the cognitive dimension, Habermas differentiates them by suggesting that strategic action is almost never

*Thompson's (1982) fine essay in the collection he edited with Held first drew this statement to my attention.

thematized. This is what makes it, in his view, instrumentally rather than communicatively rational—a distinction that, as we will see, plays a central and often problematic role in his understanding. The third distinct mode of action is expressive, referring both to emotional and aesthetic statements. The claim put forward here is not truth but "truthfulness," sincerity and authenticity in a subjective sense. The discourse that thematizes this claim Habermas sometimes calls therapeutic and other times esthetic. Finally, there is moral action, which invokes neither efficiency, truth, nor truthfulness. Its claim is to "rightness," to a normative context that is legitimate in the sense of reflecting some moral interest common to all concerned. It is practical discourse that thematizes this claim to validity.

This communication theory—to which I will return—takes up one major chunk of Habermas' book (see, especially, pp. 8–42, 75–101, and 273–337; for the first and most concise statement of this position, see 1979:1–68). Habermas' analysis of Weber takes up another. In light of Habermas' concern with the empirical immanence of rationality and his commitment to communicative argument, Weber certainly seems an appropriate reference. While Habermas has suggested that rational argument is an implicit part of everyday speech, he thinks this has not always been so. Communicative action can be more or less rational, and the further back we go in examining traditional and primitive societies the less rational it appears to have been. The point about rational communication is that understanding cannot be conceived *a priori*. It cannot—and here Habermas gives a communicative twist to Parsons' famous pattern-variable dichotomy—be "normatively ascribed" (1984:70); rather, it must be "communicatively achieved." Social rationalization, then, can be defined as the elimination of factors that "prevent conscious settlement of conflicts" (p. 119). Here lies the significance of Weber. His historical analysis of the cultural and social processes that produced rationalization can be seen as describing the movement toward communicative rationality. Habermas' communication theory leads him to incorporate Weber and, equally important, to correct him.

II

Although his reading of Weber's corpus is by no means systematic or complete, Habermas presents a sophisticated and original interpretation of certain key sections. In the positive phase of his reading, he focuses on elements of Weber's cultural history which have not yet received sufficient attention, particularly on "The Social Psychology of World Religions" and "Religious Rejections of the World" as they relate to *The Protestant Ethic*. His interpretive perspective is unique because it combines his interest in communication with a late Parsonian interest in cultural differentiation. Here he is influenced by Schluchter, whose own work reflects a similar orientation. While Habermas uses the culture/society/personality distinction as an overall framework, he focuses less on differentiation among these three systems than on differentiation among the cognitive, expressive, and moral dimensions of cultural life. He suggests that this separation (see Parsons 1961) has allowed processes of justification to occur in more rational, less ascribed ways. Cultural differentiation has meant that objective knowledge, expressive/aesthetic life, and morality increasingly can be conceived without reference to an overarching religious cosmos. "The devout attachment to concrete orders of life secured in tradition," Habermas writes, can "be superseded in favor of a free orientation to universal principles" (p. 213).

Yet whereas Parsons always felt that Weber had sustained this level of insight throughout the breadth of his work—his only failure having been the occasional resort to "type atomism"—Habermas sees significant reductionist tendencies also at work. I have suggested that Weber's reductionism emerges forcefully in the historical sociology of pre-capitalist societies (Alexander 1983). Habermas, in contrast, historicizes the reductionism, seeing it as emerging only in Weber's work on the transition from the earlier phases of cultural differentiation to modernity itself.* In a marvelous passage, Habermas suggests (1984:217) that there were three paths that Weber could have taken after he had established the rational potential of Western cultural development. First, he could have studied the social movements, like democratic revolutions and socialist movements, which sought to institutionalize such rationality. Second, he could have developed a cultural sociology of this new, more rationalized contemporary order. Third, he could have studied the institutionalization of one subtype of modern rationality, e.g., of purposively rational action.

---

*Here Habermas relies too heavily on the Parsonian tradition's reconstruction of Weber's pre-modern cultural history, rather than examining Weber's writing in its own light. He does so, ironically, because he follows Marx's radically historicist approach to "the transition," an acceptance that, we will see, eventually creates major difficulties.

He suggests that Weber took up only the third possibility, concentrating on the origins and operation of instrumental capitalism and bureaucracy. This decision was an unfortunate one because it meant that "Weber takes into consideration the horizon of possibilities opened up by the modern understanding of the world only to the extent that it serves to explain the core phenomenon he identified in advance" (1984:221). In other words, by focusing only on the purposively rational institutions of capitalism and bureaucracy Weber drastically narrowed his thinking about the nature of modern understanding, an issue whose possibilities had been genially opened by Weber's analysis of cultural differentiation in the earlier period.

Is there empirical justification for Weber's choice, or did it result from a theoretical mistake? Some of each, in Habermas' view. Certainly, the institutionalization of purposive-rational entrepreneurial activity is, from a function point of view, actually of central importance for modern societies. At the same time, however, there has been "a noticeable and consequential narrowing of the concept of rationality in Weber's action theory" (1984:221).

By exploring the presuppositional reasons behind Weber's narrowed treatment, Habermas offers an extraordinary account of what Weber's cultural sociology of modernity might have been. The pessimism about modernity was, in Habermas' view, as much the result of Weber's inability to understand the sources of continuing rationality as the result of his empirical insight and ideological sensibility. Weber described all the newly autonomous spheres of modern culture—science, art and sexuality, political morality—as doomed to irrationality. The earlier sense of the rationality of these endeavors, or at least their meaningful validity, had come from their connection to overarching religious principles. But with the victory of science over religion, Weber believed, they could no longer be related to any general principles at all. This is just what Habermas contests.* Why can these modern cultural spheres not be seen as related to secular rather than religious principles? His point is worth quoting in full:

[Weber's] explanation of the self-destructive pattern of societal rationalization is unsatisfactory because [he] still owes us a demonstration that a moral consciousness guided by principles can survive only in a religious context. He would have

*For my own argument with Weber on these points, see chpt. 2, above.

to explain why embedding a principled ethic in a salvation religion, why joining moral consciousness to interests in salvation, are just as indispensable for the *preservation* of moral consciousness as, from a genetic standpoint, they undoubtedly were for the *emergence* of this stage of moral consciousness. (1984:229 original italics)

Weber, in Habermas' opinion, offers no empirical justification for this claim. His research program, which was supposed "to make it possible to estimate 'the cultural significance of Protestantism in relation to the other plastic elements of modern culture,' was never carried through" (p. 229). If it had been, Weber would have had to include the ethical influence on modern culture of humanism and of both philosophical and scientific empiricism. Combined with the influence of Protestantism, these traditions "flowed into the rationalism of the Enlightenment and promoted a secularized, lay morality in bourgeois strata." This latter development promoted what Weber claimed was impossible: the emergence of a "principled ethic that is removed from religious contexts, and through which the bourgeois strata set themselves off from both the clergy and from the common people caught up in naive piety" (p. 230).

Indeed, as we have seen earlier, Habermas himself demonstrates that principled ethics do survive in a post-religious context, that substantive rationality is pervasive in the modern world. To reintroduce this argument, Habermas argues (p. 249) that "Weber goes too far when he infers from the loss of the substantial unity of reason, a polytheism of gods and demons struggling with one another, with their irreconcilability rooted in a pluralism of incompatible validity claims." Habermas suggests, to the contrary, that if one looks closely at differentiated cultural life, one can see that there is a "unity of rationality in the multiplicity of value spheres." Though each sphere is anchored in concretely different values—hence their immediate irreconcilability—each conceives itself as justifiable via rational argument. Science seeks justification through propositional truth, expressive and artistic life through sincerity and authenticity, morality through its claim to normative rightness. The medium for common understanding between these spheres—the source of their higher reconcilability—is precisely the fact that they make such claims to validity, and they can thematize these claims through rational argumentation. This is not to say that the interrelationship between these spheres is smooth or integrative. There remains "the problem of where, in the communicative practice of everday life, 'switching stations' have to be brought into operation so that individuals can shift their action orientations from one complex to another" (p. 250).*

This is the general argument through which Habermas demonstrates that, in his words, Weber "does not apply the comprehensive concept of rationality upon which he bases his investigations of cultural tradition" to his own sociology of modern life. He builds a more concrete case for this criticism through his detailed consideration of Weber's approach to modern law. More than any interpreter since Parsons, Habermas sees the absolute centrality of law to Weber's theory of modern society. If Weber is to make a convincing case that purposive-rational action can, indeed, be cut off from higher moral grounding, he must show that the self-regulation and stability of rational systems can be achieved through an equally rational and value-less law. If Weber wants to sustain his narrowed conception of modernity, therefore, he must succeed "in uncoupling the development of modern law from the fate of moral-practical rationality and conceptualizing it as just a further embodiment of cognitive-instrumental rationality" (p. 242).

Weber accomplishes this by focusing exclusively on how the systematicity, formality, and logicality of modern law allow it to be eminently calculable (p. 254ff). But Weber is mistaken. While the formal qualities of modern law are functional for instrumental systems like the economy, this says nothing about how such legal structures are constituted in

---

*Habermas explores here precisely the issue that was at the center of Parsons' late work, *The American University* (Parsons and Platt, 1973). In that work Parsons argued that, as modernization proceeds, the differentiated subsystems of societies increasingly become coordinated by different versions of the "rationality" value. In fact, he suggests that this becomes the major mode of inter-system coordination. Parsons argued that cognitive rationality—the theoretical standard of empirical truth—was the cultural medium through which coordination occurred and that the university was the crucial institutional vehicle. The differentiated value and institutional spheres of modern society, then, are coordinated because each depends upon the university's "outputs" of rationality, e.g., in the training of their personnel, the evaluations of their products, and the justification of their performance. Parsons identified four different types of coordinating rationality: economic, political, integrative, and value. On the one hand, this discussion indicates an extraordinary convergence on a detailed and profoundly significant empirical point. For example, like Parsons, Habermas pinpoints the crucial role that professionals play as mediators and carriers of modern rationality (1984:253), and his emphasis on the uncoerced equality of the communicative situation can be seen—in light of this reference to professionals—as parallel to Parsons' later emphasis on the emergence of collegial in contrast to hierarchic and market organization in modern societies. (On this point, see Sciulli's [1985] far-reaching analysis of the Parsons/Habermas convergence.) On the other hand, Parsons' understanding of rationality remains more cognitivist and limited than the one developed by Habermas.

themselves. To understand the latter, it is necessary to see that contemporary law embodies certain kinds of moral justifications. Weber resisted the connection of law and morality on the grounds that it denies what is precisely the major innovation of modern legality, namely its differentiation from any explicit substantive moral position. Habermas replies, ironically, that this separation can be maintained only by justifying it with reference to a more general abstract moral conciousness.

The particular accomplishment of the positivization of the legal order consists in *displacing* problems of justification, that is, in relieving the technical administration of the law of such problems over broad expanses—but not in doing away with them. Precisely the post-traditional structure of legal conciousness sharpens the problem of justification into a question of principle that is shifted to the foundations but not thereby made to disappear. (P. 261)

Habermas lists a whole series of extralegal principles that form the justifying foundation for modern law, characterizing them under the general Piagetian rubric or "post-conventional" morality: the notion that a compact between free and legal partners makes contractual obligations possible, the concept of the abstract legal subject's general competency, the very distinction between norms and principles, and so forth. This insistence on the substantive foundations of legal rationality leads him, quite rightly in my view, to emphasize the significance of political constitutions, institutions that Weber almost completely ignored. "The catalog of basic rights contained in bourgeois constitutions," Habermas suggests (p. 261), is one of the "expressions of this justification that has become structurally necessary." He criticizes Schluchter for presenting Weber's legal sociology as if it implied such legal principles and for suggesting that these principles supply a link in Weber's work between his theory of positive law and his discussion of the ethic of responsibility. Such principles, Habermas counters "are a foreign element within Weber's systematic construction" (p. 438 n. 34).

This completes Habermas' reconstruction of what Weber's cultural sociology of modernity might have looked like if Weber had not unduly narrowed his conception of rationality. To explain the impoverishment of Weber's actual account of the contemporary order, Habermas faults Weber's understanding of social action. Weber, he suggests (p. 280), operated with an intentionalist rather than a linguistic conception of action. He saw meaning as the result of actors trying to gain the understanding of others in a purposive way. From such an intentionalist perspective, action is rationalizable only in terms of means/ends relations, invoking the criteria of actual effectiveness and empirical truth. Value and emotion-related actions are, then, not rationalizable by definition; it was for this reason that Weber so sharply opposed *Zweck* to *Wertrationalität*.

What is the alternative to such an intentionalist, utilitarian view? We have seen it clearly if we have followed Habermas' argument all along. It is the understanding of action as, in the first instance, an act of communication. Action must be conceived on the model of ordinary language, either as carried on through the medium of language or as modeled upon it. For ordinary language, we have seen, is almost always carried on within the restricting framework of implicit modes of validation. Even if it is strategic, therefore, it is subject to some extra-intentional control. It is these moral foundations that provide the basis for rationalization in something other than an instrumental sense.

III

In light of the matters discussed thus far—they take up nearly the first two-thirds of the book—it may come as a surprise to the reader to learn that there is not much communicative rationality in the modern world after all! Beginning with the fourth section (I will consider the short, but highly interesting third section below), Habermas seems to bring his theoretical enterprise of the first 270 pages to a screeching halt and to change directions laboriously. He now suggests that communicative rationality is actually limited to a very small section of contemporary society called the "lifeworld." His definition of this lifeworld is distressingly vague—it certainly differs from Heidegger's and Schutz's—but he does indicate that it is where "everyday practice" and "everyday communication" occur. Whereas it had seemed to be his intention in the first two-thirds of his work to suggest that such "lifeworld" practices as ordinary language are the basis for institutional behavior, he is now intent on isolating these practices. He portrays them as vulnerable islands of feeling and thought surrounded by hostile oceans of rationalized "systems." Systems are defined as organizations of purely strategic actions, organizations that employ a "functionalist" form of reason that has nothing to do with human norms or concerns. The capitalist economic system, the legal-rational political system, even the modern mass communications system (p. 372), Habermas claims, do not rely on the medium of language but employ media like money and power (and influence?) in a coercive, anticommunicative way. At first, Habermas speaks of the relation between systems and lifeworlds as "counteracting tendencies" (p. 341). Almost immediately, however, he puts the relation into the stronger, Marxian language of "contradiction." "The contradiction arises," he writes (p.342), "between, on the one hand, a rationalization of everyday communication that is tied to the structures of intersubjectivity of the lifeworld, in which language counts as the genuine and irreplaceable medium of reaching an understanding, and, on the other hand, the growing complexity of subsystems of purposive-rational action, in which actions are coordinated through steering media such as money and power." Soon he is speaking about the "colonization of the lifeworld" by modern society's rationalized systems: "An unleashed functionalist reason of systems maintenance disregards and overrides the claim to reason ingrained in communicative sociation and lets the rationalization of the lifeworld run idle" (p. 399).

An abrupt change indeed. If Habermas were to seek to justify this shift in a thorough-going way, he would have to go back and refute, point by point, his entire discussion of Weber. In that discussion, he himself developed a systematic argument against an instrumental reading of modern social institutions. It was he who argued against Weber that instrumental rationality was not the only form of rationality to be institutionalized in the modern world, and he pointed directly to political systems and their legal foundations as his foremost examples. Is he not now arguing directly against this earlier stance?

Although Habermas does not try to refute himself, he turns to earlier members of the Frankfurt school to do much the same thing. In the volume's fourth and concluding section, "From Lukacs to Adorno: Rationalization as Reification," he presents this strand of Western Marxism as, simultaneously, a reading of Weber and an accurate description of Western society. This Frankfurt tradition, of course, did rely heavily on Weber's work, but its reading of him was precisely the one-sided, instrumentalized version that Habermas warned us against. Armed with the earlier interpretation, we are in a position to say that these Western Marxists picked up on the wrong Weber. By doing so, moreover, they allowed their picture of Western society to become so heavily instrumentalized that they missed the opportunity to root their own alternative vision of rationality in an immanent, empirical way. The latter, of course, is precisely the ambition of Habermas' new work. Yet Habermas applauds them. He uses this earlier generation of Marxists—the criticism of whose very approach to critical theory has been the implicit starting point for his own work—to steer Weber back to Marx. I said earlier that the Frankfurt theorists seemed to stop reading Hegel's *Phenomenology* after his chapters on the Enlightenment. In the earlier parts of his book Habermas used Weber to develop an empirical way to join Hegel in his post-Enlightenment discussion. But after showing us this promised land, Habermas wants to take us back to the desert. To do this, he must distort Weber's understanding of modern rationality as badly as the Frankfurt school distorted Hegel's.

"Capitalism" now becomes a satisfactory way of defining the present era, and Lukacs becomes the theorist who succeeded in producing the best definition. Lukacs ([1923] 1971) claimed that Marx's conception of commodity fetishism, which conceptualized the capitalist world as totally dominated by the instrumental value of exchange, meant much the same thing as Weber's rationalization theory. Habermas welcomes Lukacs' convergence thesis and tries to restate commodity fetishism in terms of his own communications theory. He writes (p. 359) that Lukacs "conceives of the reification of lifeworld contexts, which sets in when workers coordinate their interactions by way of the de-linguistified medium of exchange value rather than through norms and values, as the other side of a rationalization of their action orientations." In other words, (1) Weber demonstrated that modern actions are only purposively rational and that action orientations have been rationalized and do not appeal to values or norms; (2) Lukacs showed that the interrelation of workers through an exchange of commodities—the "de-linguistified medium of exchange"— rested on the same thing; (3) Lukacs' conclusion, that the lifeworld of capitalism is reified, is valid. Habermas praises Lukacs for showing that in capitalist society association is so instrumental that it can form only systems, not lifeworlds: "He makes the system-forming effects of sociation established through the medium of exchange value intelligible from the perspective of action theory" (p. 359).

To the degree that the commodity form becomes the form of objectivity and rules the relations of individuals to one another as well as their dealings with external nature and with internal subjective nature, the lifeworld has to become reified and individuals degraded—as systems theory forsees—into an 'environment' for a society that has become external to them, that has abstracted from them and become independent of them. Lukacs shares this perspective with Weber. (P. 361)

Does he? Only to the degree that Weber himself is guilty of reducing his presuppositions about action to an instrumental form. Once this has occurred, collective order, be it capitalist or socialist, can hardly be portrayed as anything other than external and coercive (cf. Alexander 1982). Habermas proves this when he demonstrates that Weber external-ist perspective on the rationality of contemporary political and legal insti-tutions can be challenged dramatically if his conception of action is made more compatible with the multivalent, "communicative" approach of his writing on cultural history. The critical theorists, from Lukacs onward, picked up precisely on Weber's theoretical mistake; given their own pre-dispositions, they saw this mistake as a statement of empirical fact.

We might say, then, that there is an empirical error behind Habermas' abrupt reversal. Modern political and economic life are never simply instrumental. They are always coded by deep structures of cultural life. To mistake this is to confuse the fact of differentiation, which allows relative strategic freedom from ascribed value positions, with the absence of moral foundations. Neither are the modern worlds of values, norms, and solidarities ever such simple, intimate, and intuitive lifeworlds as Habermas describes. They are themselves also systems subject to organi-zation on levels that individuals scarcely intuit. Moreover, they are inter-penetrated with cultural and strategic areas of social life through processes which can be analytically reconstructed as exchange.

But there is probably also an ideological source for Habermas' insis-tence on the modern isolation of the lifeworld. This is the continuing influence on his work of German Idealism (Alexander 1984), which has, of course, deeply affected Western Marxism in all of its forms. This tradition is organized around the dichotomy of ideal versus material things, and it has always perceived the threat to post-traditional society to be one of deracination. Habermas follows this tradition. Despite the occasional avowals about the positive character of differentiation in his work, the oppressive and dangerous parts of modern society are almost always portrayed as merging from rationalized, material systems, whereas the "good parts" are associated with the personal intimacy of moral life. For those who do not accept the premises of the Idealist tradition, how-ever, this ideological dichotomy has little intuitive appeal. The problems of modern society have emerged as much from the lifeworlds of intimate relations—from the authoritarian family, religious sect, and peer group —as they have from administrative and economic systems. They have been rooted as much in values and norms—in *Volk* culture, racism, and submissive beliefs—as in force and coercion. Indeed, in the history of Western societies it has often been the case that a society's "idealistic" refusal to allow the depersonalization of economic and political life has signaled its decline into irrationality and despair.*

Finally, it seems that Habermas has made an error on the theoretical, presuppositional level, an error, moreover, much like the one for which he criticized Weber. It is a problem in the conception of action—more specifically, in the manner in which his communications theory is conceived. We turn here to the "Intermediate Reflections" on "Social Action, Purposive Activity, and Communication" which completes the third section of Habermas' book.

IV

In this third section, Habermas offers his own theory of communicative action. The discussion serves two purposes. On the one hand, it supplies the communicative approach to action that Habermas has just finished chastising Weber for being unable to provide. On the other hand, it is a transition to Habermas' argument, which unfolds in the section that follows, about the contradiction between system and lifeworld produced by the instrumentalization of the modern world. These purposes, however, are incompatible.

How can a theory of communicative action buttress and elaborate Habermas' critique of Weber? It can do so by demonstrating (1) that virtually all action assumes communication, (2) that communication assumes some extrastrategic understanding between actors, and (3) that this understanding usually makes an inherent claim to rational justification. As I have suggested earlier, this is just what Habermas argues in the discussions of communication theory that precede the Weber analysis (pp. 8–42, 75–101). In this third section, which is a more technical return to communications, Habermas continues to insist that communication involves understanding and that understanding implies rationality (points 2 and 3 above). In this sense, he expands his critique of Weber's approach.

*Indeed, in chapter 3 above, Loader and I argued that this was precisely Weber's own critique of the *Gesellschaft-Gemeinschaft* dichotomy in German social thought.

But considered as a whole, this later discussion actually points in quite a different direction. Rather than elaborating on the role of communicative rationality, Habermas now devotes himself to communication's limited domain (contradicting point 1 above). He does so by developing the contrast between communication and instrumental behavior. In his earlier discussion, he had allowed that strategic, instrumental behavior, though conducted with reference to justifying criteria like efficiency and effectiveness, is not, in fact, usually subject to thematization and rational argument. The point of that earlier discussion, however, was that most action was so subject. Now, in contrast, it is the purported lack of argumentation in strategic behavior that preoccupies him. Instead of presenting a theory of communicative action to supplement Weber, he produces a concept of anticommunicative action to supplement the antinormative description of modern life which is to be the focus of his concluding section.

To argue that substantive rationality does not often occur in the principal institutional spheres of contemporary life, as he does in the fourth and final section, Habermas must demonstrate that communicative action is sharply bounded. He must show that instrumental-strategic action involves neither shared understanding nor the intent to communicate which depends on understanding. It is the attempt to so argue that the section with which we are presently concerned—section 3—is all about. Habermas constructs an ideal-typical dichotomy of "instrumental-versus-communicative action," and he overloads this contrast with heavy conflationary baggage. All actions can be distinguished, he insists, according to whether they are oriented to success (i.e., strategic considerations) or oriented to understanding (i.e. communication). If action is oriented to understanding, he maintains, it is motivated by the desire to create a harmonious relation between the actor and his environment: "In communicative action participants are not primarily oriented to their own individual successes; they pursue their individual goals under the condition that they can harmonize their plans of action on the basis of common situation definitions" (p. 288). To communicate, then, is the same as to agree: "Reaching understanding is considered to be a process of reaching agreement among speaking and acting subjects" (p. 288). Now, because strategic, instrumental action implies competition and often conflict, it cannot be termed communicative. Habermas describes it as the "noncommunicative employment of knowledge" (p. 10.)

This dichotomy does not seem valid. It seems to reflect a theoretical overreaction that conflates empirical, ideological, and epistemological issues. First, the distinction has a clear ideological intent. Habermas maintains (p. 398) that "the utopian perspective of reconciliation and freedom is ingrained in the conditions for the communicative sociation of individuals." His definition of communication, in other words, is a scarcely concealed translation of the requisites for ideal political democracy. In contrast to strategic action, where force and deception may be used, in communicative action participants are said to persue their aims "without reservation in order to arrive at an agreement that will provide the basis for a consensual coordination of individually pursued plans of action" (p. 295–296). Or again, as Habermas writes at an earlier point (p. 10), "this concept of communicative rationality carries with it connotations based ultimately on the central experience of the unconstrained, unifying, consensus-bringing force of argumentative speech."

My point is not that such ideological ambitions are illegitimate. Far from it. Rather I am suggesting that Habermas' desire to achieve such unconstrained and cooperative social relationships is not presented as an evaluative position but as part of the very definition of his presuppositions about action. Communications = Agreement is a wishful equation. Shorn of the ideological hopes placed in it, communication qua communications does not necessitate cooperation. Nor do conflict and strategizing necessarily imply a lack of understanding. Certainly there are some acts, like war and murder, that do not "depend upon" understanding in the traditional sense. A bomb can be dropped and murder committed against people who do not have the slightest idea what the meaning of this act is for the perpetrator. But, even in these physically coercive acts, understanding still plays a vital role. Murder and war are usually carried out within a "meaningful" perspective because even murderers and soldiers must understand and typify their actions in concrete and particular ways (e.g., Fussell 1975). The issue, then, is not lack of understanding but lack of reciprocal or mutual understanding. Habermas claims the distinction is an epistemological difference: does knowledge involve understanding? But what is really at stake is an empirical difference: to what degree is understanding mutual and supportive? Interpretating and strategizing are analytically interpenetrated even in war—the type case of dissensus. But clearer illustrations of interpenetration are acts that are not physically coercive, for example, strategic actions like hucksterism and deceit. The success of these actions depends not only on the perpetrator's intricate understanding of the meaning of his victim's actions, but also on the victim's understanding of his interlocutor's actions in an "objectively interpretable" way. Again, what is lacking is not understanding or communication, but reciprocal understanding and supportive communication.

Actions form an empirically variable continuum in which constant analytic dimensions are given different weights. Understanding is a component of all action; so is strategic consideration.* Whether action will be cooperative or conflictual depends on how these dimensions are filled in, on what concrete empirical form they take in specific historical situations. We can understand, now, why Habermas goes out of his way to reject an "analytic" approach to the distinction between understanding and strategizing. "In identifying strategic action and communicative action types," he writes (p. 286), "I am assuming that concrete actions can be classified from these points of view. I do not want to use the terms 'strategic' and 'communicative' only to designate two analytic aspects under which the same action could be described" (see also p. 292).

It is as if Habermas misconstrues the very distinction between cultural and social systems that informed his discussion of Weber. For Parsons these were analytic distinctions, culture referring to the meaningful organization of the symbols which inform human action and society to the actual behavior of real people. To abstract the "understanding" of partners in a real interaction is to point toward the analytic dimension of the cultural system. To describe their degree of conflict or cooperation is to refer to issues that result from the organization of the social system itself. In his discussion of communication, it seems, Habermas wants to tie social system processes directly to cultural ones. He erases the analytic distinction by a rhetorical device which occurs throughout his third section. Writing about speech, he is inclined to refer to its "binding (or bonding) effect" (see e.g. p. 294). Speech not only binds people to an understanding (through their participation in the cultural system); it also bonds them together in solidarity (through their integration in the social system). In his first systematic elaboration of his communication theory, written in the mid-1970s, this conflation is already apparent. "I shall speak of the success of a speech act," he wrote (1979:59), "only when the

---

*I have elaborated this analytic approach to strategization and interpretation, relating them to rationality and social institutions, in Alexander 1988.

hearer not only understands the meaning of the sentence uttered but also actually enters into the relationship intended by the speaker." But, while meaning is cultural; relationships are social. Success on one level by no means implies success on another.

It is not at all clear that this radical distinction is justified by the very analytic philosophy upon which Habermas draws. The philosopher whose early work had such an influence on Habermas, Karl-Otto Apel, has recently tried, for example, to support the instrumental/communicative distinction from the perspective of the synthesis of *Geisteswissenschaft* and ordinary-language approaches I mentioned earlier.

The notion of pure strategical rationality of interaction between opponents in a game indeed implies reciprocity of rule-following actions and thus implies the equal status of the partners; but it does not imply, but pragmatically presupposes and thus excludes, the notion of coming to agreement about the rules of the game, i.e., of agreements about possible purposes, means and conditions of relevant actions within the game. Now this is the same, I suppose, as the claim that the notion of strategical action excludes and presupposes the notion of coming to agreement about, and thus sharing, the meanings . . . of linguistic . . . utterances by communication. (1980:124–25)

This statement actually seems to deny the validity of the dichotomy it ostensibly supports. Apel is acknowledging that strategic, game-playing behavior relies upon understanding. In noting that such strategic action excludes the possibility of coming to an explicit agreement about rules, he is not denying the existence of such understanding but classifying the rule-following it implies as conventional and concrete rather than post-conventional and formal. In the Piaget/Kolberg sense, strategic action may be said to "presuppose" an agreement to follow rules, and, one might add, the ability to understand them, but to exclude the awareness that these rules are constructed by people consciously agreeing to them. The lameness of Apel's "I suppose" in his final reference to understanding underscores the ambiguity of his point. His earlier work, we recall, was built precisely on his opposition to the antagonism of strategy and under-standing. "Only when we are dealing with psychotics or with people of a very strange culture," he wrote in the important essay of 1967 (p. 22), "do we get the idea of doing without an immediate understanding of their motives." As a general rule, he insisted (p. 23), "objective explanation of facts and intersubjective communication about what is to be explained are . . . 'complementary' aspects of human knowledge." Even in the later article he cannot avoid this analytic, synthesizing intention. "A single person," he admits (1980:123), "could not understand the intentions of his purposive-rational actions (or even the rules of means-ends rationality) without presupposing already the intersubjective, i.e., common, general and, as it were, time-less, meaning that is fixed by the sign-types of a language."

It is Austin, however, upon whom Habermas draws most strongly for the philosophic justification of his dichotomy between strategic communicative action. Austin, one of the pioneers of ordinary language philosophy, developed the contrast between illocutionary and perlocutionary speech acts. Habermas equates illocutionary with communicative and perlocutionary with strategic, suggesting that Austin's dichotomy parallels, explains, and supports his own. Two questions immediately present themselves. First, does Habermas' dichotomy fairly capture what Austin meant to do? Second, is Austin's original intention relevant anyway? Without claiming to present an authoritative interpretation of what remains an enormously complex philosophical discussion, I would like to suggest that the answer to the first question is no, but to the second, yes.

It is very important not to forget Austin's original claim that speaking is doing. It was for this reason that he introduced into language philosophy the term "performative utterances" (Austin 1962:233–252), and it is this notion that forms the background for the famous set of lectures, *How to Do Things with Words,* which provides the most significant reference for Habermas' work. Austin insists at the outset of these lectures that "the issuing of the utterance is the performing of an action" (p. 6). In performing speech, actors have intentions, and they want to achieve goals. Because they speak in circumstances, or situations, they must communicate in ways that are appropriate. To do so, their purposive action is thoroughly enmeshed in convention.

If Austin never abandons this basic conception, why dos he introduce the distinction between actions that are illocutionary and those that are perlocutionary? Perhaps because he starts from the assumption that most acts are speeches and not simply that most speeches are acts. He wants, therefore, to distinguish, within the rubric of performative utterances, different kinds of acts (see e.g., pp. 108, 109, and passim). Illocutionary acts refer to utterances, such as informing, ordering, warning, and undertaking, that have in themselves—as words enmeshed in conventions—a certain force. Perlocutionary acts, by contrast, are utterances which by being said bring about or achieve something outside of the speech situation. Thus, an illocutionary act can be captured in the statement "In saying it I was warning him" whereas a perlocutionary act is described in the statement "By saying it I convinced him, or surprised him, or got him to stop" (p. 109). Austin himself remarks that "it is the distinction between illocutions and perlocutions which seems likeliest to give trouble" (p. 109), and his attempt to make the distinction initiated an argument that has by no means subsided. For our purposes, however, certain points seem relatively clear.

While the differences between these categories relate to their intended reference to extra-speech act effects, this is not the same as the distinction that Habermas evokes to separate strategic and communicative action. In the first place, the extra-speech effects of perlocutionary actions depends on a listener's understanding of the content of the speech. This means that strategic action, which Habermas equates with perlocutionary, could not, in fact, succeed without commmunication and understanding. To establish just such a connection actually seems to be Austin's intention when he first introduces the distinction. There is a sense, he writes (p. 101), in which to perform "an illocutionary act, may also be to perform an act of another kind."

> Saying something will often, or even normally, produce certain consequential effects upon the feelings, thoughts, or actions of the audience, of the speaker, or of other persons: and it may be done with the design, intention, or purpose of producing them; and we may then say, thinking of this, that the speaker has performed an action in the nomenclature of which reference is made either only obliquely, or not at all, to the performance of the illocutionary act. We shall call the performance of this kind the performance of a perlocutionary act. (P. 101)

The gist of this statement is that illocutionary and perlocutionary acts can only be analytically differentiated. Illocutionary acts "normally" have consequential effects on the environment. If these effects are the principal intention of the speaker, if the act of creating understanding is significant to the speaker only as a vehicle for realizing this effect, then this act can be called perlocutionary.

But if the strategic or perlocutionary acts are intended by Austin to include understanding, so also are communicative, or illocutionary, acts intended to include strategizing. Whereas Habermas defines communicative understanding as completely divorced from the strategic calculation of effects, Austin defines illocution as a type of performance. "I must point out," he insists after an initial effort at distinguishing perlocution from illocution, "that the illocutionary act as distinct from the perlocutionary is connected with the production of effects in a certain sense" (p. 115). He goes on to emphasize that "unless a certain effect is achieved, the illocutionary act will not have been happily, successfully performed" (p. 115). True, successful effect is defined here as "bringing about the understanding of the meaning and of the force of the locution" (p. 116), rather than as an effect on the environment separated from speech. But Austin insists that in illocution "an effect must still be achieved." Illocutionary understanding, then, can never occur without the calculation of effects and the purposive direction of action toward that end.

Because Habermas is an acute reader of texts and himself a philosopher, it is not surprising that one can find in his discussion the implicit recognition that Austin's categories may not, after all, support his own. For example, introducing Austin's statement (which I quoted above) that illocutionary acts "normally produce certain consequential effects," Habermas (1984:289) alters the meaning of this statement by writing that Austin is suggesting that this happens "sometimes." And he turns it quite inside out by describing the phenomenon that "sometimes" occurs as illocution having a role within perlocution rather than vice-versa. Then, after developing the argument that he present as following on Austin's own illocution/perlocution distinction, Habermas suggests that Austin was confused because he did not make the distinction as cleanly and radically as Habermas himself. "Austin confuses the picture," he suggests (p.294), "by not treating those interactions . . . as different in type." But was this a confusion on Austin's part or a justified insight? In attempting to justify his own claim, Habermas inadvertently justifies Austin's position. "Austin did not keep these two cases separate as different types of interaction," he writes (p.295), "because he was inclined to identify acts of communication, that is, acts of reaching understanding, with the interactions coordinated by speech acts." This was, indeed, exactly Austin's point. Most speech acts are performative, and illocutions certainly are concerned with interactive effects.

It can even be argued that Habermas recognizes, in spite of himself, the validity of Austin's logic, for in the course of criticizing Austin he introduces residual categories that undermine his effort to make a more radical distinction. Describing an actor engaging in different types of illocution, for example, Habermas suggests that the person "is acting communicatively and cannot at all produce perlocutionary effects *at the same level of interaction"* (p. 294, original italics). Does this not imply that rather than distinguishing types of actions, one should distinguish among different levels within an action? If illocution and perlocution are simply different levels of a single act, is this not an analytic rather than a concrete distinction? In fact, Habermas later acknowledges the "problem" of "distinguishing and identifying in natural situations actions oriented to understanding from actions oriented to success" (p. 331). The problem seems to be that "not only do illocutions appear in strategic-action contexts, but perlocutions appear in contexts of communicative action." In an apparent effort to explain this anomaly, he introduces the notion of "phases" of the interaction process, trying to convince us that "strategic *elements* within a use of language oriented to reaching understanding can be distinguished from strategic *actions"* (original italics). Such ad hoc reasoning may avoid explicit acknowledgment of the analytical interpenetration of strategy and communication, but it amounts to implicit recognition of this point. In substance if not form, Habermas' argument resembles the anti-dichotomy position ascribed to Apel above.

V

In my discussion thus far I have sketched both a positive and a negative side to Habermas' effort to ground critical rationality in ordinary language. In a positive vein, his insight into the validity claims of ordinary language allows him to see how substantively rational behavior actually permeates the modern world. This insight allows Habermas not only to transcend the reductionist and ultimately elitist approach of the orthodox Frankfurt school but also—in combination with the other theoretical traditions that he employs—to move beyond Weber's rationalization theory in a decisive sense. All of this allows him to insert a more critical edge into the normative-evolutionary tradition associated with Parsons. We have just seen, however, that there is also a negative side to Habermas' communication theory; he also uses it, ironically, to reduce the scope of rationality; first by eliminating understanding from strategic action and second by idealizing understanding in an impractical way. Instead of elaborating the potential of Weberian theory and transcending "critical" orthodoxy, this negative utilization of language theory undermines Weber's rationalizaton theory by pushing it backward to orthodox critical theory itself.

However, Habermas' communication theory also, in my view, suffers from quite another problem, even when it embraces rationality in the more acceptable, expanded sense. By considering what might be called the 'cultural weakness' of Habermas' work, I will not only offer a final interpretive criticism; I will, in addition, try to show how his theory's most far-reaching points must be extended in an important way.

From the beginning of his work on communication Habermas has claimed that engaging in communication assumes the capacity for reaching rational agreement. Understanding is identified with agreement, and agreement is identified with "unconstrained cooperation." Agreement, understanding, and the lack of constraint add up to rationality. Lack of constraint is a crucial qualification, for it implies that the actors involved in rational communication are fully conscious of what they say and do.* Not only are they free from external material constraints; they are also free from internalized controls that would place the meaning and the origins of their behavior out of their conscious reach. If they are not depicted as the complete masters of their behavior, they cannot confidently be described as able to alter it in a manner that can ensure cooperative understanding.

Why does Habermas make this claim and how does he justify it? In the background, of course, there is his commitment to traditional democratic theory about voluntary cooperation: people must be endowed with conscious rationality if their contracts are to be conceived as having been voluntarily entered into. A more direct justification for this insistence comes from Piaget. The point of Piaget's formal-operational stage, and the stage of "moral consciousness" that Kohlberg associated with it, is that individuals become capable of rethinking the foundations of their actions and are no longer subordinate to socially given meanings as such. In this sense, Piaget is part of the rationalist tradition that starts with Descartes, his contribution having been to revolutionize our understanding of the social and mental background, the learning processes, upon which the rationality of an adult depends.

Habermas shares this rationalist emphasis on conscious activity. His

---

*Recall Habermas' statement that rationalization can be defined as the elimination of factors that "prevent the conscious settlement of conflicts" (1984:119).

early description of "thematization," the ability to argue rationally about the foundations of behavior, strikingly resembles Piaget's. "Moral conciousness," he writes, "signifies the ability to make use of interactive competence for *consciously* processing morally relevant conflicts" (1979:88, original italics). What is left unsaid, but remains, in my view, enormously important, is that this conscious thematization does not have a cultural base. It is rooted in the cognitive and moral capacities of actors, capacities that are the result of developmental encounters that have, pragmatically and experientially, changed the objective structure of the self. In this same early discussion, for example, Habermas finds a parallel to his own notion of communicative agreement in Gouldner's theory that reciprocity underlines all interactions. Given his own commitment to the capacity for absolute conciousness, however, Habermas feels compelled to qualify even Gouldner's theory in an anticulturalist way. He insists that Gouldner's expression, "the norm of reciprocity," is not "entirely apt." Why not? Because "reciprocity is not a norm but is fixed in the general structures of possible interaction" (p. 88).

If understanding means unconstrained, conscious, rational agreement, can it be related to systems of signs, to symbols that are patterned by deep structures or codes? It would seem that it cannot, and for this reason, it seems to me, communications theory has an antagonistic relationship to the theory of culture. This antagonism becomes paramount in the second volume of Habermas' book, where he interprets Durkheim not as the originator of a symbolic sociology that formed a central reference for structuralism and semiotics (see chapter 5, above) but as a theorist who explained how modernity's "communicative liquification" of the sacred allows rational discourse. The elements of such an antisemiotic approach can already be seen in the volume under review, particularly in the early discussion of the contrast between "mythical" and "modern" modes of thought.

Habermas turns to this contrast to demonstrate that his communication theory is not ahistorical, as some Marxist critics have claimed. What he actually succeeds in demonstrating, in my view, is that his theory is overly historicist. He portrays the movement of modern society away from mythical thought in a manner that supports his contention that communicative rationality allows conscious mastery of thought and action. The problem with mythical thought, he believes, is that it fuses, and therefore confuses, the personal world of the actor, the objective world of society, and the subjective world of thought and ideas. Myth, for example, is based on "the concretistic relation between meaning of expressions and the states-of-affairs represented [by them]" (1984:49). This confusion is clear in magic, where the names of objects are invoked as if they were directly connected to the objects themselves. This confusing intermingling of worlds is also evident in the mythical belief that "moral failure is conceptually interwoven with physical failure, as is evil with the harmful, and good with the healthy and the advantageous" (p. 48). The problem with such intermingling is that it prevents the differentiation of self, morality, and society upon which all critical thinking is based. "A linguistically constituted worldview," Habermas writes, "can be identified with the world-order itself to such an extent that it cannot be perceived *as* an interpretation of the world that is subject to error and open to criticism." In this sense, "the concept of the world is dogmatically invested with a specific content" (pp. 50–51, original italics). Rational rather than mythical communication becomes possible, Habermas believes, only when such mythical intermingling has ended. "Actors who raise validity claims," he writes (pp. 50–51), "have to avoid materially prejudicing the relation between language and reality." Only if this prejudice is avoided can "the content of a linguistic worldview . . . be detached from the assumed world-order itself." At a later point, Habermas makes this antithesis between rationality and mythical thought even more pointedly. The cultural tradition, he writes (p. 71), "must be so far stripped of it dogmatism as to permit in principle that interpretation stored in tradition be placed in question and subjected to critical revision."

But this antithesis, like several others Habermas has described, is overdrawn. It is true and not true at the same time. There has certainly been an enormous differentiation of culture, society, and personality, and it is this differentiation that has allowed conciousness and rationality to emerge in the modern sense. The problem for social theories of modernity, however, is that the arbitrary, unconscious, fused, and, yes, irrational elements of culture have not at the same time disappeared. Language and worldview continue to predefine our understanding of the object world before we even begin to subject it to our conscious rationality. Nor can we regard our linguistically-structured worldviews simply as humanly constructed interpretations, which are therefore transparently open to criticism. Our "regard" is, ineluctably, conditioned by the pre-

conscious world itself. It follows, then, that there is an inevitable investment of the world of things and the world of ideas with some kind of
dogmatic, uncritical status. Modern, rational people continue to infuse
values, institutions, and even mundane physical locations with the mystery and awe of the sacred. It is for this reason that physical, social, and
moral reality is organized into centers and peripheries. Even for modern
people, moreover, there continues to be some intermingling of biological
and social life. We "concretize" moral rules by equating their violation
with pollution, dividing the "forces" of morality into the pure and the
dangerous. We also concretize abstract relationships by evoking metaphors and other tropes. Finally, there seems to be abundant evidence that
moderns still seek to understand the contingency of everyday life in terms
of narrative traditions whose simplicity and resistance to change makes
them hard to distinguish from myths.*

None of this implies the elimination of rationality in Habermas' sense.
What it does mean is that there is much, much more besides. It means
that deeply held conceptions of self, nature, society, beauty, and goodness
continue to structure modern action in a relatively arbitrary way. Yes,
these convictions can be thematized and subjected to rational argument,
but such demands for justification must proceed within the confines of
some given cultural parameters. Rationality, moreover, is not simply the
psychological capacity for such arguments. It is itself a system of significations. For rationality to develop it must be invested with cultural
power. This is usually done by connecting "rationality" to the sacred
centers of a modern society through mythical stories about the society's
"rational" origins. The Maoist conception of rationality connected its neo-
Confucian understanding of value and will with a revolutionary Marxist
theory of material inequality as producing change. The French left's
conception of rationality is more solidaristic, linking communal notions
from Catholicism and the guild tradition with more universalistic principles from the revolution. American rationality cannot be separated from
commonwealth ideas about republican virtue, Puritan ideas about individual rights, and revolutionary distrust of power. These examples are
only suggestive. The relation between rationality and tradition is a complex problem. The ideological complexes of "enlightenment" and "reac-

---

*This is exactly what I have documented in my symbolic analysis of the Watergate crisis
in the preceding chapter. Americans pursued critical rationality in "culturally arbitrary"
ways.

tion" have ensured, moreover, that the problem has scarcely begun to be understood.*

That the relation exists, however, points to a serious weakness not only in Habermas' account of contemporary society but also in his theory of communicative action itself. We are not faced with a contrast between, on the one hand, constraint through institutional coercion (established via media like money and power) and, on the other, voluntary cooperation freed from constraint altogether. To the extent that cooperation is achieved, it is voluntary only in a very conditional sense (Alexander 1978). It is always mediated by cultural constraints outside any single actor's conscious control and, for that matter, by institutionally coercive processes that can never be completely superseded. We are fortunate that rationality has recently become more available for resolving disputes, but it is neither theoretically justifiable nor politically necessary to envision this rationality in a culturally and institutionally free-floating way.

Conclusion: The Marxian Dilemma

In the second volume of *Theoretical Logic in Sociology* (1982:345–370), I suggest that the most original theorists of twentieth century Marxism have been caught inside the "Marxian dilemma." Faced with Marx's instrumental approach to action and his deterministic understanding of order, these theorists have sought a more normative and subjective theory of action and a more voluntaristic, multidimensional theory of order. It is from this desire that the notions of action as "praxis" and superstructures as "relatively autonomous" have emerged. But if these theorists were to remain within the Marxist tradition, they could not step entirely outside the boundaries of Marx's thought. To avoid this, they have done two things: first, they have usually introduced some notion of determinism "in the last instance"; second, they often have left their revisions of Marx so extraordinarily ambiguous that these revised versions can be construed

---

*Gadamer (1975:245) states the problem well, though his work does not go far toward resolving it. "Does the fact that one is set within various traditions mean really and primarily that one is subject to prejudices and limited in one's freedom? Is not, rather, all human existence, even the freest, limited and qualified in various ways? If this is true, then the idea of an absolute reason is impossible for historical humanity. Reason exists for us only in concrete, historical terms, i.e., it is not its own master, but remains constantly dependent on the given circumstances in which it operates."

only as residual categories. These options form the horns of the Marxist dilemma. In this century, Marxist thought has careened between the Scylla of indeterminacy and the Charybdis of the last instance. The dilemma can only be resolved, and a systematic multidimensional theory obtained, by stepping outside Marxism itself.

With the publication of *Theory of Communicative Action,* Jürgen Habermas intends to do just that. He seems to step outside Marxism and create a new theoretical tradition. In his earlier work, he struggled with the Marxian dilemma, his loyalty eventually leading him down the path of the last instance and indeterminacy. His theory of communication, in contrast, allows him to offer a systematic alternative to the impoverished "action" of traditional Marxism, and his developmental theory of normative rationality—which brings together Piaget, Parsons, and speech theory—allows him to describe social order in a much more rich and complex way. These presuppositional revisions have also allowed him to avoid one of the central ideological embarrassments of twentieth-century Marxism, for he can root his critical perspective in immanent processes that are both empirical and "rational" at the same time.

My complaint has been that Habermas does not go quite far enough. There remains in his work a strong residue of the *Weltanschauung* of the Frankfurt school. This leads Habermas to reintroduce themes of instrumental rationality and the determination of lifeworlds by material systems (in the last instance to be sure). His multidimensional theory is qualified, so much so that at various points his conceptual innovations become ambiguous, and sometimes simply residual, to his analysis of modern society. But if Habermas has not gone far enough for me, he has certainly gone much too far for others. It is far enough to have created a remarkable book, one from which every effort at creating a democratic and critical social theory must certainly learn.

REFERENCES

Alexander, Jeffrey C. 1978. "Formal and Substantive Voluntarism in the Work of Talcott Parsons: A Theoretical and Ideological Reinterpretation." *American Sociological Review* 43:177–198.
—— 1982. *The Antinomies of Classical Thought: Marx and Durkheim,* Volume 2 of *Theoretical Logic in Sociology.* Berkeley and Los Angeles: University of California Press.

—— 1983. *The Classical Attempt at Theoretical Synthesis: Max Weber.* Volume 3 of *Theoretical Logic in Sociology.* Berkeley and Los Angeles: University of California Press.

—— 1984. "The Parsons Revival in German Sociology," *Sociological Theory* 2:394–412.

—— 1988. "Action and Its Environments" In *Action and Its Environments,* pp. 301–333. New York: Columbia University Press.

Alexander, Jeffrey C., ed. 1985. *Neofunctionalism.* Los Angeles and London: Sage.

Apel, Karl-Otto. 1967. *Analytic Philosophy of Language and the Geisteswissenschaften.* Holland: Reidel.

—— 1980. "Three Dimensions of Understanding Meaning in Analytic Philosophy: Linguistic Conventions, Intentions, and Reference to Things." *Philosophy and Social Criticism* 7(2):115–142.

Austin, J. L. 1962. *How to Do Things with Words.* Cambridge: Harvard University Press.

—— 1970. *Philosophical Papers.* 2d ed. London: Oxford University Press.

Fussell, Paul. 1975. *The Great War and Modern Memory.* New York: Oxford University Press.

Gadamer, Hans-Georg. 1975. *Truth and Method.* New York: Crossroads.

Giddens, Anthony. 1982. "Labour and Interaction." In John B. Thompson and David Held, eds., *Habermas: Critical Debates,* pp. 149–161. London: Macmillian.

Habermas, Jurgen. 1971. *Knowledge and Human Interests.* Boston: Beacon.

—— 1979. *Communication and the Evolution of Society.* Boston: Beacon.

—— 1981. *Theorie des Kommunikativen Handelns.* Frankfurt: Suhrkamp.

—— 1982. "A Reply to My Critics." In Thompson and Held, eds. (1982):219–283.

—— 1984. *Theory of Communicative Action.* Volume 1: *Reason and the Rationalization of Society.* Boston: Beacon.

Hegel, G. W. F. [1807] 1977. *Phenomenology of Spirit.* New York: Oxford University Press.

Lukacs, Georg. [1923] 1971. "Reification and the Consciousness of the Proletariat." In Lukacs, *History and Class Consciousness.* Cambridge: MIT Press.

Parsons, Talcott. 1961. "Introduction to Culture and Social Systems." In Parsons et al. *Theories of Society,* pp. 963–993. New York: Free Press.

Parsons, Talcott and Gerald Platt. 1973. *The American University.* Cambridge: Harvard University Press.

Piaget, Jean. 1972. *The Principles of Genetic Epistemology.* London: Routledge and Kegan Paul.

Sciulli, David. 1985. "The Political Groundwork for Critical Theory: Bringing Parsons to Habermas (and Vice-Versa). In Alexander, ed (1985):21–50.

Thompson, John B. 1982. "Universal Pragmatics." In Thompson and Held, eds (1982):116–133.

Thompson, John B. and David Held. 1982. *Habermas: Critical Debates.* London: Macmillan.

Index of Names

Subject Index